SAS Ghost Patrol

Damien Lewis

W F HOWES LTD

This large print edition published in 2018 by
W F Howes Ltd
Unit 5, St George's House, Rearsby Business Park,
Gaddesby Lane, Rearsby, Leicester LE7 4YH

1 3 5 7 9 10 8 6 4 2

First published in the United Kingdom in 2017
by Quercus Editions Ltd

A CIP catalogue record for this book is available
from the British Library

ISBN 978 1 52880 371 7

Typeset by Palimpsest Book Production Limited,
Falkirk, Stirlingshire

Printforc￼ ￼erlands

For all who took part in the raid on Tobruk
and never returned.

AUTHOR'S NOTE

This book is entitled *SAS Ghost Patrol.* I have chosen that title because many of those serving with the Special Interrogation Group (SIG) – the unit that lies at the heart of this story – also appear to have served with the SAS. These include Maurice Tiefenbrunner, who by his own account joined the SAS in July 1941, Lieutenant David Russell, the SIG's second in command, and Captain Henry Cecil Buck, the founder of the SIG.

The SIG was deeply enmeshed within SAS desert operations, and at the time of the missions related in this book the unit was formally under SAS (then called L Detachment) command. Prior to that, the SIG appears to have been utilized on many occasions to enable SAS patrols to cross into German territory undetected. Indeed, this appears to have been the unit's prime function.

The SIG was chiefly a brainchild of the Special Operations Executive (SOE), and the close relations between the SAS and SOE have been well documented. Once the SIG was disbanded, the handful of survivors returned to the SAS and many soldiered with them to the war's end. Of course, with a unit of the SIG's nature – utterly deniable and top secret – nothing is ever absolutely certain, if for no other reason than that many of the official papers concerning the SIG have been destroyed.

There are sadly few if any survivors from the World War Two operations depicted in these pages. Throughout the period of the research for, and the writing of, this book I have endeavoured to contact as many as possible, plus surviving family members of those who have passed away. If there are further witnesses to the stories told here who are inclined to come forward, please do get in touch with me, as I will endeavour to include further recollections of the operations portrayed in this book in future editions.

The time spent by Allied servicemen and women as special forces volunteers was often traumatic and wreathed in layers of secrecy, and many chose to take their stories to their graves. Memories tend to differ and apparently none more so than those concerning operations behind enemy lines. The written accounts that do exist also tend to differ in their detail and timescale, and locations and chronologies are often contradictory. That said, I have done my best to provide a proper sense of place, timescale and narrative to the story depicted in these pages.

Where various accounts of a mission appear to be particularly confused, the methodology I have used to reconstruct where, when and how events took place is the 'most likely' scenario. If two or more testimonies or sources point to a particular time or place or sequence of events, I have opted to use that account as most likely. Where necessary I have re-created small sections of dialogue to aid the story's flow.

In earlier press reports and publications about the SIG pseudonyms have been used to protect their identities. With the passage of time the real names of those involved have emerged, and I have used those real names here. The one exception is the German POW and SIG trainer Bruckner, whose real name was very possibly Brockmann. As Bruckner is the official cover name that he was given by British intelligence during his time with the SIG, that is the name I have used in this book.

The above notwithstanding, any mistakes herein are entirely of my own making, and I would be happy to correct any in future editions. Likewise, while I have endeavoured to locate the copyright holders of the photos, sketches and other images and material used in this book, this has not always been straightforward or easy. Again, I would be happy to correct any mistakes in future editions.

It is not only the 'highwayman' tactics that appeal to us, but the fact that the men were able to make the journey at all over such hazardous country. Free and easy it may be to these gallant men, but there is a quality of daredevil romance in the exploits of this group which thrills the imagination in these days when warfare has become only grim and horrible.

From a 14 March 1941 news cutting,
source unknown

PREFACE

A good few years ago I crossed the Sahara desert – once from north to south, and once in the other direction. I did so with the benefit of a relatively modern vehicle and navigational technology, decent maps, and – mostly – generous food and water supplies. I was travelling with a few good friends, we had decent guidebooks and were often accompanied by local guides. We journeyed through Morocco, Algeria, Niger, Nigeria, Tunisia, Libya and one or two other African countries. We did so at a time of relative peace, when the desert wasn't convulsed by war and those operating in it hunted from pillar to post, watched from the skies by avenging warplanes. Even so, it was still a challenging and at times even fearful undertaking.

Perhaps that is why for many years I've been fascinated by the story of the autumn 1942 attack on Barce aerodrome in Axis-held Libya by Allied special forces. The Barce raid was a spectacular mission almost without parallel and it is generally recognized as one of the most successful 'beat-up' raids ever carried out. The attackers had to navigate some 1,900 miles of the world's most inhospitable and hostile terrain in order to carry out their mission, penetrating deep into the dune seas and burning wastes of the Sahara. The Barce raid, code-named Operation Caravan, remains one of the longest – if not *the* longest – missions in the history of special forces, an epic of against-all-odds desert survival.

As I began to study the raid in more detail, I asked my superlative researcher, Simon Fowler, to have a peek in the files held in the UK National Archives, searching for the war diary and any other official documents relating to Operation Caravan. Thankfully, a reasonable body of records has survived. It was in the process of perusing those files that a quite extraordinary and hidden narrative began to emerge – a layer of secret history underpinning the Barce raid itself.

Operation Caravan was part of a larger spread of special forces missions, all of which were executed on the night of 13 September 1942 with varying degrees of success. They involved a variety of elite units operating across much of Axis-held North Africa. The most important mission of all – indeed, the absolute *raison d'être* for that night's audacious series of attacks – was the raid on Tobruk. And to carry off that breathtaking mission a very special unit had been formed, one steeped in utmost secrecy.

Barely a platoon in size, this unit bore various names during the war, but it was most commonly known as the Special Interrogation Group, or SIG. The SIG's role is touched upon in some of the files held at the National Archives. The papers reveal how the unit – part Special Operations Executive, part SAS – was founded to perpetrate one of the greatest deceptions and subterfuges of the entire war.

The platoon of men who made up the SIG consisted entirely of fluent German speakers, who were recruited for one purpose, and one purpose only: to pose as a unit of German soldiers, with the aim of enabling our elite warriors to penetrate the enemy's lines. The SIGs were to be the masters of deception, disguise and bluff, and they were to use such skills to spirit the desert raiders to their targets.

In doing so they were to break every known rule of war.

On the night of 13 September 1942 they were the Trojan horse that took Allied special forces through the series of supposedly impregnable defences that encircled General Rommel's key stronghold in North Africa, Tobruk. Indeed, the raids on Barce and the other attacks of that night were but decoys designed to blind the enemy to the real target – the port fortress that was the key to victory in the desert.

The story of the raid on Barce is thus inextricably linked to that of the SIG and the mission to destroy Tobruk.

During the various operations carried out that

night the heroics performed were almost beyond belief or compare. Those recruited into the SIG and the elite forces that accompanied them knew that they were almost certainly going to their deaths. They went anyway, willingly. All were volunteers.

Every book has an evolution, a path that leads the author to finally put pen to paper. From the starting point of perusing those papers in the National Archives, this proved one of the most surprising and compelling, not to mention edifying journeys. It took me back to the Sahara, a place that I had grown to know, love, fear and respect at first hand. It took me to a stack of musty World War Two documents, some of which have been revealed for the first time as a result of Freedom of Information requests filed with the Archives.

It took me to the war diaries of some of those who took part in the drama revealed in these pages, and to the personal accounts some had written of the roles they played, penned long after the war came to an end – material which has mostly remained unpublished and largely forgotten with the passage of time. And it took me to the last few survivors from those storied times. I am so grateful for the privilege of meeting those to whom I managed to speak.

Nevertheless, I am certain there is more to be revealed about the raids of 13 September 1942 and of the wider histories of the units involved, which were populated by real do-or-die heroes. Eccentrics, mavericks and free-thinkers, I remain humbled and in awe of their daring and exploits. I look forward to whatever revelations may result from the publication of this book.

But first, let me take you to a parched and weary soldier stumbling alone through the barren, war-torn desert, in the early spring of 1942.

CHAPTER 1

The heat rose in shimmering waves off the sun-blasted desert terrain. A lone figure stumbled through the harsh, boulder-strewn landscape. It seemed impossible that anything could survive here, yet somehow this man had, although to the watchers – alert and tracing his every step through their rifle sights – he was clearly on his last legs.

It was just after dawn on 21 February 1942, and already the air was thick with heat from the rising sun. The war in North Africa was not going well for the Allies. Reeling from a succession of defeats at the hands of Erwin Rommel, the commander of the Afrika Korps, British forces had learned a grudging respect – if not fear – for their adversary.

Indeed, in recent months Rommel and his Afrika Korps had earned an almost mythical status. Their reputation for invincibility went before them, their lightning armoured thrusts striking repeatedly at the flanks of the British and Commonwealth troops, forcing a series of desperate retreats across miles of unforgiving desert, mountain and scrub.

Over the weeks of bitter fighting Rommel had acquired a nickname among the British: the Desert Fox. Wily, quick-thinking and smart, who knew what ruse the German general might attempt next? Which made it all the more worrying that a mysterious figure – seemingly a lone Afrika Korps soldier – was making his way towards Allied lines.

What could he be intending, the watchers wondered? Was this some new and cunning deception by Rommel, one designed to confound the British front-line commanders? Was this something altogether more innocent: an enemy soldier lost in the desert – parched, exhausted and hopelessly disorientated? Or was he perhaps a deserter, somehow intent on delivering to them a choice piece of intelligence?

The first sign of the incoming figure had been a dust cloud on the horizon far to the west of the British positions, as a vehicle traversed the main coastal highway running east towards the Allied stronghold of Tobruk. It had advanced thus far, but then the cloud had dissipated. In due course a stick-thin figure had emerged, mirage-like, from the early-morning haze, trudging along the lonely road that snaked through the rocky hills making up this war-blasted no-man's-land.

Moment by moment the figure drew closer. Finally, a group of British soldiers broke cover, scuttling forward, weapons held at the ready. The enemy soldier was dressed as an officer and maybe this boded well. Perhaps he *had* made the perilous journey across the lines carrying a crucial piece of intelligence, one that he wished to hand over to Allied commanders, although what his motives might be no one could yet imagine.

Under close guard the stranger was brought into the checkpoint that straddled the road. He was laid in the shade and given some water, which revived him somewhat. As little by little the captive began to recover his composure, several things became obvious to his captors. First, the Afrika Korps officer looked incredibly young to the British soldiers, who themselves were mostly in their late teens or early twenties. Second, there was something distinguished – almost haughty-looking – about his demeanour, with his thick shock of coal-black hair and the calm, level gaze in his dark eyes. He certainly didn't have the subdued air of a captive. Third, and most shocking, when this man of mystery managed to utter his first words he did so in fluent English and with a decidedly upper-crust accent. Whoever this soldier might be, he sounded more like an Oxford don or a BBC broadcaster than any Afrika Korps officer.

Once he'd regained strength enough to relate the basics of his – utterly incredible – story, a force was sent out to fetch the vehicle in which he had been travelling. If he was telling the truth, it contained nine of his fellows who could verify his extraordinary tale. As for the man himself, he was placed in a jeep and rushed to Allied forward headquarters in Tobruk. If he was to be believed, the captive promised a potential bonanza in terms of intelligence.

Upon arrival at Tobruk the prisoner repeated his riveting story. He was given a stiff drink to fortify himself for the journey that lay ahead and put on a vehicle for the long drive to British Middle East headquarters in Cairo, from where the entire North Africa campaign was being orchestrated. Seemingly he didn't just have some choice intelligence to impart to Allied high command; he also had a plan, one born of his unique background, innate intellect, cunning and eccentricity, and informed by his life-or-death experiences over the past few days.

As he was whisked the 500 miles east along the Mediterranean coast towards Cairo, the captive reflected upon the singular nature of the war being fought in North Africa and how it had led him to conceive of his great idea. There was no other theatre of warfare like it.

Egypt, Libya and Tunisia – the battleground over which the Allies and Axis were waging war – were largely alike geographically: huge desert basins and arid mountain ranges with only a thin strip of fertile land running along the Mediterranean coast, where the towns, villages, farms and ports were concentrated. With over 90 per cent of the land being desert or semi-desert, and inhospitable in the extreme, fighting was restricted to this narrow coastal strip and concentrated around the

4

one navigable highway. Inland lay the Sahara – an expanse of fearful wilderness the size of India, consisting of flat sandy plains (*serir*), rocky plateaus (*hammada*), deep dry watercourses (*wadis*), treacherous salt marshes (*shott*) and massive deathly dune seas (*erg*).

In the depths of the desert it never rained, and temperatures soared to 55 degrees Celsius in the shade. No army – Allied nor Axis – strayed far into the scorched wastes that lay to the south of the coastal strip. The terrain was barren, flyblown, ridden with exotic diseases, featureless, waterless and hostile to human habitation as nowhere else on earth.

But the 'captive' knew of one or two small bands of fighters who were starting to venture into this wasteland. They were making the desert their own, emerging from it to take the Axis forces by total surprise, after which they would melt back into the wilderness. And the 'captive' had himself just conceived of the most audacious plan to spur the fortunes of these desert warriors.

Upon arrival at Cairo headquarters he proceeded to relate his story in great detail. By his own account he was no Afrika Korps officer. Quite the contrary: he was Captain Henry Cecil Buck of the 5th Battalion, 1st Punjabi Regiment – a redoubtable infantry unit consisting of Indian troops led by British officers, which had seen some of the fiercest fighting in the battles to repulse Rommel's forces.

Captain Buck hailed from Camberley, in leafy Surrey. The only son of Lieutenant Colonel Cecil Buck, he'd spent much of his early childhood in India, where his father was serving, before going to Oxford to study politics, philosophy and economics. Prior to the outbreak of war he'd joined the British army and been posted to an Indian regiment, only to have his commanding officer lament the twenty-two-year-old's woeful lack of soldierly capabilities. 'Has not developed military qualities and can hardly be described as a potential cavalry officer,' he complained of the young Buck. 'Of average physique and a thinker rather than a doer.'

If Captain Buck's story was to be believed, he had just proved his former commanding officer very, very wrong.

On 1 February – twenty days previously – Buck had been commanding B and D Companies of the 1st Punjabis, who were dug in around the highway at Derna, a coastal settlement west of Tobruk. Buck also had with him an artillery troop equipped with 25-pounder field howitzers and another with anti-tank guns. A gifted linguist, he spoke numerous Indian languages and was loved by the men of his command.

Buck's orders were to hold the line for twenty-four hours against Rommel's armour, buying the main body of the 4th Indian Division time to retreat to new defensive positions. Despite suffering heavy casualties as Rommel threw waves of tanks and motorized infantry against them, the 1st Punjabis did as they were asked and held firm.

Then at last light on 2 February Buck and his men spied a column of British armour approaching their positions. In the fast-moving battles favoured by Rommel, and with Allied forces falling back on all sides, Buck presumed this was the remnant of a retreating British unit. Radio communications were hit-and-miss at the best of times, and amid the confusion of battle it was little wonder that no one had called through a warning.

In the half-light, by the time Buck and his men realized their mistake it was too late: the uniforms worn by those riding in the – captured – British vehicles were those of the Afrika Korps. Fifteen minutes of intense combat followed, but all was lost. Only one platoon, from Buck's B Company, managed to escape; the rest were captured, wounded or killed.

Buck himself was injured in the fighting and taken prisoner. But he quickly reasoned that what was sauce for the goose was surely sauce for the gander. If the Germans could make like Allied troops to bluff their way through the British lines, surely he could do the same in an effort to escape? Over the next seventy-two hours he watched, eagle-eyed for an opening, warning his men to be ready to rise up and make their getaway.

By acting more seriously injured than he actually was, Buck managed to avoid being included in the first shipment of captives trucked to the POW cages, at Tripoli, 600 miles further away from Allied lines. On the evening of 5 February he teamed up with a highly resourceful would-be fellow escapee, Lieutenant John 'Jock' McKee of the Royal Scots. They were being held in a POW camp built by the Italians, who were fighting alongside the Germans in the battle for North Africa.

As darkness fell, Buck and McKee managed to secure permission to use the wash house. They slipped inside and proceeded to knock out several bricks, opening a hole in the wall that lay adjacent to the camp's perimeter. This consisted of a heavily guarded fence and watchtowers. Buck and McKee timed the sentries' patrols along the perimeter. Immediately after one passed, Buck clambered through the hole in the wall, McKee following. It seemed to take an age, but in the thick darkness they managed to worm their way beneath the wire. They crawled for several minutes, coming upon a road crammed with Italian tanks, but in the night they managed to slip away.

By dawn they were well into the scrub-covered hills, the prelude to the desert proper. McKee had managed to hide a map on his person, which would prove invaluable. Over six days and moving during the hours of darkness, they made their way east-wards, flitting through the hills like ghosts. There were troops everywhere and they were constantly dodging patrols. At one stage they had to dash across an enemy airfield as Allied warplanes rained down bombs, setting the hangars aflame. Here and there they encountered Bedouin tending flocks of sheep. McKee had served in North Africa for several years, and he knew the desert well, speaking basic Arabic. The Bedouin proved friendly, leading the two fugitives to their black-tented camps for rest, food and water.

Finally, they hit a heavily wooded section of the coastal highway. There they lay in hiding, poised to execute the next stage of Buck's audacious plan. They waited until a lone vehicle – a captured Ford truck – came trundling along. Then Buck, clad in clothing scavenged from dead Afrika Korps soldiers – a German waterproof; a leather jerkin; and one of the distinctive Afrika Korps forage caps – stepped forward into the road.

When not in India, Buck had spent much of his childhood being schooled in Germany, and he spoke fluent German. He felt confident that in his attire he would appear like any other Afrika Korps soldier. In his pocket was stuffed a heavy spanner. He flagged down the vehicle. The driver was alone in the cab, which was perfect for what Buck intended.

Pulling his best imperious German officer's act, Buck demanded to see the driver's pass and to know where he was heading. As the man fumbled for his papers, Buck raised the spanner in his pocket to appear like a concealed weapon. Menacing the driver with his 'pistol', he ordered him to dismount. 'Get down from the truck. Down! And don't resist, or it'll end badly for you!'

Bang on cue McKee appeared from behind Buck, a scavenged German rifle levelled at the unfortunate driver. Neither man was a cold-blooded killer. Not yet, anyway. 'There was no point in killing him,' McKee would remark of the hapless driver, 'so we tied him up and left him near the road, where we knew he would be discovered in the morning. For miles we travelled in a German gun convoy and nobody noticed us.'

After covering some fifty miles they pulled over to take stock of their fortunes. The priority now was fuel. If British forces had held firm on the day that Buck and his unit were captured, they would be east of Derna, holding the Gazala–Bir Hacheim line, several hundred miles away. During the retreat dozens of tanks, field howitzers and anti-aircraft guns had been lost, but on their new defensive line Buck's parent unit, the 4th Indian Division, had been bolstered by incoming South African, Polish and Free French troops. He and McKee just had to hope that they had held their positions and halted Rommel's advance.

Buck and McKee resolved to make for the Gazala–Bir Hacheim line, for which they would need a full tank of fuel. They opted to head south on a little-used desert track, aiming to reach a petrol dump that they knew of. But in the course of scouting that location they were spotted and came under a barrage of fire. They were forced to abandon the truck and make their getaway using the cover of some thick scrub.

During the week that followed they collected together an assortment of fellow escapees: there were two officers of the Norfolk Yeomanry, five men from the Welch Regiment (motto Better Death than Dishonour), plus an RAF flight sergeant. Together they now numbered ten, and Buck was determined that all should make good their getaway.

On the evening of 20 February he led the group back to the main coastal road, with highwayman business again in mind. They went to ground some 400 yards east of a German army camp, at a point giving a good view of the route in both directions. At the approach of the first vehicle Buck stepped forward, forage cap pulled low and rifle slung over his shoulder. As luck would have it, he'd pulled over a staff car crammed with Afrika Korps officers. He waved it through: it was too risky and the vehicle too small for their purposes. Then a German truck rumbled out of the darkness. This was more like it.

Buck flagged it down. 'Where are you heading, soldier?' he barked. 'And how many are you?'

'Two, sir, and we're headed that way,' answered the driver, indicating the nearby army camp as his destination.

Excellent, Buck told himself: there was no one else in the rear of the vehicle. He stepped back and raised his rifle. 'Hands up! Get your hands in the air!'

Instantly, McKee and one of the other escapees

appeared at his shoulder, weapons at the ready. The two German soldiers were forced out and the truck was backed off the road, whereupon the remainder of Buck's ad hoc force climbed aboard. Leaving the two Afrika Korps soldiers trussed up and hidden in the scrub, Buck and McKee clambered into the cab, each now sporting items of uniform taken from the truck's previous occupants. It was around 9 p.m. on 20 February when they set off east on the main road, intent on making good their escape. This time they were in luck: the vehicle was carrying a full tank of fuel.

Nine hours later – having bluffed his way through a series of German checkpoints – Buck had made it back to British lines.

Following his epic breakout Captain Henry Cecil Buck would be awarded the Military Cross. The citation would read: 'Captain Buck's escape is remarkable as an example of gallant, consistent and ingenious efforts to get away in spite of tremendous odds, supported by some extraordinary quick-thinking . . . His powers of leadership in this direction were amply displayed when he led his little band of escapers back so gallantly to British territory.'

Buck was recommended for the decoration by Lieutenant Colonel Dudley Clarke of MI9, a department of the War Office established to facilitate the escape of Allied prisoners. Dudley Clarke ran MI9's Middle East section, heading up the top-secret and mysterious Force A, which sought out escapees deep inside enemy-held territory.

Buck's daring and singular escape had brought him to the attention of Dudley Clarke and his Force A people, and this dashing British officer was about to propose one of the greatest deceptions of the entire war. To Buck it was clear that if he could slip out of Axis-controlled territory, a force similarly disguised and blessed with the right linguistic skills and nerve, could slip back in again to wreak all kinds of havoc behind the lines.

The Special Air Service (SAS) and the Long Range Desert Group (LRDG) – the Allies' desert raiders – had to travel hundreds of miles through the hostile interior to launch their hit-and-run attacks. But what if a deception force could be formed, capable of simply driving straight through the German lines? It would require the right combination of daring and bluff, but Buck believed his own escape proved that it was possible.

The key challenge would be to find the right kind of recruits: men with a hatred of the enemy so absolute that it would propel them to undertake what would prove near-suicide missions, for discovery would mean certain death at the hands of the enemy. Plus they would all need to be fluent – ideally native – German speakers. It was a tall order, but as it happened Buck had an idea as to where he might seek out his first recruits.

The previous summer he had been riding in a truck in Palestine, where his Punjabi regiment was undergoing desert training. He'd ordered his driver to stop to pick up two pretty female hitchhikers. One, Leah Schlossberg, was just thirteen years old, but already she was an aficionado of the burgeoning Tel Aviv cultural and music scene. Buck declared a love of opera, and Leah invited him to visit the Schlossbergs' home for tea.

At twenty-five years of age, Buck had already proved himself an accomplished scholar at Oxford. A fine musician and poet, he was so gifted intellectually that at times he could appear reserved and aloof. Even senior officers could appear uneasy in his presence. But those who knew him well could tease him about his somewhat distant manner – a bringing-down-to-earth that he would take well. Plus they knew that when he chose, Buck could be utterly charming.

Leah never actually expected the young British captain to take up her invitation, but offering home hospitality to the Allied forces was very much in vogue right then. A letter arrived at the Schlossbergs', announcing Captain Buck's acceptance of Leah's kind invitation. Her parents were somewhat taken aback. 'Leah, what kind of relationship have you established with this British officer?' they demanded.

Upon calling at the Schlossbergs' home, Buck – known affectionately as Bertie – set about captivating Leah's parents. Well travelled and cosmopolitan – with his love of India and foreign climes, adventure was in his blood – he quickly won them over. He

14

charmed them with his fluency in German, the family's first language, for the Schlossbergs were refugees from the dark predations of Nazi Germany. Jews from Königsberg (now Kalilingrad and in Russian territory), the Schlossbergs had emigrated to Palestine in 1933, immediately after Hitler came power. By doing so they had escaped the horrors that were even then unfolding across the Reich, but not all of their wider family had been so fortunate.

Over the course of his visit Buck took a shine to Aviva, Leah's older sister, although apparently she didn't fall head over heels for him. But he also became intrigued by the unwitting discovery that he had made in picking up the Schlossbergs' hitch-hiking daughter: there were native German speakers resident in the region who had every reason to hate the Nazis with a vengeance. The more he probed, the more Buck realized how extensive their numbers were. Thousands of German Jews had fled to the comparative safety of the British Mandate of Palestine, then under British protection.

Of course, the Jews had not been made entirely welcome, the local Arabs resenting the sudden influx. Conflict had sparked, and the Jews had formed Haganah – Hebrew for 'Defence' – a paramilitary organization that even had a German-speaking section. With the outbreak of war thousands of Jews had signed up with the British military, aiming to strike back at the hated Nazis. There were also numerous German-speaking Czechs,

Poles and other nationals serving with the British. Surely, Buck reasoned, from their number he could muster the deception force that he now had in mind.

Buck was forever restless and searching for new inspiration, forever hatching plans. But he was also a man of action. Beneath his scholarly demeanour there lay a core of steel. His daring escape had given the lie to his former commanding officer's characterization of him: 'a thinker rather than a doer'. Buck was both a thinker *and* a doer, plus he had the raw courage to undertake the founding of a unit that might well prove as terminal for him as for all his recruits.

Rommel had declared his campaign in North Africa '*Krieg ohne Hass*' – a war without hate. The conflict was to be chivalrous and honourable. Buck had been captured and many of his men wounded and killed through an act of deception – an attack with captured British armour to the fore. Chivalrous and honourable this was not. At Oxford he had been a member of the ju-jitsu squad and a champion fencer with the university team – the aptly named Assassins. The warrior tradition ran deep in the Buck family blood.

There was to be no war without hate for him any more.

CHAPTER 2

Went the day well? many might have been forgiven for wondering as they nursed pounding hangovers and worried about what trouble they were in now.

It had all started in the finest of traditions. A blistering 23 August 1942 day in Cairo, it was the custom for this battle-hardened unit to have a last lunch and a few drinks before heading into the unforgiving desert. A final taste of luxury – carousing in the city's noisy bars or the fleshpots of the seedy Berka district – before embracing the weeks of hardship and privation to come.

Whatever one's predilections, Cairo catered admirably for British servicemen on leave. The city's downtown Melody Club boasted the best belly dancers this side of Beirut, who performed on a raised platform protected by barbed wire. In the drinking dens a lady of the night – *bint* in local parlance – would hang on a young soldier's every word, as long as he kept the cherry brandies flowing.

Generally, leave in Cairo was strictly segregated between officers and 'other ranks'. Not so far from the Berka district were a clutch of officer-only institutions: Shepheard's Hotel, the Sporting Club, the Turf Club and the Anglo-Egyptian Union. But today's gathering of desert warriors would observe no such privileges: Winchester-College-educated Captain David Lloyd Owen, their commanding officer, was very much one of the boys.

They'd started drinking in a café adjacent to the Continental Savoy, an arched and pillared edifice of stunning opulence which had hosted T. E. Lawrence before he rose to fame as Lawrence of Arabia. It was an entirely fitting setting for a new generation of desert wanderers such as these. But as the afternoon wore on and the beer flowed, these tough-looking sun-bronzed men with their distinctive keffiyehs – the flowing Arab headdress that their unit, and theirs alone, favoured – got increasingly out of hand.

The first sign of matters going seriously awry had come when the unit mounted their Willys Jeeps and Chevrolet light trucks and set out south-west for their desert oasis headquarters. A traffic light turned red, the convoy juddered to a halt, and a figure at the front cried out that his truck had become bogged in soft sand – a regular occurrence in the furnace of the open desert, but not so common on the busy streets of Cairo.

He vaulted out of his seat, unlashed the sand rails – tough sheets of serrated metal roped to the side of the truck – and launched into the drill for freeing a heavily laden sand-bogged vehicle. From the length of the convoy voices roared a chorus of raucous encouragement: 'Man the sand rails! Man the sand rails!' Normally the sand rails were shoved under the wheels, providing the truck with firm ground upon which to haul itself out of the baking mire – not something that was entirely necessary here in Cairo. Even so Captain David Lloyd Owen couldn't help but be amused.

At just twenty-four years of age Lloyd Owen was younger than many of his men, but he was already vastly experienced. He knew well what lay before them: a top-secret mission of an ilk that had never been tried before, and not even by this unit, the Long Range Desert Group (LRDG), nor their sister outfit, the SAS, who would also be involved.

Indeed, so secret was the operation that only he among his men was privy to its exact nature. Those under his command knew only the very basics: the expected duration of the mission – crucial for packing the vehicles with sufficient supplies – and their supposed destination, the Libyan town of Derna, where there was a busy enemy airbase. But even that was a deliberate falsehood: as Lloyd Owen knew well, they were not heading for Derna at all.

The LRDG and the SAS lived by the mantra of need to know. What a soldier didn't need to know to function properly he would never be told, because what you didn't know you couldn't tell if captured by the enemy. Lloyd Owen's indulgence of his men's high jinks was rooted in what he knew was coming. Creeping past the enemy's southern flank in terrain that was utterly merciless, they would be under constant threat of discovery, death or capture.

The lights changed, and the convoy lurched into motion once more, its occupants cheering wildly. But their capers had drawn the attention of the Allied troops who thronged the streets, attracting the disapproval and envy of many of the more conventionally dressed and rule-bound soldiers. There was an exoticism and romance to these desert warriors that earned them few friends, least of all among the British military high command.

The convoy pressed on, before hitting the area of the Pyramids, on Cairo's southern fringes. As the Ancient Egyptian monuments loomed large, so a collective decision seemed to have been reached: Something Had To Be Done About The Pyramids. On this day these desert warriors were compelled to pay tribute to an ancient civilization that had also gained a certain mastery over the desert.

The first vehicle turned off the main highway, heading directly for the Great Pyramid. As was the patrol's wont, the others followed. In short order the drivers began to execute crazed circuits around the base of the fabulous structures, unleashing volleys of multicoloured Very lights – military flares fired from Very pistols – and girding the Pyramids in fluorescent brilliance.

The spontaneous lightshow was undeniably spectacular. So too was the response from the Military

Police (MPs), who happened to be stationed nearby. The fun and games came to a sudden halt as the enraged redcaps surrounded the LRDG patrol. The commander of the MP unit demanded to know what in God's name was happening.

The initial response came from Lloyd Owen's driver, a diminutive but hard-as-nails former Somerset farmer, who left the redcaps in little doubt as to what he thought of their unwelcome interruption. Just when it looked as if the entire patrol was to be rounded up by truncheon-wielding MPs, Lloyd Owen intervened. He volunteered his rank and explained that he was in charge of the patrol.

The redcap officer fixed Lloyd Owen with a baleful glare. 'What do you think you're *doing*?' he demanded, incredulously. 'And where d'you think you're *going*?'

Lloyd Owen pondered this for a moment, then decided honesty was probably the best option. He jerked a thumb westwards. 'Tripoli. More or less . . .'

The officer's eyes bulged. Tripoli was a thousand miles behind Rommel's front line, then lying at El Alamein, a good way into Egypt itself. Obviously, this unit of hooligans could not be headed for Tripoli, he reasoned, and it was all the more enraging to be lied to. Fuming, he invited Lloyd Owen to join him in his office. Still feeling remarkably well fed and well watered, the LRDG captain did as asked, seemingly without a care in the world.

On one level the officers and men of the LRDG

felt they had little to fear in terms of disciplinary action. They were poised to head into the desert, and no MP was about to follow them there. Indeed, most Allied commanders viewed the Sahara as no fit ground for a professional army. To them the idea of special forces such as the LRDG and SAS ranging far and wide across the desert wastes was an affront to proper soldiering. After all, what made them so special?

The desert warriors were viewed as maverick risk-takers who poached the best men for their private armies. They committed good soldiers and valuable machines to madcap adventures with very little prospect of success. Even worse, these freewheeling units – apparently devoid of proper military order or of discipline – were being unleashed upon the enemy pretty much at will, and operating so far behind the lines as to obviate all forms of formal command or control.

The special forces knew they weren't popular. Without the spirited backing of Winston Churchill, they might well have been disbanded before they had even got properly started. It was only the British prime minister's determination to strike back hard against the Nazis – to 'set the lands of the enemy aflame' – that gave them the where-withal to operate as they did, but even so they knew how insecure was their existence.

By the time Lloyd Owen was released by the MPs and the convoy got under way again, the high spirits were starting to dissipate. Until recently the

LRDG had been based at Siwa, an isolated oasis steeped in history set to the far west of Egypt. Just forty miles short of the Libyan border, Siwa was ideally placed for mounting both recces and hit-and-run offensives against the enemy. It was also the perfect point of return after a long desert patrol. The LRDG operators would dive from ancient stone parapets into Cleopatra's Pool, a deep lagoon of bubbling water where the queen of the Nile herself was said to have bathed. With its magical setting shaded by palm trees, Siwa was utterly captivating. The men had nicknamed it Pollywood, parodying its film-set ambience and walled pools.

But after the recent defeats at the hands of the Afrika Korps, Siwa lay in enemy hands. Instead of heading due west, Lloyd Owen's men had to push south out of Cairo, making for their new base at El Fayyum, a huge depression set in the desert and thick with crops irrigated by the waters of the Nile. Mud dredged from the great river was used to fertilize the fields. Siwa it was not, and the retreat to El Fayyum mirrored the fortunes of the wider British military. Right now Rommel's armoured legions were massed just 150 miles west of Cairo.

The German commander looked set to seize the city itself – Britain's headquarters in North Africa – and an air of panic had set in. The retreating British army was fast losing the respect of the locals. Egypt's reigning monarch, King Farouk, had refused to pledge his loyalty to the British crown, and nervous British officials were burning secret documents, the ash from which rained down like snow upon the streets. If Cairo fell, the Nile Basin and the all-important Suez Canal would follow, an unmitigated disaster for the Allies.

Suez provided a comparatively short sea route for the transport of vital Middle Eastern oil to fuel Britain's ships, tanks and warplanes. It also offered a crucial link to Britain's far-flung colonies – India, Australia and New Zealand among others. In short, the canal was essential to Allied naval superiority. If it were lost, supplies of men, raw materials and fuel would have to be routed via South Africa and the Atlantic, a far longer voyage that was more vulnerable to U-boat attacks.

That was why the Allied line at El Alamein had to hold and Rommel's hitherto lightning advance had to be thrown into reverse. The mission of Lloyd Owen and his men – risky and daring in the extreme though it might be – was a vital part of the wider plan to overturn Rommel's fortunes. Getting arrested for lighting up the Pyramids wasn't perhaps the most auspicious of ways to get started.

By the time the convoy reached El Fayyum, high spirits were fading into hangovers. Throats were parched, eyes squinted against the burning sun and heads were pounding. More to the point, there was a growing sense of unease as to what kind of trouble they might have landed themselves in. They knew that the case of the Very-lighted Pyramids was to be reported to the LRDG's commanding officer, Major Guy Lennox Prendergast.

Major Prendergast had a legendary status among the men. During the inter-war years he had been one of a small band of explorers and adventurers who had mapped the vast wastes of the desert, using the most rudimentary of motor vehicles to do so. At war's outbreak Prendergast and fellow desert explorer Ralph Alger Bagnold had recognized that if the war for North Africa was to be won, the Allies would need to dominate the desert.

Conceiving the idea of the LRDG, they'd fought tooth and nail to bring the unit into being. No one had seemed willing to listen. Then in early 1940 General Archibald Wavell, a craggy-faced veteran of the World War One, had taken over command of the North Africa campaign. Bagnold and Prendergast had explained their plans for the LRDG, which boiled down to behind-the-lines reconnaissance and intelligence-gathering, coupled with 'some piracy on the high desert'.

At the mention of desert piracy, Wavell's stern features had cracked a smile. Within six weeks the LRDG was up and running. Volunteers had answered a call for men 'who do not mind a hard life, scanty food, little water, lots of discomfort, and possess stamina and initiative'. Tough, self-reliant soldiers were recruited, those who would feel at home in the vast desert wilderness.

Countrymen, farmers, gamekeepers, poachers and hunters flocked to the call.

New Zealanders and South Africans seemed peculiarly suited to the harsh rigours of life in the LRDG, as did – rather counter-intuitively – British Guards officers. Of course there were significant compensations. LRDG soldiers had to endure few of the mindless rules, bull and mucking about of regular army life. They were led by men who lived and breathed the desert. For them it held no fear; indeed, they thrilled to its brilliant starlit nights and the cool of a desert dawn.

Bagnold's early plans were for a self-sufficient long-range reconnaissance and raiding unit. 'Every vehicle . . . with a crew of three and a machine gun, was to carry its own supplies of food and water for three weeks, and its own petrol for 2,500 miles of travel across average soft desert surface.' His patrols were to carry 'a wireless set, navigating and other equipment, medical stores, spare parts and further tools'.

General Wavell referred affectionately to the LRDG as his 'mosquito army', pricking and stinging the enemy in the most unexpected and inconvenient of places. Before long they had earned a fearsome reputation among the Italians, the original foe in North Africa before Rommel's forces arrived in theatre. To the Italians they became known as the *pattuglia fantasma* – ghost patrol.

Prendergast was a harsh taskmaster and hugely protective of his creation. Doubtless he would have to do something about the 'Pyramid assault'

26

charges, but the men had every confidence that Lloyd Owen would have their back. They felt certain that he would find a way to shield them from any consequences, most likely by shipping them off for an extended period of desert raiding. One thing seemed certain: getting the hell out of Egypt would do them no end of good right now. It would allow the proverbial dust to settle, and by the time they returned from the coming mission, with luck the incident of the Very-lighted Pyramids would have been forgotten.

Lloyd Owen himself had once come perilously close to being rejected by the LRDG. He'd volunteered as a young captain from the Queen's Royal Regiment, but was judged wholly unsuited to desert soldiering. He had little experience of the terrain, few mechanical or linguistic skills and wasn't familiar with the LRDG's weaponry. Never one to beat about the bush, Prendergast had told him as much, but he had been persuaded to give the young captain a second chance.

Since then Lloyd Owen, known as 'the skipper' to his men, had helped build the LRDG into an outfit that blended the elite warrior spirit with a large dash of maverick derring-do. Their speciality was the beat-up – a shoot-and-scoot attack, striking by surprise from the direction the enemy least expected it and melting away just as rapidly.

In the dark days of summer 1942 the secret exploits of the LRDG – whispered in Cairo bars and across front-line trenches – gave the average

British soldier something to be proud of. They were a huge boost to morale, which was exactly what Churchill had intended of his special forces.

At Fayyum, tired eyes red with partying turned to the distant horizon. A mystery force was supposed to be heading for their base, one that the LRDG were tasked with ferrying deep into the Sahara. Finally they spotted a billowing dust cloud. All were keen, if not a little apprehensive, to lay eyes on their charges: sheepdogs eager to appraise their flock.

'Skipper!' someone called. 'They're coming.'

Lloyd Owen stepped down from his command vehicle, the nearest the LRDG had to a permanent field headquarters. He too studied the horizon. Tall, dark-haired and blessed with rugged good looks, Lloyd Owen was heavily bearded, as were all his men. This alone marked them out as being outsiders; as being 'other'. But it wasn't for effect. With the kind of strictures on water consumption all would soon be facing, they could spare little to wash, let alone shave.

Lloyd Owen cast an indulgent eye around the men of his unit. Dress was largely a matter of personal choice, and many sported items of uniform from their home nation's militaries. Lloyd Owen favoured a battered woollen cap-comforter as headgear – akin to a Commando woolly hat. Others sported pith helmets or wide-brimmed Aussie bush hats, but the vast majority wore the Arab keffiyeh headdress.

Some accused the LRDG of affectation, as if

sporting the keffiyeh was a T. E. Lawrence pose. Certainly, it did mark them out as being different, but it was also an extraordinarily useful piece of kit. Nothing rivalled the keffiyeh's ability to shield a neck from the burning sun, and when the desert wind got up, coruscating sandstorms blasting across the scoured wastes, it could be wrapped around the face to shield exposed skin.

Even so, Lloyd Owen appreciated what kind of initial impression his men tended to make. He was apprehensive about this first meeting. The British military was famously tribal, and two units from very different traditions and cultures were going to have to co-exist in close proximity, over extended periods of hardship and extreme duress.

He stepped forward to where he could receive the commander of the incoming unit. A column of heavy trucks – eight in all – thundered out of the heat haze. They ground to a halt in a strict line, the lead vehicle stopping adjacent to where Captain Lloyd Owen was standing. A figure emerged from the cloud of dust. Tall, crisp, erect – dressed in the spotless tartan of a hodden grey kilt – this was Major Colin Campbell of the London Scottish regiment.

Hodden grey, a tough, coarse dun-grey cloth, had been chosen by the regiment's founder, Lord Elcho, for the following reason: 'A soldier is a man-hunter. As a deer-stalker chooses the least visible of colours, so ought a soldier to be clad.' In the coming days Major Campbell would prove just as tough and unyielding.

Older than most, Campbell was a strict disciplinarian, but he was also iron-willed and indomitable, and a brave and courageous leader. Lloyd Owen was well aware of this: the two had shared each other's company while planning the present mission back in Cairo.

Campbell's force consisted of seventy-seven officers and men, and a hard-looking bunch they were. Bigger than your average soldier, they had the air of an elite fighting unit. All had volunteered for the present mission – described to them only as an extremely hazardous special operation – and the majority were commandos. These were men who could be rough and dangerous when it came to a fight, and they knew it.

Of those who weren't commandos, most hailed from the kind of outfits that needed to be attached to a special operation such as this: signallers, sappers (demolitions experts), gunners and the like. Oddly for a desert mission there was also a detachment of the Special Boat Service (SBS) – the water-borne special forces, and sister unit to the SAS. Why were what amounted to sailors being taken deep into the desert? Not even the SBS unit's commander, Lieutenant Thomas 'Tommy' Bennett Langton, knew the answer to that. It was just one of the many mysteries surrounding the present mission.

Langton, a square-jawed Cambridge rowing blue, was a towering giant of a man and a veteran of numerous behind-the-lines seaborne raids. An accomplished sportsman prior to the war, his first love was rowing, but he'd also boxed at a good standard, was a fine swimmer and had played rugby at club level. Langton had studied law and was working as a barrister when war was declared. The twenty-six-year-old had signed up for officer training in the Irish Guards, but he'd soon tired of regular soldiering and had volunteered for the commandos.

Posted to North Africa, he'd fallen in with David Stirling and others of a like mind, and had been recruited into special forces. He'd gone on to win a mention in dispatches in 1942 for a seaborne raid on one of Rommel's key ports. More recently, Langton had been ordered to hang on to the rear rail of a speeding motor torpedo boat (MTB) and lob sticky grenades – an explosive device covered in glue and encased in a removable metal casing – onto enemy barges. On paper the mission was a fine idea. In practice the mines had tended to stick to Lieutenant Langton as much as they had to the targets. It was a miracle that he had escaped with his life.

Despite his rank and battle-experience, Langton knew precious little about the coming mission. But one thing was clear: this was a bespoke force, one that their commanders had put together for a very specific task.

Lloyd Owen shook hands with Major Campbell, and the two men turned towards the command vehicle, heading for a chat in the shade. The commandos, meanwhile, did what they always did when there was nothing obvious to do. From each truck a can of sand was produced, doused in petrol and set alight, so that the men could boil water to brew tea.

As they supped their brews the two forces – LRDG and commandos – eyed each other warily, each weighing up the other. The commandos wondered what good this scrawny, scruffy, unshaven bunch might be in a fistfight. For their part, the men of the LRDG wondered how these big, beefy commandos with their cumbersome three-ton army trucks might fare once they hit the first of the burning desert sands.

As commandos tended to, these ones cherished their identity, and they were immensely proud of the war record of their unit. They wore their crisp uniforms, berets and cap badges with unabashed pride. But in truth the unit they hailed from had only survived due to an eleventh-hour reprieve, one delivered by the personal intervention of Winston Churchill himself. Their original units, 50 and 51 Commandos – known collectively as the Middle East Commando – were sadly no more.

In July 1940, as Britain had stood isolated and besieged, Churchill had called for the creation of irregular fighting units to take the war to the enemy. The men of 50 and 51 Commandos – all volunteers – were some of the first to respond to that call, being sent to North Africa to combat the growing menace from Italy. Mussolini had poured over half a million troops into the region, whereas Britain's General Wavell had an army of 50,000. The Italians also boasted a fast and modern navy and a well-equipped air force. On paper Wavell barely stood a chance.

The commandos had been dispatched to even up the odds a little. As matters transpired, Wavell drove the Italians back into the sea, with the commandos playing a leading role in a series of lightning victories. But then had come the Desert Fox, with his Afrika Korps and his panzers, and a complete reversal of Allied fortunes had followed.

In the intense fighting the commandos had suffered terrible losses, their ranks being decimated. Cairo headquarters responded by disbanding the Middle East Commando, but not on Churchill's watch. When the British premier learned of their fate, he'd ordered the unit reformed, but now under the direct command of the Special Operations Executive (SOE).

A 5 April 1942 'Most Secret' memo decreed that Middle East Commando would become a 'fifth-column organization under SOE'. They would specialize in 'all forms of subversive or sabotage work, in or out of uniform, in territories occupied by the enemy, or, in certain circumstances, neutral territory . . . Parties to be in disguise or uniform according to circumstances.' In one fell swoop Churchill had removed the Commando from top brass predations and wrangling, freeing them up to do the utterly unexpected.

'How wonderful it would be if the Germans could be made to wonder where they were going to be struck next,' he had declared in early 1940. Shortly thereafter he'd formed the Ministry for Economic Warfare – a cover name for the Special Operations Executive. SOE was charged with doing the unthinkable, making 'stabbing attacks . . . between the chinks of the enemy's military and economic armour'. Sabotage of every sort was to be the order of the day. Shadowy, deniable and secretive, the SOE would become known as the 'fourth armed service', hiding its activities behind a series of cover names, including the innocuous-sounding Inter-Services Research Bureau, the Firm and perhaps most suitably the Racket.

From the very first the SOE was charged with overturning every known and accepted principle of warfare. Churchill's first minister in charge of this new outfit was Dr Hugh Dalton, a Labour member of his coalition government. Despite their differences in politics, Dalton rose to Churchill's challenge, keen to consider any means of striking back at the enemy, no matter how unorthodox.

'We have to organize movements in enemy occupied territory comparable to the Sinn Fein movement in Ireland . . .' he declared. 'We must use many different methods, including industrial and military sabotage . . . terrorist acts against traitors and German leaders . . . We need absolute secrecy, a certain fanatical enthusiasm, and willingness to work with people of different nationalities.' The force now brewing tea in El Fayyum oasis had been formed in that image.

The commandos had retained their unit designation, 'partly as cover and partly because the prime minister wanted the name "Commando" to continue'. In keeping with the SOE's mandate, their coming mission with the LRDG would break every known and accepted rule of warfare. Not that any among them – barring Lloyd Owen and Campbell – knew that yet.

They were in the dark, and for now at least it was very much better kept that way.

CHAPTER 3

It was hard to tell who resented whom the most, or on which side resided the greatest suspicion. While the commandos were an elite unit, they were steeped in the traditions of smartness, rank and military formality. They had little experience of the deep desert, and even less familiarity with the informal, bearded, Homeric *esprit de corps* of the LRDG.

The LRDG were the unchallenged lords of the Sahara. The bone-dry wastes were their domain and they did not welcome trespassers. There were moments when this legendary unit did seem to deliberately dramatize their otherness and their feeling of superiority over all who wandered into their realm. They were also protective of their hard-earned reputation. Events shortly after leaving Fayyum were set to prove their concerns well founded, or so Lloyd Owen's men would argue.

There was an undeniable mismatch between the two units' vehicles. The LRDG used the 30-hundredweight (1.5 ton) Chevrolet pickup as their ship of the desert, a very different beast to the commandos' 3-ton army trucks. Two-wheel drive only, the Chevy was relatively light and fast and not too greedy on the juice, which was crucial when traversing thousands of miles of desert. On the LRDG-adapted models, its curved bonnet and graceful lines were augmented by machine guns and heavier weapons mounted in the cab and on the pickup-style rear.

Once the LRDG crossed into enemy territory, they needed to be poised to fight at the drop of a hat: enemy warplanes might swoop from the skies at any second, and German or Italian patrols might appear. The Chevrolets were their mobile gun platforms, and restraints both of combat and of load-carrying meant that they were only ever crewed by three people: two riding in the cab and one – the lead gunner – in the rear. Loaded to the gunwales, the Chevys could carry two tons of petrol, ammo, explosives, food, water and personal supplies. But even thus burdened they were far faster, less crowded and more nimble than the commandos' overloaded and cumbersome army trucks.

It was the morning of 24 August 1942 when the combined force departed from El Fayyum, and the LRDG vehicles promptly shot off ahead. There was only one road to follow south along the bank of the Nile, so there was little chance of their charges getting lost or otherwise coming to grief. In fact, trouble was soon coming.

Not an hour into the journey, a commando officer decided to take a turn behind one of the trucks' wheels. The road ran along a raised embankment. In a momentary lapse of concentration the officer lost control of his vehicle, which mounted the kerb and crashed down the far side.

The entire convoy ground to a halt, as men rushed to the scene to discover what had happened. The hapless truck was lying on its side in an irrigated field, wheels spinning crazily and with its load strewn into the thick, clinging mud. Those who'd been riding in the rear hauled themselves out of the mire, cursing furiously. By some miracle no one had been killed, but the truck was done for.

They salvaged what kit they could, and the men and materiel were crammed aboard the remaining vehicles, which were now more crowded than ever. It was day one of their journey and already this had happened. But these men were commandos and they'd seen countless vehicles shot to shreds, bombed and torched in previous battles. They shook themselves down, scooped off the mud as best they could and got under way again.

A little later the convoy juddered to a halt: time for a tea break. As the oil-drum burners were broken out, a curious incident unfolded on the banks of one of the nearby irrigation channels.

A massive, barrel-chested bear of a man was seated beside the water, separate and brooding. He took something out of the pocket of his drill shorts. For a second he hefted it in the palm of his hand, before hurling it far into the water. He

removed a second item and repeated the performance. More objects were thrown. It turned out that
they were keys with large brass fobs attached, of the
type you generally only find in hotels. For some
reason the mystery soldier was hurling a collection
of hotel keys into a tributary of the Nile.

It was only after the final one was thrown that
the morose figure – who wore the uniform of a
lieutenant – seemed to shake himself out of his
dark reverie. He rose to his feet to discover that
he had attracted a small audience, mainly of
fellow officers.

He glanced around defiantly. 'What a bloody
stupid thing war is!' With that he turned and
stalked away.

Only one explanation made any sense: most
likely, each key was a keepsake from the room in
which the mystery lieutenant had entertained his
sweetheart. Now he was heading into the desert's
uncertain embrace, having been forced to leave
his love behind. This was his last goodbye.

It was late afternoon by the time the depleted
convoy of trucks pulled into the small settlement
of El Minya, a cluster of mud-walled houses lying
beside the palm-fringed Nile. In spite of the
mishap, the commandos had covered some 200
miles, each turn of the wheels taking them further
from Cairo and deeper into the heart of the African
continent. At around 4,300 miles the Nile is the
world's longest river, and if they chose to follow

it all the way south it would take them deep into east Africa, to its source in Lake Victoria. But shortly after El Minya the entire force would swing west, away from the beckoning Nile and into the waterless wastes of the desert.

As the 3-tonners rumbled into town a waiting Chevy pulled out of the shadow of a high wall and took up the lead. The LRDG vehicle weaved through the narrow streets, before coming to a halt in a yard surrounded by large, hangar-like buildings. But this was no military installation; it was a cotton mill, and the commandos were told to bed down among the soft bales of cotton.

But not just yet; first there was to be a party. As if by magic crates of ice-cold beer materialized, plus dishes of local fare that were a far cry from British army rations. Cheers went up as the commandos got busy. Whoever this LRDG bunch might be, they certainly seemed to be well connected and to know how to live in Africa!

The officers were taken to a white-walled colonial-style villa, set on the banks of the Nile. This, it turned out, was the residence of one Lieutenant Colonel John Edward Haselden, of the Intelligence Corps and the SOE, a man whose reputation went before him. Haselden had already won the first of two Military Crosses he would earn during the war, for a solo operation deep behind the lines.

He'd win his second MC partly as a result of Operation Flipper, a November 1941 mission to assassinate General Erwin Rommel. In Op Flipper a team of commandos had been dropped by submarine off the Libyan coast, and guided into the beach by Haselden, who had already spent weeks on the ground disguised as a local, gathering intelligence. As matters transpired they failed to nail Rommel, but that took nothing away from what was a gallant and daring undertaking.

Not by coincidence, sticky-grenade-wielding Lieutenant Tommy Langton had been one of the SBS assault party on Operation Flipper. Right now, Langton was part of the present mission because Haselden had asked for him specifically. He needed Langton to perform a very specific and vital part in the coming action. Although few of the men gathered at El Minya yet knew it, their present mission was largely of Haselden's conceiving.

The Haselden family had spent three generations in Egypt, growing cotton along the Nile. Though his final years of schooling were at King's School, Canterbury, John Haselden had grown up mostly in Egypt, and he spoke Arabic like a native. Tall, strong and charismatic, Haselden's English father had married an Italian beauty called Maria Ester Cazzani. John had inherited her dark complexion and deep brown eyes. He was one of the few Englishmen in this war who could pass as an Arab, making him perfectly suited to behind-the-lines intelligence-gathering.

Wearing local clothes, he could pass from one Arab encampment to another without the Germans or Italians suspecting anything. He seemed to thrive on the raw danger of such missions. On one occasion he'd resorted to driving a flock of goats across an aerodrome, to get a closer look. He'd calmly paced out the airstrip's dimensions as the Italian guards gazed in bemusement upon an apparently foolish Arab shepherd.

On more than one occasion Lloyd Owen had been charged to take out an LRDG patrol to collect Haselden from some deep-desert mission. The two men were close, and Lloyd Owen had come to think of Haselden as possessing an almost mythical invincibility. Haselden, he believed, could thrive in terrain that would kill any other man. Like many gathered at the villa, he would follow the thirty-nine-year-old lieutenant colonel into the very jaws of hell, if called upon to do so.

As Haselden hosted tonight's dinner, which was served in the beautiful villa gardens at long tables clad in linen, the esteem the locals held him in was clear. When he passed by they prostrated themselves and tried to kiss his hand or his jacket hem. Yet Haselden remained courteous and humble, speaking kindly to everyone no matter who they might be.

Even in the official history of the War Cabinet – itself a secret account and hardly known for hyperbole – Haselden is described as 'a very remarkable man with a great influence over the Desert Arabs'. Known to some as the 'Lawrence of World War Two', he was an extraordinary figure even among the party now assembled. He served with an outfit known only as G(R), which was in truth the specialist raiding department of the SOE.

There was a power struggle presently under way over the special forces units. Much as the military high command might resent the desert raiders their freewheeling existence, they weren't keen to fully relinquish command and control. At the same time the SOE were courting the raiders assiduously, but seeking to draw them into ever darker and more Machiavellian undertakings – the present mission being one of the first such operations.

The officers now gathered at Haselden's dinner tables included some of the finest the British Isles had to offer. Tartan-clad Major Campbell's second in command was Lieutenant Graham Taylor of the Wiltshire Regiment. Taylor had himself received training from the masters of desert warfare – the New Zealand section of the LRDG. Forceful, aggressive and impatient for action, he was ideal commando material.

Third in command was Lieutenant Hugh Davidson Sillito, originally of the Argyll and Sutherland Highlanders and another man resplendent in tartan. The kilted Sillito was known to be recklessly brave in combat, but there was a charm to him and a depth of intellect that came to the fore when away from the battlefield.

Second Lieutenant William 'Mac' MacDonald was one of the real characters of the Commando. A New Zealander, Mac had travelled the world and battled Franco's fascist forces during the Spanish Civil War. MacDonald fought from the heart for the things he believed in, and stopping the march of Nazism was at the very top of his list right now.

Lieutenant M. 'Trolly' Trollope, of the Royal Corps of Signals, was the unit's chief signaller. A descendant of the Victorian novelist Anthony Trollope, Trolly was a character to rival MacDonald, if for no other reason than the utter strangeness of his being there at all. Trollope hated the desert, wilted in the sun, expressed no burning desire to fight and yet had *volunteered* for this special mission. He cheerfully admitted that he had no idea what he was doing with the commandos. At every possible juncture he'd jam a wide-brimmed hat onto his head and attempt to get out of the sun, but he never complained and would prove a huge boost to morale.

In contrast to Trolly, Lieutenant Hugh 'Bill' Barlow – a hulking artillery officer – thrilled to the open wastes and luxuriated in the desert heat. He'd spent two years fighting his way back and forth across North Africa, and he seemed most at home when in the midst of combat. A giant of a man who hated his birth name – hence the adopted 'Bill' – he was another larger-than-life character. Though they would never accuse him to his face, some suspected Barlow of being the officer seen hurling hotel keys into the Nile.

The commandos' medic was an equally

distinctive individual. Tall, mustachioed and with a quick, dry sense of humour, Captain John Gibson hailed from the Royal Army Medical Corps and was of Canadian origin. A stunningly cool customer under fire, Gibson was to earn a certain infamy among the men for the quirkiness of his supposed medicinal cures.

On that balmy late evening the diners gazed out over the Nile, as local musicians serenaded their last night of luxury. An army of servants brought one rich dish after another. Midnight boating on the Nile rounded off an evening of high spirits tainted by a certain poignancy. Here was so much water, but all knew they were poised to disappear into an arid hell.

Back in the cotton sheds the other ranks were draining the last of their beers. By far the most physically imposing – indeed, the biggest man in the entire Commando – was the squadron sergeant major (SSM), Arthur Swinburn. Typical of his breed, Swinburn was a grim-faced disciplinarian who looked aghast at the men of the LRDG. To him they were a bunch of ruffian pirates, even if they could rustle up chilled beers and fine food in the midst of the bush. With his smart slicked-back hair, protruding ears and prominent nose, Swinburn believed that Major Campbell was the finest, most upstanding officer he had ever had the good fortune to serve under. The two men shared a certain unbending constancy and austere fortitude. But even Swinburn had a secret, softer side: he fancied himself as a something of a trombonist.

There were five other sergeants in the Commando, including the quick-witted and steadfast Paddy O'Neill, from Tipperary in Ireland. Then there were the junior ranks, who hailed from the length and breadth of the British Isles. Men like Allardyce of the London Scottish, a rugby player of international repute; the gnarled, war-bitten figure of Hogan of the Irish Guards; or Ted Ashford, who was the spitting image of Clarke Gable, the 1940s king of Hollywood, but a whole lot tougher.

Major Campbell could not have wished for a finer bunch of men to lead into battle. Often troublesome around camp, they had volunteered for hazardous duties in part to escape the rigours of regular army discipline. Rowdy in a Cairo bar, bad boys after a few too many beers, they were exactly the kind of material his Special Operations Executive Commando called for.

Early the following morning the entire force of commandos and LRDG mounted their vehicles. Most had presumed that their host Lieutenant Colonel Haselden would be joining their number, but no such luck; he was there only to bid them farewell. This was more than a little curious, for he'd seemed to exude such a natural sense of command over, if not ownership of, the mission.

All morning the convoy nosed south on a dirt track that hugged the meandering course of the

Nile. But when they reached the riverside settlement of Asyut, Captain Lloyd Owen signalled the vehicles to leave the road. Following his lead they took to a minor track that snaked through bush and scrub, the calm serenity of the Nile soon being left behind them. At first spirits among the commandos soared: at last they had turned towards the direction of the enemy. It felt as if the mission proper had begun. But the going quickly worsened. Soon they were jolting along a barely visible track, deep ruts carved into the mud set hard as concrete by the burning sun.

Conditions were worst for the commandos, who were perched atop piles of kit in the open-backed army trucks. As the heavy vehicles rocked wildly, the cargo worked free from its lashings and crashed about on the smooth metal floors. Holding on for dear life while trying to prevent the heavier loads breaking free proved tough and exhausting work.

This was the beginning of the Asyut–Dakhla leg of their journey, which would take them 200 miles south-west and deep into the wilds of the Egyptian desert. They were now following a track that camel trains had used for millennia, and as Lloyd Owen's men knew well, this was actually fairly good going. Compared to what lay beyond the Dakhla oasis, they were having it relatively easy right now. Although marked out by the passage of myriad camels' feet, in places the desert sand had encroached upon the track, obliterating it completely. At those moments the commando drivers were wholly reliant upon the men of the LRDG, keeping about 500 yards in front and scouting the way ahead.

The heavily laden army trucks proved as cumbersome over such terrain as the LRDG's Chevys were nimble. It wasn't long before the first got bogged down in one of the patches of soft, clinging sand. Everyone had been briefed on the procedure should this happen: no vehicle was to stop and help, for to do so invited disaster. Keeping up momentum was the key to not getting mired. It was up to the immobilized vehicle's occupants – in this case ten young and muscle-bound commandos – to dig and shove the errant truck free.

As the sweating commandos laboured under the merciless sun, they began to have a new appreciation for the force shepherding them across the desert. It was well known that LRDG patrols regularly crossed thousands of miles of such terrain, which right now seemed nigh-on impossible. Shovelling sand and shoving heavy trucks was exhausting, mind-numbing work, made all the worse by the raging thirst that each was developing.

As soon as they'd turned into the desert proper, the men of the Commando had been put on to desert water rations, which amounted to just a few pints per man per day. In such heat and under such conditions it was nowhere near enough, but there was a resolute stoicism about the commandos and no one bitched or complained.

Shockingly, it was the iron-willed Major Campbell who seemed to be suffering the most. It soon became clear that his malaise was no normal reaction to the exertions and the desert sun. The major appeared to be seriously sick. He was displaying worrying signs of dysentery, an infection of the intestines causing bloody diarrhoea.

The LRDG had learned to master the desert by bending to its ways. No one had ever conquered it and no one ever would. The dark fate that befell those who tried was typified by the story of the lost army of Cambyses. Cambyses II was a member of the Persian Achaemenid dynasty. Around 550 BC, in an effort to expand his empire, he'd led an army of 50,000 men to capture the Siwa oasis – the LRDG's erstwhile base. According to the Greek historian Herodotus, he'd marched his men halfway across the desert before a massive sandstorm blew up. Cambyses' entire army died of thirst or were buried alive.

Explorers have searched in vain for the lost army in the centuries since they met their grisly fate. Wherever they may have perished, the LRDG had no desire to join them or to lead the commandos to a similar doom, which was why desert survival discipline was like a religion to these men. The rules governing water use were set down in the logbook – the desert survival bible – that each LRDG patrol carried.

'The summer water ration (for all purposes, including radiators) is one gallon per man per day

. . . Except when camping at a waterhole, no extra water is available for cooking purposes. Tinned food is heated up by standing the tins in the water used for making tea. The period of actual boiling must be reduced to an absolute minimum in order to save water.' Eight pints of water were allocated to each man per day, but that ration also had to be used for topping up the Chevys' radiators when required.

'Rapid drinking during the heat of the day must be avoided,' the logbook continued. 'Nearly all the water is merely thrown off again in excessive perspiration . . . Moistening the mouth and throat lessens the first cravings . . . No water will ever be drawn from any drinking water container except at regular issue times under the supervision of an officer . . .' Water discipline informed every action, even down to how to clean eating utensils. 'The intense dryness causes food remains, especially syrup from tinned fruit, tea dregs, etc. to solidify so much that it has to be chipped off. All utensils used for food must be cleaned in sand (drifts of blown sand, not the dried clay of the desert floor) immediately after use.'

Not drinking even when parched with thirst; scrubbing dirty plates in a handful of desert sand; heating tinned food in the water used to brew their precious tea – to the commandos, this was sacrilege. It was as if they had stepped into an alien land, but to the men of the LRDG this was the norm and the absolute key to survival.

Yet even the experienced could still get caught out in the desert. Fierce swarms of hornets – giant wasps with debilitating stings – stalked the hot air. If a leading vehicle unwittingly disturbed a nest, the swarm would set upon those that followed. Vehicle sumps could be damaged by rocks that lurked beneath the surface of soft sand. It was how the men adapted to and overcame such challenges that marked them out as special. On one occasion an LRDG jeep hit a boulder, ramming the sump up into the crankshaft. The patrol's vehicle mechanic calmly removed the sump, hammered out the dent and sealed the cracks by soldering on a flattened-out tin of peaches that he'd just finished eating.

In addition to the heat, the thirst, the dust and the mind-numbing exertion, the commandos had much else to learn if they were to master desert warcraft. Lloyd Owen called a halt that first evening and drew the assembled party in close. Though they were still many miles from hostile territory, the newcomers needed to be ready. Here in the open desert a column of dust could mean only one of two things, Lloyd Owen explained: either a fellow LRDG or SAS patrol on the move, or the enemy. If it was the latter, the trucks of the Commando were to keep moving, but head directly away from the threat, leaving the LRDG to engage their adversaries. Lloyd Owen and his men would buy the commandos some time. They could always follow their tracks and catch up with them later.

The LRDG's Chevys packed a serious punch. On the passenger side of the cab was fixed a machine gun – commonly a .303 Lewis – while on the rear of the pickup a heavier weapon – a .5-inch Browning machine gun or a water-cooled Vickers .5 – was mounted on a pivot, giving all-round firepower. One of the favourite weapons was the Vickers K .303 machine gun, mounted in pairs. The Vickers K had been retired from service with the RAF, and the LRDG and SAS had taken as many of the hand-me-downs as they could. The rapid-firing weapons could deliver devastating broadsides, especially when loaded with a mixture of standard ball, armour-piercing and tracer rounds.

To accommodate such a weight of weaponry, the standard Chevy had been pared down to the bare minimum. Windscreens, roofs, front wings, doors and even driving mirrors were removed. Specially designed condensers were fitted to the radiators to recycle evaporating water. The suspension was strengthened and brackets were fitted on the vehicle's sides to carry the 5-foot sand ladders.

Two vehicles in each twelve-vehicle patrol also sported a heavier weapon. In February 1941 British forces had overrun the Italian positions at Beda Fomm, on Libya's eastern coast. There they had captured scores of Breda 20-millimetre cannons, a highly effective anti-armour weapon with a comparatively fast rate of fire. Any number of these had been grabbed by the LRDG, whose 'gun trucks' now boasted rear-mounted Bredas. When a Breda was fired from a Chevy, the recoil was so powerful that it could lift the wheels off the ground. It offered the LRDG a real defence against German armour and limited protection from their warplanes.

Yet it was from the air that the LRDG – and now too the Commando – remained most vulnerable. Dust clouds could be seen for miles, drawing hostile aircraft to investigate. The standard operating procedure if set upon from the air was to disperse in as many different directions as possible, relying upon speed and mobility to escape, vehicles jinking and swerving to avoid the enemy's fire. Only in extremis should they stand and fight.

Once the sun dips below the horizon, the open, bare terrain of the desert can become bitterly cold. Day one of their journey proper complete, the commandos bedded down on the hard sand beside their vehicles. They were starting to appreciate just what they were getting into. It would be a miracle if the burning heat, raging thirst or the freezing nights didn't kill them, let alone marauding enemy warplanes.

Their target – whatever it might be – had never felt so far from their grasp.

CHAPTER 4

Day two of the desert journey would find
the convoy swinging due west at the
remote Kharga oasis, the most isolated of
Egypt's five desert oases, but only if the LRDG's
navigation was spot on. Finding the correct track
among the many that crisscrossed the desert was
like searching for the proverbial needle in a
haystack.

The LRDG navigated by a method known as
dead reckoning. Every man in a patrol had to
master the technique, for it could prove a matter
of life and death in such conditions. Again, the
LRDG logbook outlined in detail how it was to
be done, stressing that navigation was each and
every soldier's personal responsibility.

'One NCO is responsible for noting the compass
bearings and speedometer readings and for
keeping the course plotted on the map . . . It is
very important that every man should know how
to use the sun compass should his truck become
separated from the main patrol. He should be
able to note bearing and distance . . . and know
the speedometer correction of his vehicle.'

At its most basic, dead reckoning involved noting the distance travelled on a certain bearing at a certain speed, and plotting that on the relevant map. For this the so-called sun compass was vital. Consisting of a vertical spike set at the centre of a calibrated dial, direction was indicated by wherever the spike's shadow fell, with an adjustment for the sun's movement throughout the day. With a sun compass bolted to each Chevy's dash, accurate bearings could be taken on the move, whereas a traditional magnetic compass would be thrown off true by the metal of the vehicle.

Ease of navigation was dictated by the terrain. On the rare occasion when a patrol was traversing *serir* – smooth, hard-packed gravel plain – a dead-straight course could be maintained and navigation was relatively easy. But most time would be spent crawling over broken ground or weaving around dramatic formations of wind-sculpted rock and towering sand dunes.

The strict discipline of desert navigation had to be maintained no matter what. These wilderness warriors had to endure incredible physical hardship, coupled with the psychological stress of a level of isolation and loneliness few British soldiers ever experienced. Desert operations meant weeks and weeks away from civilization or the company of others. It meant living in sweat-soaked, stinking clothing and rarely washing or shaving.

It meant long days exposed to the Saharan sun in open-topped vehicles – days in which the mind-numbing monotony might be punctuated at any moment by savage bursts of combat. It meant always keeping alert to one's location, and mastering complex navigational formulae, when the sun-addled brain craved nothing more than mindless stupor and oblivion.

It meant trying to keep alert to danger despite the stultifying heat. It meant enduring companions whose company had seriously started to grate. But most of all it meant suffering the all-consuming, agonising torture that was a constant companion of such desert warfare: thirst. The rarely satiated craving for water sapped energy, spirits, resolve and morale like nothing else.

And now the commandos were being exposed to the same debilitating privations. The experience must have come as a real shock, and the LRDG veterans worried about how their charges would cope.

Long periods of boredom and hardship, interspersed with the odd bloody bout of violence: that was the life of a desert warrior. Lloyd Owen's last mission reflected the harsh realities of such work. It had involved five weeks of torturous desert travel, followed by two of 'road watch' – lying prone on a ridgeline observing the movement of enemy traffic on the main coastal highway, and radioing back detailed reports, down to the number and types of vehicles seen. Secreted just a few hundreds yards from the Afrika Korps' main resupply artery, the slightest movement might spell discovery or death. Road watch, maintained unbroken by a rotating roster of LRDG patrols, was the most reviled of missions.

Of course they understood that this was vital intelligence for drawing up a picture of Rommel's strength, but it was still a fearful, crushingly monotony. And in truth none of them appreciated the extraordinary, war-changing work they were doing. The real purpose of road watch concerned the Allies' highest level of security classification possible: 'Ultra'. Ultra covered the single greatest Allied secret during the war – the work of Bletchley Park in breaking the German's codes.

Since the spring of 1940 the British had been intercepting and decrypting the Third Reich's most sensitive coded messages. This extraordinary breakthrough afforded Allied commanders 'the unique experience of knowing not only the precise composition, strength and location of the enemy's forces, but also, with few exceptions, of knowing beforehand exactly what he intended to do'. Knowledge of Ultra was restricted to the prime minister, key generals and senior intelligence figures.

German signals were encoded upon the Enigma machine, an encryption device that resembled an oversized semi-electric typewriter. A wonderful piece of technology perfected prior to the war, Enigma relied upon a series of wheels, rotors and drums, coupled with complex electronic circuitry, to churn out thousands and thousands of unique ciphers. It was fast, efficient and reliable: messages could be encoded within a matter of seconds and spirited across the airwaves. Its codes were so complex as to be utterly unbreakable, or so the Germans and their Italian and Japanese allies believed.

But at Bletchley Park, to the west of London, a team of cryptologists, mathematical wizards, linguists and others had worked feverishly to achieve the impossible. Gradually they had broken the Enigma codes. Yet in North Africa Ultra had not yielded the victories that Churchill and his generals had hoped for, and one of the main reasons for this was Erwin Rommel.

In his eternal struggle with Berlin for greater resources, Rommel had deliberately sent pessimistic reports regarding his strength in armour, fuel, ammunition and troops. He had consistently put forward his worst case, gambling it would win him more men and supplies. But in doing so he had unwittingly deceived the British as to his true strength, which had led the cryptologists to worry. Had they somehow got their code-breaking wrong? Or was the enemy feeding them a diet of subtle but battle-changing misinformation? And if so, had Ultra backfired in such a way that it was being used against them? In short, had the Germans somehow rumbled Ultra and turned it against the Allies?

The answer to such questions lay in the LRDG's road watch. Its real objective – the one that could not speak its name – was to verify Ultra. If the actual numbers of war machines and troops moving on the main highway could be married up with the Bletchley intercepts, then the code-breakers could be relieved of their gnawing fears, and Churchill and his generals with them.

That was exactly what Lloyd Owen and his ilk were there to provide: *verification.* Of course, he and his men knew nothing of Enigma, Bletchley Park or Ultra. To their way of thinking road watch was a mind-numbing, if necessary, chore. It was not until long after the war that their success in authenticating Ultra was finally revealed.

By contrast to road watch, their present mission with the SOE Commando offered the chance of real adventure and action.

Having successfully navigated the convoy through the low-lying basin of the Kharga oasis, Lloyd Owen steered a hard right – making due west for Dakhla, their first significant milestone and stop-over. With the approach of evening, he drew the vehicles into an isolated wadi – a dry watercourse – in which he had on occasion camped before. The LRDG men slipped into their evening leaguer routine, prior to which no one could break for rest or a meal.

Truck commanders checked their vehicles' vital statistics – fuel, water and stores – and reported these to the patrol headquarters. Gunners stripped, cleaned and oiled the vehicle-mounted machine guns, which would be full of a long day's drive of dirt and grime. They double-checked their position with the patrol navigator's dead reckoning: his map was tacked up somewhere convenient for all to see. Then they triple-checked by taking a reading from the stars.

Meanwhile the radio operator was firing up the wireless, which was mounted in a side compartment of the signals vehicle – raising Cairo headquarters was always something of a challenge. And while all this was going on all hands were prepared to make the fastest possible getaway in case of trouble.

Radio operators were in high demand and were attached to whichever patrol needed them. One of the youngest in the LRDG was nineteen-year-old Jack Mann. Schooled outside Britain, Mann had a gift for languages, including German and Italian. Originally he'd been recruited to infiltrate Italian POW camps posing as an Italian prisoner, so as to listen in on gossip and glean intelligence. But he'd pointed out that his Italian wasn't fluent and his cover would soon be blown.

Instead he'd volunteered to join the ranks of the desert raiders. He found the LRDG a truly international brigade. From a Welshman Mann had learned to sing hymns in Welsh, and from a Russian he'd learned to speak Russian. He faced one problem in the unit. Unlike most of the LRDG, the youthful Mann had found it impossible to grow a proper beard.

'Put some chicken shit on it,' one of the veterans

had joked. 'It'll grow thick as a bush.' Mann still couldn't muster a beard, so he'd compensated by growing his hair 'thick as a bush' instead. 'We could be out on operations for weeks on end,' Mann remarked, 'and of course we had no barbers.'

In the LRDG he learned 'the value of total self-reliance, plus the value of your fellow raiders . . . who quickly became your closest mates'. The radio operator had to erect a pair of twelve-foot poles between which to sling antennae. In theory this would provide a 1,000-mile-plus range, more than enough for reaching Cairo. But securing a connection could be hugely time-consuming and left the patrol vulnerable to detection.

'We had to send all messages in Morse, never in voice,' Mann explained. 'With messages being doubly encoded, this took real time and effort to get right. All codes can be broken, but the theory was by the time the Germans had cracked a double-encoded cipher signal sent in Morse, we would be long gone.'

Rommel appreciated that the vast distances that the desert war was being fought over meant radio communications were the key to battlefield supremacy. He described the radio as 'a medium as dangerous as it was valuable, and the British used it more carelessly than ever'. He'd ensured that the Afrika Korps had a highly effective signals intercept and direction-finding unit – the Nachrichten Fern Aufklärung Kompanie 621, or NFAK 621 for short.

The superbly efficient and technologically accomplished NFAK 621 stripped the Allied signals from the air, and fed them back to Rommel, giving him a fingertip feel for strategy and battle. The men of NFAK 621 referred to themselves as the Circus, due to the gaggle of nondescript busses and radio trucks they operated. Civilian vehicles commandeered mostly in France, they looked nothing like the rest of Rommel's very businesslike Afrika Korps transport. Among the unit's number were scores of fluent English speakers, who scoured the airwaves for the juiciest snippets.

But on 10 July 1942 a surprise attack by Australian troops overran the Circus. In fierce fighting all of its operators were either killed or captured. Upon hearing the news Rommel was furious: he had been deprived of his window into the inner workings of the Allied war machine. Rommel's loss was the Allies' gain: they knew for sure now what lengths the Afrika Korps commander would go to, in order to eavesdrop on their communications.

For the LRDG and now, also, the commandos, the threat was two-fold. Having their signals to Cairo headquarters intercepted was bad enough, but if an operator remained on the air for too long he risked betraying the patrol's very location. The Germans were using direction-finding (D/F) equipment to track down the desert raiders operating under their very noses.

Permanent D/F stations consisted of a skein of aerials set atop the roof of an isolated building.

When a LRDG patrol started trying to raise Cairo HQ, a German D/F station would pick up the signal and attempt to triangulate it with a sister facility. Where the intercept bearings crossed, there would be the transmitter. More worryingly for the desert patrols, both the German and Italian air forces were equipped with airborne D/F units. In the game of cat and mouse that was the deep desert war, the enemy baulked at sending in men and machines on the ground, but if the British raiders could be hunted down from the air, so much the better.

Evening radio signal sent – and hopefully not intercepted – it was finally time to eat. Typical LRDG rations included 'Bacon, biscuits, cheese, fruit – dried, fruit – tinned, herrings, jam, lime juice, pickles, oatmeal, onions, potatoes – tinned, sardines, sugar, tea, vegetables – tinned, Marmite, rum, cigarettes, cocoa, curry powder, mustard, pepper, salt.'

At their present location, some 400 miles from the nearest enemy base, Lloyd Owen's men knew they could afford to cook on open fires, which saved fuel. Wood had been collected during the day, and the flames were soon dancing and crackling, throwing ghostly shadows over the rough rock walls of the wadi. In the cool of the night, with the silent desert all around them and the overarching heavens above, the men could shake off the trials and tribulations of the day. They were still dirty, exhausted and thirsty, but a meal was coming, followed by tea and the much-prized rum ration. It was now that the desert took on a magical quality, and tired minds wondered if that day's journey really had been as harsh as it had seemed.

The cool of evening ushered in the desert's own inimitable smell – the dry, clean, pure scent of thousands of miles of terrain devoid of human-kind. Cooking fires, pollution, human waste, vehicle exhausts; none of that encroached upon the vast wilderness of the Sahara. The air – when it wasn't so baking hot as to burn the nostrils – was a joy to breathe. Once the evening rum ration was distributed, boots wrapped in a shirt were formed into a pillow, and tired heads tumbled into a deep sleep just as soon as they hit the sand.

No movement was possible the following morning before the sun was at least twenty degrees above the horizon; any lower and the sun compass failed to cast a workable shadow. There was little point in setting forth if the convoy lost its way. As the sun continued to climb they moved out heading due west. Furnace-like, it bored into them on this, their third day in the desert. Eventually the sun seemed to fill the entire sky. Exposed skin seemed to sizzle and crackle. The commandos eyed the LRDG's keffiyehs appreciatively: it seemed those Arab headdresses weren't such an affectation after all.

As midday approached driving became impossible; unbearable. To all sides a burning white glare possessed the desert, flattening everything and ironing out treacherous dips or wadis. The harsh light threw the ground into a glaring homogeneity: everything looked the same. There was no option but to pull over for an hour or so. It seemed impossible even to breathe. All the men craved was to find some shade, any shade, and hide.

LRDG and commandos alike crawled into the only shelter available: the shadows beneath their vehicles. The trucks' sides were burning hot to the touch. Skin would stick to flat metal surfaces and scorch badly. A scanty lunch was eaten, but no one wanted food; all craved moisture. Figures eyed each other, wondering how much of their daily water ration they might dare to drink. They could probably spare a pint, but no more.

From beneath the Chevys and the army trucks, dry red eyes gazed out balefully over a landscape crawling with heat. There was no shadow, no colour and no variation in the blinding light. The men found their vision played tricks. The desert was a shifting universe where the heat haze seemed to dance and gyrate in the distance, evoking waves of rippling water in a cold, fresh lagoon. It shimmered invitingly. Enticingly.

The day turned. The heat dissipated slightly. Shadows sprung from where before there had been only fire and light. Lloyd Owen clambered into his vehicle. The rest of the LRDG followed suit. The commandos stirred, shaking themselves from their torpid stupor. It was day three, they reminded themselves. Only day three. And they could tell from the rations loaded aboard their vehicles that they must have weeks of this ahead of them. How would they endure?

It was a blessed relief – to put it mildly – when the feathery tops of palm trees hove into view late that afternoon: the Dakhla oasis, to which the LRDG had navigated the convoy across 400 miles of featureless desert. They had described Dakhla as 'not much of an oasis'. It was no Siwa, certainly. But the commandos didn't much give a damn. It would have taken an entire panzer division to keep them away from its deep wells and shady pools. Dakhla was paradise, and nothing had ever tasted as good as the long draughts of water they imbibed, or the countless mugs of tea they brewed long into the evening.

When a wind blew through the oasis it swayed the palm trees above their heads, their dry fronds clacking together, making a noise like a giant wooden rattle. The commandos began to associate the noise with water, and somehow it sounded comforting. When the breeze rattled the palm fronds all was good with the world.

But Lloyd Owen and Major Campbell knew they couldn't pause here for long. From across the desert the raiding forces were converging: from one direction another LRDG patrol, from another a brace of SAS squadrons, and from others units whose existence was even more secret than their own. All would need to arrive at their targets on the exact same day and hour, if a decisive blow against Rommel was to be struck.

Unfortunately, Major Campbell was in a sorry state by now. He definitely had dysentery, which if left untreated could kill. It sapped a man's strength and drained him to a withered husk. But the hodden-kilted major wasn't complaining and he would brook no delay. Lloyd Owen knew he was right; they had to push on. Their schedule was horrendous. To bring so many specialist units to their targets at the exact same hour, having crossed thousands of miles of desert, was one hell of a challenge and there was no time to lose.

The following morning they bade farewell to the Dakhla oasis, the thirteen vehicles setting out due south once more. To the west the way was impassible, for there lay the Great Sand Sea. Consisting of an undulating mass of towering, friable dunes, the Great Sand Sea straddles the border of Egypt and Libya, covering an area the size of Ireland. There was no way through it for a convoy such as this, with its heavy army trucks. Instead, they would have to loop lower, aiming to carve a way across the southernmost fringes of the dunes.

They were into the depths of the Sahara by now and needless to say the going was about to get a whole lot tougher. There was no track to follow any more, not even the faintest of indentations. The way ahead was a mass of hilly, broken ground strewn with rocks. It made for spine-shattering going. Chevys and army trucks alike were reduced to a painful crawl. At times they had to inch up precipitous slopes, engines screaming in the heat and wheels fighting for grip on the rough, broken ground.

The punishment meted out to both vehicles and men was hellish. The hours blurred into one long cacophony of vibrations, crashes, violent lurches and deafening noise. No one spoke. No one could hear themselves think even. Minds were focused on surviving the sheer, bone-shaking punishment of inching forward across such terrain.

Come nightfall, they had experienced their harshest day's driving since leaving Cairo, and they had covered the shortest distance of all, barely sixty miles. It was a sobering realization.

On day five things grew marginally better, or maybe worse . . . The convoy hit soft sand. They were traversing the southernmost limit of the Great Sand Sea, where the *erg* itself petered out into individual dunes, each like a thick finger groping southward. Here the terrain made for softer, smoother going, but driving tactics had to change completely.

No more the orderly progress of follow-my-leader. Across soft sand, speed was everything. The vehicles spread out, each driver gunning his engine and going hell for leather across whatever route he could determine. It was akin to a cavalry charge, and woe betide anyone who flagged. If a vehicle slowed it became bogged, with the inevitable digging and grunting and cursing and *perspiring*. Precious water was wicked away.

Clouds of powdery white dust were thrown up

by the speeding vehicles. It stuck to sweaty skin like a funeral shroud. It got everywhere, coating eyebrows, irritating eyes, clogging nostrils and transforming parched mouths gasping for breath into a choking, gritty dryness. As all the glass had been removed from the cabs of the army trucks, to prevent it flashing in the sunlight and alerting enemy aircraft, even the drivers had no relief from the billowing dust clouds.

And so the crazy charge continued.

The lighter Chevys rarely got stuck, and every hour Lloyd Owen would call a halt on firmer ground and wait for the commandos to catch up. Gazing north into the Great Sand Sea was like looking out over a vast frozen ocean. The parallel lines of dunes ran almost north–south, rising to some 500 feet above the desert floor. Here and there, the smooth 'whale back' dunes reared into sharp, knife-edge crests, falling away almost sheer on the lee side.

Sculpted and shaped by the wind over thousands of years, the dunes were impassable by vehicle, or so it had long been assumed. But the LRDG had managed to forge a secret passage through the Great Sand Sea and to master the art of dune driving. Lloyd Owen had been forced to avoid that path: the commando trucks would never make it. But there was another LRDG patrol crossing via that route right at this very moment.

Somewhere among the serried ranks of dunes resembling the great Atlantic swell – long rollers with plunging troughs between – a convoy of Chevys and jeeps was threading its way west, making for the heart of enemy territory. Within the Great Sand Sea all would be lifeless and dead apart from that LRDG patrol: not a blade of grass nor any shrub would break the uniformity of golden sand and burning blue sky.

On one level Lloyd Owen and his men resented the slow and unwieldy progress of their present charges. But it was no fault of the commandos, who worked like slaves to shove, haul and nurse their heavy trucks through the worst of the sand. Without them Lloyd Owen's patrol could have shaved days off their journey. But equally, they knew that the Commando was their ticket to some real action. In reminding themselves of that, they could shake off the short temper and irritableness that the Sahara brings on in even the most experienced travellers.

One thing was clear to Lloyd's Owen's men by now: their immediate destination. It could only be Kufra, a magical oasis that lay beyond the Great Sand Sea, at the meeting point of two other similarly giant *ergs* – the Rabiana and Kalansho Sand Seas. Positioned over 600 miles south of the Mediterranean and far into Libya, Kufra should by rights have been Axis-held territory. But once the LRDG had wrestled the oasis off the Italians they weren't about to give it up any time soon. Right now it was the most forward Allied outpost in North Africa, and it was a place to which the unit had a special, romantic kind of attachment.

Until the 1930s few outsiders had ever set foot in Kufra. Then Mussolini – whose forces had colonized Libya – decided to take the remote oasis by force of arms. The Arabs who lived there stood little chance against the Italians' modern weaponry. Kufra fell and the Italians built a fort in the centre of the oasis, mostly using Arab slave labour.

For the next decade the Italians had ruled Kufra unchallenged. Then the LRDG teamed up with the Free French forces of Colonel the Viscount de Hautecloque, or Colonel Leclerc as he was more commonly known, the Free French commander in Equatorial Africa. In February 1941 the two forces launched their assault on the Italian positions. They shot up and torched the Italian aircraft at Kufra's dirt airstrip and dynamited the Italian's D/F station.

Witnessing the carnage, the Italian garrison had retreated to the fort, leaving the Free French and LRDG to occupy the wider oasis. A siege had ensued. Though the Italians were well armed and well provisioned, they finally decided enough was enough, and a white flag was run up the flagpole. The LRDG proceeded to make the beautiful oasis their forward base. They'd even built a circular, freshwater swimming pool.

After Kufra there would be only hostile terrain and war. But for now at least that magical oasis offered a last sanctuary.

The urge to get to Kufra spurred everyone on. On day six the convoy slipped past the most incredible feature they had yet to encounter: a bald, flat-topped red sandstone plateau that reared suddenly out of the desert plains. This was Gilf Kebir – the Great Barrier – a massive block to any easy passage further south. But as Kufra lay due west the convoy suffered little inconvenience. Indeed, the LRDG led the commandos to the base of one of the Great Barrier's towering sandstone walls. In a shadowed cave amid the red cliffs Lloyd Owen's men had established a fuel dump.

With a certain pride they flashed torches across the cave walls, pointing out its remarkable features for the men of the Commando. The walls were a mass of ancient cave art. So old were these magical and evocative murals that they portrayed a very different kind of desert, where spear-brandishing natives hunted rich herds of game. One wall was bedecked with the silhouettes of hands, as if paint had been blown onto the rock face around them. The hands were interspersed with long-legged ostrich-like birds. In times past the desert had bloomed. Civilizations had flourished here: the art alone was testimony to that.

The afternoon of day six marked the final run into Kufra. The convoy was moving on *serir* – hard-packed golden sand, which proved as good as any motorway. The surface seemed to mute all sound, and the vehicles whispered and purred along. Compared to what had gone before, it was sheer heaven.

Spirits soared.

But then the peace of that magical late afternoon was pierced by a sharp warning. Eyes swept the horizon. Up ahead of the Commando trucks Lloyd Owen was gesticulating from his Chevy, which flew a distinctive pennant marking it out as the command vehicle. Within moments the startled commandos saw the LRDG vehicles wheel around and speed off, slipping into a V-shaped attacking formation. Engines screamed under the punishing demands for greater speed.

A figure in the Commando pointed north-east, back the way they had come. A boiling cloud of dust was fisting up from that direction. *Dust: dust meant vehicles.* And the LRDG had warned them that they were expecting no other company in this stretch of desert. It could only be the enemy, and it looked as if they had been tracking the British convoy.

As suddenly as that their fortunes had turned. Out of the blue they were under attack, and all the commandos could do in their big, unwieldy army trucks was run. It went against the very essence of all they stood for. It was in their blood to fight – to meet fire with fire – but all they could do was turn towards Kufra and gun the trucks' tired engines.

They pushed westward, necks craned to watch the LRDG going into action, but Lloyd Owen's speeding vehicles were quickly swallowed by their own wake of dust. Far in the distance the men of the Commando could just make out the approaching enemy column. There were scores of speeding vehicles, and the LRDG looked to be hopelessly outnumbered. But as the commandos had learned, Lloyd Owen's men were masters of their trade, and they'd vowed to buy their charges the chance to escape.

It was a race against time now.

CHAPTER 5

Minutes after the adversaries had closed in a cloud of swirling dust, the six vehicles of the LRDG came racing back out again. They thundered west, swiftly catching up with the heavier trucks of the Commando. Lloyd Owen passed across the good news: the mystery column had turned out to be a friendly patrol.

It was a unit of SAS that was also making for Kufra, another element in the forces gathering to strike a knockout blow against Rommel. They were well behind schedule, which is why Lloyd Owen and his men had presumed they were hostile and intent on mounting an attack.

It was good to have the SAS link up with the force now assembling at Kufra. The SAS's founder David Stirling was a tall and dashing Guards officer of a singularly unconventional mindset. Battling officialdom, Stirling had formed a parachute-borne raiding force designed to wreak havoc behind the enemy lines. His fledgling force was christened L Detachment, Special Service Brigade, which latterly became the Special Air Service.

In November 1941 fifty-four men had set out

on the first ever SAS mission, aiming to parachute into Axis airfields deep behind the lines in Libya. Bad weather led to disaster: one planeload was dropped onto the airfield itself and most were captured. The other was released over the Great Sand Sea and few survived. Only twenty-one men returned at mission's end, yet Stirling remained undeterred. Parachute operations were abandoned in favour of vehicle-born missions.

The SAS linked up with the LRDG, who ferried them to their targets. Over time the SAS learned the craft of desert navigation and survival from the LRDG, who were their foremost teachers. 'We came to owe the Long Range Desert Group a deep debt of gratitude,' Stirling would remark of this time. 'The LRDG were the supreme professionals of the desert and they were unstinting in their help.'

The SAS acquired their own vehicles – chiefly the Willys Jeep. They specialized in raiding airfields, and in the first six months of 1942 scored phenomenal successes: approaching 150 enemy warplanes were destroyed. As Stirling noted, 'By the end of June [we] had raided all the more important German and Italian aerodromes within 300 miles of the forward area at least once or twice.'

The three forces converging on Kufra – the LRDG, the SOE Commando and now the SAS – constituted a potent combination. They formed up as one unit to complete the last few miles to the Kufra oasis itself. When the first palm trees hove into view, the speedometers on the LRDG vehicles indicated that they had just covered a 997-mile journey.

The oasis was like a magical apparition, bathed as it was in a fine evening light. It was an utterly arresting sight for the men of the Commando. They had expected a small, compact slice of paradise – clumps of palm trees anchored to a scattering of pools. Instead, Kufra extended as far as the eye could see. In parts it was fifty miles across, stretching from horizon to horizon.

Set in a low-lying bowl a good few feet below sea level, the oasis was entered via a narrow track that descended from the high *serir*. The vehicles were forced to slow their precipitous pace, which gave ample time for the men to feast their eyes upon the captivating scene. They swore they could smell the water on the cooling breeze that wafted through the palm trees.

Everywhere palms laden with dates bowed their graceful heads, casting long shadows in the dying rays of the sun. To left and right lay strips of greener ground – cultivated land. The fields were irrigated with freshwater drawn from wells and hauled by donkeys, glistening leather buckets strapped to their haunches. Here and there lay mud-walled Arab villages, the streets twisting, shadowed and labyrinthine, and seemingly as old as time itself.

In the distance a lone mosque towered above the earth-brick buildings of El Giof town; in its shadow clustered the low-rise wooden shelters of the El Tag marketplace, thronged with traders. The lush greenery and vegetation was particularly welcome to those who'd just spent six days in the desert, and the combined force swept into the heart of Kufra in jubilant mood.

The column of vehicles pulled to a halt in the shade of a palm grove overlooking a dirt airstrip. In between the palms were scattered tin sheds and small hangars, and this was clearly a busy, working aerodrome. At one end squatted a pair of ageing Bristol Bombays, a dual-role transport aircraft and bomber. Obsolete in the European theatre, the Bombays were being used by the RAF's 216 Squadron to ferry troops and war materiel across the North African battlefield.

But of chief interest to the new arrivals were the bathing facilities. They had been told to make the most of Kufra, where they would have several days' rest and recuperation. They needed no second urging. There was the swimming pool custom-made by the LRDG – a tin-lined circular affair, filled with freshwater. Mud-bottomed, it proved blissfully refreshing and cool to sun-scorched bodies.

There was also a natural lake, sapphire-blue and as intensely salty as the Dead Sea. These men, who had spent days in the scorching desert, digging and hauling heavily laden trucks through the burning heat, were plagued by the sweat rashes and sand sores such exertions inevitably cause. Immersion in the lake's saltwater proved an agonising yet powerful balm for such ills.

After an exquisite – if pain-racked – bathe, the men settled down under their scratchy army blankets to an exhausted sleep. They awoke to the light of dawn filtering through palm fronds, their blankets dusted with fresh dates that had fallen during the night hours.

After breakfast the men of the Commando, curious about this new and mystifying location, were free to wander at will. A massive-walled fortress dominated all. Set on a low hill, this was the Italian citadel built by Arab forced labour following Mussolini's seizure of Kufra. It now served as the makeshift headquarters for the ragtag band of private armies who operated out of here: LRDG, SAS and now also the SOE Commando.

The fortress was garrisoned by a company of the Welch Regiment – there being perhaps no stranger place to stumble upon the soft, lilting accents of Swansea or Cardiff. Lloyd Owen, and the long-suffering Major Campbell established their temporary base at the fort. It proved to be awash with rumour as to what the raiding forces now converging on Kufra might be up to.

In fact rumours were swirling around the length and breadth of the oasis. But neither Lloyd Owen nor Campbell were about to breathe a word. The full nature of their operation was to be revealed shortly, and by none other than the man who had first conceived of such a daring – some might argue, suicidal – undertaking.

* * *

So secret was the present mission that David Stirling had been warned to keep his lips buttoned tight, even in the company of Winston Churchill himself. In early August 1942 Churchill had paid a visit to Cairo, en route to a meeting with Stalin in Moscow. Each evening the British premier enjoyed a lavish dinner party, to which the rising stars of the war in North Africa were invited. Stirling had received just such an invitation, but it had come with an unexpected health warning: he was not to discuss the coming mission with the British prime minister.

'Why on earth not?' Stirling had demanded.

'Because he's famously insecure, of course,' came the reply. 'We cannot run any risks.'

Stirling had been lobbying Churchill hard about his raiders. The SAS commander was well connected, and he'd managed to get a 'Most Secret' memo into Churchill's hands, outlining 'certain proposals for the employment of special forces'. It told of how the SAS lived in 'constant fear of being disbanded', in spite of the victories they had scored against Rommel's forces.

Over dinner in Cairo Stirling regaled Churchill with stories of the SAS's derring-do. Already he was being referred to in Axis radio traffic as the 'Phantom Major'. The Phantom Major had caused no end of trouble, but would soon be captured or killed, the enemy boasted. He was firmly on Rommel's radar. The German general had written in his diary of Stirling, describing him as the leader of 'the commandos' who cause 'considerable havoc and seriously disquieted' Axis troops.

Over dinner Stirling impressed Churchill with his light heart and cool courage. The prime minister thrilled to his daredevil cock of the eye and the stories of the SAS's luck and pluck endeavours in the deep desert. Churchill declared himself 'delighted' by such tales, and, quoting Byron's *Don Juan*, he referred to the SAS commander as 'the mildest mannered man that ever scuttled ship or cut a throat'.

Stirling used the opportunity to raise with Churchill the vexed issue of his unit's impermanent – some might argue endangered – status. He was invited back for a second night's carousing and discussions, after which he was reassured that he would be granted all that he'd asked for. He would get more jeeps, more men and arms, plus his unit would be given a more permanent and official status.

In the short term the SAS and SBS were to operate as one cohesive unit, and in close collaboration with the LRDG. In essence, the special forces raiders were being moulded into one tight-knit group, in preparation for their enlargement to regimental status under Churchill's direct purview. That was slated to take place in September 1942, but only if Stirling and his fellows survived the coming mission.

By the third day of their sojourn at Kufra the men were becoming restless. They were impatient for news. For action. They began to sense that they were waiting for someone to arrive at Kufra, at which time all would be revealed.

Sure enough, on the morning of 4 September – their fourth day at the oasis – a lone Bristol Bombay beat its slow and laborious course across the hot air, before touching down in a cloud of dust on the dirt strip. Its arrival drew many a curious eye, but as the door to the cargo bay swung open little did any expect what was to follow.

Two British officers – one a captain, one a lieutenant – stepped down, leading what appeared to be a column of *German troops*. As the assembled British soldiers gawped in amazement, the Afrika Korps unit was marched across the airstrip to an isolated stand of palms. There the British officers proceeded to issue orders to their charges in the harsh-seeming guttural tones of German.

The commandos stared in bewilderment as the officers proceeded to drill the troopers, who responded swiftly and smartly, wielding their German weaponry with practised skill. As the barked orders rang out through the oasis, they sounded a chilling note. It felt so very, very wrong to the men gathered there. Kufra was the Allies' desert redoubt; what was a force of the enemy doing here, of all places?

Their worries – their resentment – were tempered somewhat by the reception that Lloyd Owen and Major Campbell afforded the new arrivals. The two commanders had been radioed a warning regarding the unusual nature of the force that would be flying in to Kufra. The 'Secret' message told them to expect, 'Buck and six ORs [Other Ranks] . . . wearing German uniforms. Their recognition signal is "red handkerchief".'

If the newly arrived unit were to be challenged, they were to give the code word 'red handkerchief'. In spite of appearances, the code word would confirm that they were in reality friendly forces, commanded by an extraordinary individual most had only ever heard spoken about in whispers.

Following his daring escape from the enemy dressed as an Afrika Korps officer, Captain Henry Cecil Buck had worked tirelessly to bring his Great Idea to fruition. At the time General Sir Claude Auchinleck was in command of British forces in North Africa. An Indian Army officer himself, Auchinleck had looked kindly upon Captain Buck's extraordinary plan, but it was clear that no such unit could ever be formed as an official part of the British military.

Buck's force would have to be utterly deniable, which made it ideally suited to the Special Operations Executive. As a SOE outfit, the British government and military could deny all knowledge and responsibility, if ever they were challenged. So it was that the war's greatest ever deception force was formed as a special detachment to G(R) – the nerve centre of the SOE's raiding operations.

With his hawk face, aquiline nose and piercing blue eyes, high-born Lieutenant General Terence Airey was just the kind of officer Captain Buck needed to sponsor his creation. Serving in a cloak-and-dagger role with military intelligence, Airey would go on to mastermind Operation Fritzel, a clandestine meeting with SS General Karl Wolff aimed at negotiating the surrender of German forces in Italy. But in the spring of 1942 he was stationed at general headquarters, Cairo, and he'd taken up Buck's proposal with a vengeance.

'We are . . . forming a Special German Group as a sub-unit of ME Commando,' he declared in an extraordinary 1 April 1942 memo stamped 'Most Secret'. 'It is intended that this . . . unit would be used for infiltration behind the German lines in the Western Desert . . . The strength of the Special Group would be approximately that of a platoon.'

'The personnel . . . are fluent German linguists,' Airey continued. 'They are mainly Palestinians of German origin. Many of them have had war experience . . . They will frequently be dressed in German uniform and will operate under the command of a British officer who has already proved himself to be an expert in German language.'

That 'British officer' was of course Henry Cecil Buck, and the chief purpose of Airey's memo was to secure the kind of transport that his newly formed unit required.

In order to enable the Group to operate efficiently, it is essential that it should be provided with . . . the under mentioned vehicles:

one German staff car
two 16-cwt trucks

Airey signed off his memo by giving Buck's unit the proposed cover name the Special Operations Group. As if it were an afterthought, 'Operations' was crossed out by hand, and replaced with a scribbled alternative: 'Interrogation'. For better or worse that would become the name under which Buck's force would become known: the Special Interrogation Group, or the SIG for short.

At its simplest, Airey and Buck's plan was to have the SIG talk its way through German lines riding in German vehicles and bristling with hidden weaponry. Buck's men would then attack targets of opportunity, in particular German staff cars carrying high-ranking German officers. But once David Stirling got wind of the SIG, more flesh was added to the bones of the plan: the SIG could perhaps best be utilized by bluffing its way through Axis lines, 'guarding' truckloads of SAS posing as prisoners of war. Once through the enemy lines the SAS would throw off their POW shackles, cry havoc and let slip the dogs of war.

Buck recruited as his second in command a man cut from similar cloth – a fellow daredevil and eccentric. Lieutenant David Russell was a Scots

Guards officer who'd earned renown for his fear-lessness. Another gifted linguist, he was a fluent German speaker, which made him ideal for the SIG. With his slicked-back hair, luxuriant moustache and dashing good looks, Russell was also the archetypal British adventurer. He'd spent his youth astride speeding motorcycles or climbing into and out of Cambridge colleges. It was when driving that Russell truly threw all caution to the wind. He liked to keep his speedometer above the 80 mph mark, and this had earned him, perhaps inevitably, the nickname the Flying Scotsman. His greatest fear was what to do with his restless soul once the war came to an end.

Having soldiered with Stirling's SAS, Russell had come direct from there to the SIG. He differed from Buck in one key aspect: a cool, calculating officer, Russell was inclined to trust no one until he or she had proved themselves deserving of his confidence. Buck, by contrast, had a tendency to an otherworldly naivety, and he would put his faith in others all too easily. Neither man was a cool, calculating killer. Russell would write to his sister from the desert, describing his distaste at taking out Germans at close hand. An intensely family-oriented man, he had to steel himself to carry out such acts in cold blood.

From the very outset the SIG had the aura of a suicide squad. All militaries take exception to the enemy posing as friendly forces. Neither Buck nor Russell were under any illusions as to what fate might befall any of the SIG should they fall into enemy hands. A firing squad would be the least of their worries.

As word leaked out to the regular military of the SIG's existence, howls of protest could be heard. Ever since Operation Flipper – the attempt to assassinate Rommel – voices had been raised at the highest level, lamenting the indecent and very 'un-British' nature of such missions. Assassinations, subterfuge, posing as the enemy: these were not the kinds of things that soldiers in British uniform should indulge in. But Churchill had called for 'ungentlemanly warfare', and the SIG's brand of warfare promised to be ungentlemanly in the extreme.

The SIG's earliest operations had been fairly low-key affairs, designed to test the waters. Now, five months after its formation, a contingent of the SIG had arrived in Kufra to link up with the forces gathered there. Whatever their mission might prove to be, this promised ungentlemanly warfare beyond compare. But the SIG were far from universally welcome, even among the mavericks and misfits of the 'private armies'.

No one could argue with the sheer bravery of those who volunteered to serve in such a unit, wherein capture would lead to horrific torture and death. It testified to a dedication to defeating Nazism that demanded a certain respect. Yet rumours abounded about the SIG being plagued by betrayal. Traitorous behaviour had led to disaster and Allied special forces soldiers had died a terrible death as a result. Few hadn't heard the dark reports. The commandos and LRDG gathered at Kufra eyed the SIG operatives warily, as they wondered just what kind of a mission was now in the offing and what exactly they had let themselves in for.

With the arrival of the next Bristol Bombay aircraft they were about to find out.

CHAPTER 6

It was late afternoon when the lumbering Bombay set down on Kufra's dirt strip. Most of the men were away at the bathing pools, so few were around to see just whom the aircraft was carrying. But Lloyd Owen was there to greet the new arrival – the former cotton trader Lieutenant Colonel John Haselden.

That evening several of the men caught sight of Haselden, recognizing him from their night spent partying at the cotton mill on the banks of the Nile. The news spread. It looked as if they'd not been wrong when they'd presumed that Haselden was instrumental in their mission. He was here now, and clutching a very official-looking briefcase, one doubtless stuffed with a full set of orders.

At dawn the following morning the men of the Commando were called to parade. Major Campbell presented them to Haselden, who stepped forward to inspect the ranks of unshaven, sunburned, grim-faced cutthroats. Haselden must have liked what he saw, for a gentle smile creased his weathered features.

'Take a seat, gentlemen,' he commanded coolly.

Eighty-odd elite warriors settled onto the sand. 'You're no doubt anxious to learn of your destination and what work is planned. Understandably so. Now I'm going to give you the full picture.' Haselden paused, for dramatic effect it seemed. The men waited, tense and silent, as the lieutenant colonel spread out a map before them. When he recommenced speaking, few could believe what he had to say: 'Gentlemen, we're going to capture Tobruk and destroy it completely.'

Just like that Haselden had declared the utterly unthinkable.

Countless ideas had been mooted by the commandos as they debated their possible objectives, but none had ever imagined that Rommel's foremost stronghold might be their target. Tobruk: it was the fulcrum of the desert war. Whoever held it held the key to victory in North Africa, or so most argued.

Tobruk was a long way away, lying 600 miles due north of Kufra. It was arguably the finest natural harbour on the entire North African coast. The port itself was two miles long and blessed with a deepwater basin boasting numerous quays and jetties. The glistening waters nestled in the curve of a natural amphitheatre, bare and barren hills rising on three sides. Those slopes were peppered with forts, gun emplacements, trenches and bunkers, forming a fearsome defensive ring thrown around the anchorage itself. The fortifications stretched inland some eight or nine miles, reaching into the open desert. The outer cordon was made up of wire fencing and anti-tank ditches, and studded by a double line of bunkers, each linked to its neighbour by telephone and all linked thus to headquarters.

Tobruk had been the Allies' main stronghold in North Africa, before Rommel's panzers had wrested it from British hands. Rommel's *Panzerwaffe* – armoured force – was an elite unit tried and tested during stunning victories scored in Belgium and France. The *Panzerwaffe* had struck first in North Africa in April 1941, winning a string of lightning victories. Months later, after a grinding siege, Tobruk had fallen.

It was June 1942 and Churchill was in Washington, seeking to persuade US President Roosevelt to supply more tanks, warships and aircraft to the Allied war effort. The British premier was in the Oval Office, speaking with Roosevelt, when a telegram with news of the calamity arrived. It could not have come at a worse time. Suffering defeats on all fronts, Allied fortunes were at their nadir. In taking Tobruk Rommel had seized much of the Allied artillery intact, plus thousands of tons of munitions and fuel. He had also captured 33,000 troops.

It was a dark day, one that Churchill lamented bitterly. He declared it 'a bitter moment. Defeat is one thing; disgrace is another.'

Rommel considered the seizure of Tobruk the crowning achievement of his career. It provided his Afrika Korps with thousands of tons of supplies and a vital port through which to resupply his forces from occupied Europe. Hitler was equally ebullient: he promoted Rommel to field marshal to reward him for the daring venture.

Churchill railed against the loss. Determined to strike back, he demanded a counterpunch. He argued that Rommel's greatest victory was also his Achilles heel. Seizure of the port had yielded enormous war booty and eased Rommel's supply logistics immensely. Yet Tobruk was vulnerable from the sea and air, and especially to hit-and-run sabotage from the desert.

Right now those desert raiders gathered at Kufra would need some convincing. The fact that Rommel's forces had achieved the 'impossible' and taken Tobruk made Haselden's proposal seem all the more incredible. How could 33,000 Allied troops have surrendered Tobruk, only for Haselden's force of eighty souls to retake it?

A low murmur swept around the men as they gave voice to their surprise and concern. Smiling, radiating an avuncular confidence, Haselden waited for the noise to die down. He proceeded to flip open his briefcase. His orders – issued to him on 21 August 1942 and marked 'To Be Kept Under Lock And Key' – confirmed that the seemingly impossible was indeed at hand: the eighty men assembled in Kufra were to wrestle Tobruk from Axis control.

Typical of military orders everywhere, those

Haselden carried were dry and curt. 'Intention: Forces . . . will capture and hold the south shore of the harbour from Umm Es Sciausc to the Bulk Oil Tank, which is to be destroyed . . . At last light on the 12th September Force . . . less the LRDG patrol will enter the Tobruk perimeter . . .'

As Haselden well knew, what they were tasked to do was daunting in the extreme. He also knew that no dry set of orders would compel men such as these to follow him where he intended to lead them. He ran his eyes over the document one last time, before straightening his shoulders and preparing to deliver the speech of his life.

'Gentlemen, we're going to take Tobruk,' he repeated. 'I know the idea sounds fantastic, but it would also sound fantastic to the enemy, and that is our single greatest strength. We are going to do the utterly unexpected, taking the enemy by total surprise. It is for that very reason that we are going to do exactly what I have just said – take Tobruk, hold it for several hours and leave it so that it is useless as a supply port for the Afrika Korps.'

Haselden eyed the men. He could tell that his calm, confident delivery coupled with those carefully chosen words was starting to take effect. But right now the commandos would have scores of unanswered questions whirling through their minds. He intended to answer the most pressing ones right away.

'We are going to capture a bridgehead just outside of Tobruk harbour,' he continued, 'under cover of the biggest air raid this coast has ever seen. The RAF will unleash merry hell onto Tobruk's defenders. Under cover of that, and because we won't be expected, we shall establish the bridgehead with little difficulty. Then, through this little harbour that we have established, MTBs will pour in reinforcements.'

MTBs – motor torpedo boats – light, fast attack ships. That would explain the SBS unit included in the commandos' number.

Tobruk was believed to be garrisoned by low-calibre troops, Haselden explained, and to be only lightly defended. Rommel had sent the cream of his forces to the front line, to prepare for the thrust towards Cairo itself.

'Rommel has stripped Tobruk of its key defensive forces,' Haselden continued, quoting intelligence reports. 'All that remains to guard the port are a couple of battalions of third-rate Italian troops, plus a number of German technicians and ack-ack personnel.' Haselden figured that the German soldiers numbered 1,000 all told.

Low-grade Italian troops weren't something to be feared by the commandos. They'd crossed swords with, and vanquished, such forces many times before. And presumably the German ack-ack (anti-aircraft) gunners would be fully occupied with trying to repulse the Allied air raid. If the enemy could be taken by surprise, success would doubtless be theirs.

Haselden rolled off the names of the units

– Argyll and Sutherland Highlanders, Royal Northumberland Fusiliers; regiments that had earned a fearsome repute during the desert campaigns – who would land from the sea. Once reinforced, the Commando would break out from the bridgehead and seize the southern shoreline of the port, even as destroyers landed marines to take the northern side. They would then smash their way into Tobruk in a pincer movement, linking up at the centre of the fortress.

As Haselden continued speaking, his stature seemed to grow. He exuded utter confidence in their ability to do just as they had been ordered. His attitude seemed to be catching: he could detect a growing sense of assurance surging through the men before him. They'd hold Tobruk for twelve hours, he explained, during which time they'd dynamite dock installations and piers, destroy tank repair workshops and blow up ammo dumps and fuel depots. The assembled men began to comprehend the impact such an operation might have on the hated enemy: deprived of fuel, ammo, tanks and the means of resupply, this would constitute a knockout blow that could cripple Rommel's war effort.

The key would be the calibre of the troops defending Tobruk. If they were as Haselden suggested, a sudden strike delivered with maximum surprise might well prove decisive. The intelligence on the quality of the Tobruk garrisons had an impeccable pedigree: it came from Ultra intercepts. Indeed, signals decoded at Bletchley had revealed Rommel's trials and tribulations generally, as his supply lines had become ever more extended.

Ultra gave warnings of the resupply convoys setting out from Italy. Those were being hit by pinpoint RAF air strikes, sending Rommel's much-needed war materiel to the depths. Repeatedly, the German field marshal had demanded new tanks to re-equip his *Panzerwaffe*, but Bletchley intercepts revealed that not enough were getting through. As Rommel siphoned off crack troops to fill the gaps in his front-line positions, Tobruk had been left increasingly vulnerable.

In recent months the speed by which such Ultra intelligence reached Allied forces had increased massively. At first it had taken days, sometimes weeks, for signals to be decoded at Bletchley and for the information they contained to make it to the front. But in May 1942 Bletchley had started sending cryptanalysts to war. One of the first was a Lieutenant Harry Meirion Evans, an Oxford graduate who'd once been accused of having 'insufficient bloodlust' to make it as a proper soldier. Evans had been posted instead to Bletchley, where he had helped break the German cipher code-named Double Playfair. But he felt guilty about not serving in a combat role, and he was among the first to volunteer for North Africa.

When the fresh-faced Evans was deployed to Egypt, a Cairo veteran of the Auxiliary Territorial Service (ATS) – the women's branch of the British army during World War Two – had declared, 'Good God, has it come to this? They're sending us children now . . .'

Evans quickly realized that he needed to take a signals intercept team plus code-breakers right to the front, to speed up the provision of usable intelligence. In trying to locate the front-line HQ, his convoy of vehicles had almost blundered into Rommel's forces. He wrote in his diary of time spent sleeping 'in a Jerry dugout' and of being 'bothered by a Heinkel, but cloud was low and he went away'. On another occasion he and a fellow cryptologist spent the night in a hut in a remote Arab village, taking turns sleeping on the only bed or standing guard with a pistol. Through such heroic endeavours, Evans and his fellow front-line code-breakers accelerated the provision of usable intelligence exponentially.

Haselden had enjoyed the benefits of such rapid-fire intelligence, as had all the planners who had been involved in conceiving the present mission. Stirling had played a key role; indeed, many argued it was the SAS commander who had first mooted the idea of a lightning raid on Tobruk. But it was Haselden who had really taken the plan up, giving it wings.

Scores of simultaneous raids would take place all along the Axis-held coast, Haselden explained to the force gathered before him at Kufra. That would spread confusion among the enemy commanders as to the main target. In the biggest of such decoy

97

attacks, Stirling would lead some 200 SAS in dozens of vehicles, causing havoc and confusion at Rommel's second port, Benghazi. That mission, with typical SAS elan, had been code-named Operation Bigamy.

Other units would hit enemy bases, fortifications and targets of opportunity at widely dispersed points across the desert. Hundreds of dummy parachutists would be dropped at various locations, to convince the enemy that a series of airborne landings were under way. One raider unit would hit the Jalo oasis, a former Allied stronghold before Rommel's forces overran it. Another was tasked to raid Barce airfield, set to the far west of Tobruk, on a mission code-named Operation Caravan.

Having guided the Commando to its target, Lloyd Owen's LRDG patrol would attack the main radio station located on the outskirts of Tobruk's defensive perimeter. It would then raid the nearby airfield, remaining on hand should any of Haselden's commandos need to link up with the LRDG patrol to escape.

'For twelve hours we will hold out at Tobruk,' Haselden announced portentously. 'Twelve hours. There will be no retreat. Twelve hours is all the time the sappers need to do their demolitions work.'

'And afterwards?' a voice queried. 'Do we come out via the desert?'

Haselden shook his head: they would be taken off in Royal Navy warships, he explained. Getting in through the desert was going to prove challenging enough. Getting out by the same route would be nigh-on impossible. Which brought Haselden to the most most daring and audacious aspect of the coming operation.

'We are going to drive openly into Tobruk at dusk,' Haselden announced, scrutinizing the men for their reactions. He nodded in the direction of the SIG camp. 'We will enter as prisoners of war captured at the Alamein front, under the guard of what are supposedly German soldiers.'

The SIG operatives had kept themselves to themselves at Kufra, but suddenly the presence of the 'Afrika Korps' contingent was explained. The last thing the enemy would ever expect was a group of POWs emerging from the desert, who were in truth the much-feared British commandos, not that the men were overjoyed upon learning of the key deception that would underpin their mission.

Admittedly, there was no way into Tobruk without a Trojan horse such as the SIG provided. The commandos needed the SIG deception to get them through the fearsome defences, but few were keen to place their fortunes in the hands of 'Germans', even if their allegiances supposedly lay with the Allies now. In the background lurked the dark suspicion – the rumours – of previous betrayals.

There was little time to contemplate such fears. Haselden spread more maps in the sand. Most of the Commando had served in Tobruk at one time or another, and the terrain was familiar to them. Haselden jabbed a finger at a point in the south-eastern end of Tobruk harbour. It was a narrow boot-shaped inlet, enclosed with high cliffs and marked 'Marsa Umm Esc-Sciausc' – *marsa* being the colloquial Arabic word for 'bay'. Sciausc Bay lay just outside the Tobruk boom, a barrier of floating nets that closed off the harbour entrance, leaving just a narrow entry point.

'This is the bay that we are going to capture on September 13th,' Haselden announced in his quiet, self-assured tones.

September 13th: they now had a date for the coming raid. Today was 4 September. They were nine days out and counting.

'Aerial reconnaissance shows coastal defence guns positioned all around the cove, as well as ack-ack further inland,' Haselden continued. He glanced at the faces all around him. 'Our job is to capture those guns. If we fail, the Argylls and Fusiliers will be blown out of the water as they come in to land.' He paused. 'But we will not fail. We will capture those guns and turn them against the enemy. No warships of ours will be blown out of the water. No warships of theirs will be allowed to leave the harbour.'

The more the commandos listened, the more they liked what they heard. This raid on Tobruk appealed to their wilder, reckless sides. The plan was a good one and it all tied up nicely. They could see it playing out beautifully. Surprise, ingenuity and audacity would carry the day, plus they could be serving under no better leader, that was for certain.

The faith the commandos placed in any new commander was based in large part upon his reputation. In Haselden's case, it was second to none. Few hadn't heard of his exploits masquerading as an Arab deep behind the lines. Haselden seemed not to understand fear. The possibility of betrayal lurked at every juncture, but it seemed never to occur to him that things might go wrong or the enemy capture him.

The story most often told around the flickering campfires was of his role in Operation Flipper. Lieutenant Tommy Langton – the SBS veteran of sticky-grenade fame – had been on that mission, so could speak of it personally. The British submarines *Torbay* and *Talisman* had crept up the North African coast, to a point offshore of what was believed to be Rommel's headquarters. They carried a force of SBS and commandos led by Lieutenant Colonel Geoffrey Keyes, the son of the famous admiral Sir Roger Keyes.

The submarines had surfaced to discover a point of light blinking at them miraculously from the shoreline. Langton had been told to expect the landing-point marker, but he had never once believed it would be there bang on schedule. The thirty-strong commando force had paddled ashore, to discover Lieutenant Colonel John Haselden dressed head-to-toe in Arab robes, operating the signal light and to all appearances unconcerned that he was doing so smack bang in the midst of enemy territory.

Having been dropped behind the German lines by the LRDG, Haselden had spent two weeks scrutinising what Allied radio intercepts suggested was Rommel's base. Over the next three days, and, perversely, battling torrential rain, he led the raiders to the doorstep of the building they believed was the Desert Fox's headquarters.

But they met with fierce resistance, which ended in the crushing realization that Rommel was not at home. He had apparently flown to Rome unexpectedly, for his fiftieth-birthday celebrations. In the course of fierce fighting Major Keyes was killed. He would be awarded a posthumous Victoria Cross. Many commandos also lost their lives. But Haselden managed to melt back into the desert, where he was picked up by an LRDG patrol.

He earned his second MC for that daring operation. The citation would stress how Haselden had 'walked a distance of nearly 100 miles through the heart of enemy territory' to recce Rommel's headquarters. It spoke of a 'fearless action worthy of the highest praise. The success he achieved was largely due to information he had gained during his reconnaissance.'

Haselden never built himself up to be a man of mystery, or one who possessed outstanding courage and charisma, yet in his quiet, understated way he was all those things and more. Blessed with a magnetic personality, he was one of the most unconventional heroes of the war. He had already suffered tragic loss in his life, and on a level that would have excused him for putting personal interests above the call of duty.

Married in 1931 to Nadia Szymonska-Lubicz, a nineteen-year-old Polish-Italian beauty, he had lost his wife five years later to a car crash. That had left their only child, Gerald, seven, deprived of a mother and Haselden himself widowed. Nonetheless, not long after the outbreak of war Haselden had signed up for military service. He was a man who made friends easily, and then had those friends exercise themselves to win him more friends. He was a man born to lead missions such as the present one, and the men of the Commando could sense it.

He rounded off the briefing by turning to the most scintillating aspect of the coming raid. Once their objective was secured, their key task was to free the thousands of POWs held in the Tobruk cages. They would be released and armed with captured weaponry, so they could join forces with the raiders.

At mission's end the former POWs would be evacuated by Royal Navy warships or would break out into the desert, where they would link up with Stirling's SAS. Those who managed to do so would form a guerrilla army, operating in Rommel's rear. Unsurprisingly, it was this aspect of the coming operation that appealed most to the commandos.

The taking of 33,000 Allied prisoners at the fall of Tobruk had truly smarted. Those troops had fought like lions and no one doubted that they would do so again. If they could spring those

POWs and arm them, they would have a massive force of battle-hardened fighters to pit against the German and Italian forces manning Tobruk.

Now was the moment to turn defeat into victory, Haselden urged. But he sounded a final note of caution. He indicated a point on the map about twelve miles east of Tobruk on the coastal road. 'That's the danger point. The Germans have a staging point hereabouts. Those are crack panzer troops intended to reinforce the Alamein front, and they are to be feared. That's why we must fight our way into Tobruk, to hold a line that covers that road.'

The commandos remained undaunted. If they managed to block the road, no reinforcements were getting through to Tobruk, of that they felt certain. The wild card in the mission remained the 'Germans' in their midst, although most understood how and why German Jews had come to fight alongside Allied forces.

Adolf Hitler – an aggressive proponent of the so-called 'stab in the back' theory – had blamed the Jews for Germany's humiliating defeat at the end of World War One. He'd added to that the potent – and entirely flawed – concept of eugenics, claiming that the Jews weren't simply a reviled religious group, but also inherently racially inferior. The Jew, Hitler claimed, was a different species to the rest of humankind and could not be redeemed. Only annihilation would solve 'the Jewish question'.

Already the Nazi concentration camps were busy with their deadly work, which meant that the British and the German Jews had become natural allies. Churchill himself would praise the Jewish soldiers who had joined the Allied cause, lauding the units formed from 'that race which has suffered indescribable torments from the Nazis, a distinct formation among the forces gathered for their final overthrow'.

But still those gathered at Kufra were suspicious of the soldiers in their midst who spoke only in German, wore German uniforms, wielded German weaponry, marched and sang in distinctly German martial tones and kept themselves entirely apart. The men of the Commando might recognize their raw bravery and courage, but that didn't mean that they trusted the men of the SIG.

Could they really be relied upon, or were they dissemblers, awaiting the moment of betrayal? News of previous double-crosses suffered by the SIG troubled the men of the Commando. Could they really place their lives in the hands of such men? Captain Buck for one believed that they could. He had trained and briefed and readied his men exhaustively. No stone had been left unturned in preparing their cover stories.

Indeed, there was no finer deception force in the entire Allied military, or so Buck believed.

CHAPTER 7

So much hung upon the calibre of the men making up the SIG.

Buck had sought out his earliest recruits among the Middle East Commando, at their Burg El Arab headquarters, set to the west of Cairo. The Commando's war diary for 17 March 1942 simply records the arrival of 'a Capt. Buck to select German-speaking personnel with a view to certain work'. Recruiting for that 'certain work' was never going to be easy. The potential volunteers were mostly nationals of the country they were going to fight, and traitors under international law, even if their 'treason' was in the name of liberation from Nazi tyranny. They would be shot without question, if captured.

Upon arrival at the Burg El Arab camp, Buck had announced that he wanted to talk only to fluent German speakers. He told his audience that he was seeking volunteers for a very different kind of challenge, before outlining the basic objectives of the SIG. He stressed that any Jew caught masquerading as a member of the 'master race' was finished.

'If your identity is found out, there's no hope for you,' he warned. 'For any who volunteer, your lives will change completely. You will need to be prepared to cut yourself off from the rest of the British military. You will need to have as little contact as possible with your erstwhile brothers-in-arms.'

He needed independent self-starters who were happy with their own company, Buck explained. Volunteers would have to isolate themselves in a bubble of Teutonic discipline and efficiency, imbibing the Afrika Korps *esprit de corps* to the extent that they would almost begin to *believe* they were soldiers fighting in the Nazi cause. Their very survival depended upon their ability to eat, live and breathe that deception. They would need to wear their disguises faultlessly and to learn to drill as an Afrika Korps soldier.

Every volunteer who stepped forward was made to sign a declaration, acknowledging the dangers involved. It read: 'I hereby certify that I understand the risks . . . to which I and my relatives may be exposed by my employment in the British Army . . . Notwithstanding this, I certify that I am willing to be employed in any theatre of war . . .'

Not that the SIGs would be serving in the British army, of course. Buck had already been transferred into MO4, one of the numerous cover names for the Special Operations Executive. Any who volunteered for the SIG would likewise be shifted sideways on to the SOE's shadowy payroll.

One of the first to step forward was Maurice

'Tiffin' Tiefenbrunner, a German Jew hailing from Wiesbaden, a city in western Germany. One of eight children, his parents had owned a delicatessen. After school, Tiefenbrunner had worked as a fitter in a Jewish-run department store, but in 1934 Nazi storm troopers had burst in and started beating up the staff. Tiefenbrunner had stepped in, trying to defend the store manager. He ended up spending several days in hospital as a result of the beating he sustained.

Four years later his parents were rounded up for deportation to Poland. Maurice offered to take his mother Matel's place, so she could continue caring for his younger siblings. He was duly shipped to Poland along with his father, Efraim, who was blind. So began a long saga of flight from Nazi oppression, which ended with Tiefenbrunner being forced to abandon even his father. With war about to break out, he managed to bribe his way onto the *Parita*, a French pleasure boat bound for Palestine. En route the captain diverted to Cyprus, for the hopelessly overcrowded vessel was running out of food. It was crammed with over 700 Jewish refugees.

Tiefenbrunner and his fellows decided to act. They seized the ship and steamed full speed for Palestine. Upon arrival the British authorities tried to prevent them from landing, but they were not to be deterred, running the boat aground on Tel Aviv beach before smashing up her engines. Tiefenbrunner and the other refugees were interned as illegal immigrants, but at war's outbreak they were released, most signing up for the British army.

By the spring of 1942 Tiefenbrunner had already had a long and varied war. He'd fought with the British Expeditionary Force in France, escaping via St Malo in June 1940 on one of the last of the ships. On his arrival back in England he'd immediately volunteered to serve in the commandos. He'd joined the Middle East Commando, fighting in the Horn of Africa, where he was wounded while trying to rescue a fallen comrade, earning a mention in dispatches.

Tiefenbrunner described Captain Buck's 17 March 1942 recruiting pitch in the following terms: 'He said we would be trained by experienced people to behave like German soldiers, put on German uniforms and go into enemy territory and do intelligence as well as sabotage work . . . This was one step further to my aim to hurt the Nazis as much as possible . . . I and the other volunteers said we were willing to take the risk and go.'

For those who did step forward, all traces of Jewishness would have to be expunged. Maurice Tiefenbrunner chose to adopt his war nickname Tiffin as his new 'official' surname in the SIG. But with his shock of black hair, darkly intense eyes and prominent features, he remained particularly Jewish in appearance, so his cover story in the SIG would have to be flawless, if it were to be convincing.

Another commando who stepped forward was an unlikely looking recruit. Corporal Charlie 'Chunky'

Hillman was plump, cheerful, fresh-faced and barely out of his teens. The son of an Austrian butcher, Hillman had clearly overindulged in the pastries of his native Vienna. Small, stout and with gold-rimmed spectacles, he looked more like a junior professor than an archetypal paratrooper or desert warrior, but his appearance belied his true nature.

In his mid-teens Hillman had been imprisoned in Vienna for what he described happily as 'Nazi-baiting'. Among other things it had involved ringing up the fire brigade and police from public phone boxes and calling them out to emergencies that did not exist, and otherwise generally throwing a spanner in the works of the Nazi administration. After prison, he'd been forced to take a job on a chicken farm. He was to feed several thousand chickens before breakfast, to encourage them to lay eggs for the Nazi war effort. In spite of his love of food he decided to stop feeding the chickens, after which egg production dropped from around 2,000 a day to six.

Portly, even in his late teens, he would nevertheless prove to have the spirit of a lion, earning both a Military Medal and a Military Cross as the war progressed. He also had a somewhat left-field sense of humour, which endeared him to his fellows. He spoke English with a cockney accent and was in the habit of introducing himself as Baron Von Schnitzberger. Hillman chewed garlic whenever he could get his hands on it, and he cheerfully avowed that the only things he cared about in life were eating . . . and killing Germans.

Hillman was utterly fearless and would go on to be one of the most highly decorated foreigners in the British army. Towards the war's end he would be parachuted into his native Vienna on an SOE operation, and end up interrogating the head of the Vienna Gestapo. But for now the SIG beckoned.

Private Opprower, at twenty years old, was another volunteer and equally imbued with raw courage. In 1936, when he was just sixteen years old, his father was deported from their native Berlin to the concentration camps. There he was to perish alongside millions of others. Young Opprower was sent out of Berlin and arrived in Palestine at the outbreak of war, signing up right away for the British military.

Posted to administrative duties, Opprower absconded from camp three times in an effort to join a front-line unit and avenge his father's death. Three times he was brought back to face charges. Luckily, he came to the attention of someone at Special Operations headquarters in Cairo. 'This is just the kind of chap we are looking for,' he declared, and Opprower was promptly recruited into the Commando.

By late March Buck had his full complement of SIG recruits. There were thirty-eight all told, around a platoon in strength. Not all were German Jews. Some hailed from the Free Czech forces, others from the French Foreign Legion

111

and yet others from the ranks of the Free French. They shared two things in common: they were all fluent German speakers who could pass as German natives, and they had an all-consuming desire to strike back hard against the Nazi war machine.

Buck the master-planner and strategist was under no illusions as to the challenges they faced. Success – and with it the survival of those now under his command – depended entirely upon the ability of the men to carry out their masquerade to perfection. Nationality and language proficiency alone would not be enough; each and every SIG operative would need to speak the slang used by the Afrika Korps, reflecting the latest barrack-room gossip, topics of interest and military jargon.

They would need to be intimately acquainted with the German movie actors, dancehall singers, pin-ups and sports stars then most popular with Rommel's troops. Bearing, dress, drill, manner-isms, the curses and idioms they used would need to be that of seasoned veterans of Rommel's Afrika Korps.

Buck decided his men needed to train in utter isolation from any other Allied forces. He couldn't afford to have the SIG 'contaminated' by British soldierly ways or anything else remotely un-Germanic. Accordingly, he established a training camp on the shores of Egypt's Bitter Lakes, stretches of intensely salty water lying astride the Suez Canal. The SIG base was isolated, utterly secret and off limits to all but himself and other members of the unit.

There, the training regime proved relentless. Trainees wore German uniform at all times, even down to their underwear and socks. Reveille was signalled by a sharp blast on a whistle and the greet-the-dawn cry of '*Kompanie aufstehen!*' – Company, get up! This was followed by twenty-minutes of PT, after which the SIG trainees had to march to breakfast, singing lusty German martial songs along the way.

All cigarettes, chocolate or other luxuries in camp were German. The recruits were forbidden from speaking any language other than German, and when they marched it had to be in the German fashion, goose-stepping and with their hands swinging smartly across the chest. Great emphasis was placed on close-combat training, as every member of the SIG might have to fight his way out of a seemingly hopeless situation with no chance of reinforcement or relief.

They trained with the full assortment of Afrika Korps weaponry: Gewehr 41 semi-automatic rifles, Luger P08 pistols, Maschinenpistole 40 subma-chine guns (commonly known as the Schmeisser by the Allies), Stielhandgranate stick grenades and Schiessbecher 30-millimetre grenade-launchers. They handled German explosives, learned to read German maps, and were taught desert navigation They also learned to maintain and operate the German vehicles provided in response to Lieutenant

General Terence Airey's memo requesting German staff cars and trucks.

Buck's recruits had to salute officers in the German fashion and utter 'Heil Hitler' with appropriate gusto. They even had to dream in German – for a few English words uttered in their sleep might spell a death sentence. Awakened suddenly in the night by an inquisitorial Buck, they had to speak German from the off.

In his relentless quest for authenticity, Buck began to slip one or two of his men – Tiefenbrunner among them – into the POW camps around Cairo. There they were told to mix with the German prisoners, masquerading as Afrika Korps soldiers captured in recent fighting. Their mission was two-fold. First, they were to test out their own disguises: could they make it as German captives? Second, they were to soak up the essence of the Afrika Korps and bring it back to the SIG camp.

At night they would talk about every aspect of Rommel's forces, becoming steeped in the identity of the unit they supposedly belonged to. After several weeks of such intensive training, they had been indoctrinated to think and behave as Afrika Korps soldiers, if not to feel like one of their number.

To complement their new sense of identity, the SOE's forgery department went into overdrive, producing false Afrika Korps *Soldbücher* – pay books – and numerous other official papers, complete with photographs, stamps, dates and grand-looking seals. Buck secured German army typewriters, stationery and genuine *Wehrmacht* forms, to better document the force now in training.

The recruits' personal stories were refined and perfected. For those genuinely hailing from Germany, they were kept as close to reality as possible. Each was furnished with a photo of himself in Afrika Korps uniform posing with a suitably Aryan-looking 'sweetheart' – in reality volunteers serving in the Auxiliary Territorial Service, dressed in suitably Germanic clothing. The photos were even furnished with typical German backgrounds, to complete the ruse.

A member of the SIG who considered himself something of a writer penned 'love letters', which were copied by those ATS ladies on to crumbly, well-thumbed notepaper for the men to carry with them into battle. The stamps, franking and envelopes were all entirely authentic, courtesy of the SOE's documentation and forgery department.

Opprower's girlfriend was an ATS blonde bombshell. He addressed her as Lisbeth Kunz in his love letters, the name of the daughter of a well-known Nazi who had been a neighbour on his Berlin street. Even this was done for a deliberate purpose. In case of capture, it was always better to claim a real person as a sweetheart, as opposed to some flimsy creation of the imagination that might fall apart under interrogation.

Likewise, each trainee had to commit to memory his new German name and life story. He had to answer to that name instantly. He had to know intimately his family history as if he'd really lived it. He had to know when and to whom he was married, the names and birthdays of his children, and what jobs his wife was doing back in Germany to aid the Nazi war effort. Every day Buck would quiz them on such details. It was relentless, but it was also entirely necessary if the SIG deception was to hold up.

But still Buck wasn't satisfied. A perfectionist, he sought to take the SIG to the next level. He decided he needed real Afrika Korps veterans to train his recruits. He sought two junior officers as instructors. As only the genuine article would do, they would need to be sourced from the POW cages holding Afrika Korps soldiers.

The risks to security were legion, especially as the fortunes of the war were going very much against the Allies. Finding two German prisoners who were willing to swap sides was a tall order. Moreover, the SIG was slated to work in tandem with other special forces on operations to which those POWs would doubtless become privy, adding another layer of security risk.

Still Buck demanded his Afrika Korps trainers.

British intelligence worked closely with the Military Police to scour the camps for potential recruits. It took time, but eventually two candidates were identified. Both had served in the French Foreign Legion, before being conscripted into the *Wehrmacht* when France signed the armistice with Germany. They had been drafted into the 361st Regiment of the Deutsches Afrika Korps, and they had been captured in November 1941.

Unteroffizier Heinrich Bruckner was a big, fair-haired, muscle-bound sergeant. Brash, over-confident and prone to belligerence, he was in many ways a classic product of the French Foreign Legion, if not a typical Afrika Korps soldier. By contrast Feldwebel Walter Essner was a quiet, good-natured and generous staff sergeant. Between the two they typified the breadth of unusual characters – the misfits and wanderers – attracted to life in the Legion.

In fact, Bruckner and Essner were not their real names. These were the covers given to them by their recruiters and screeners, who themselves were a decidedly oddball bunch. In order to be cleared for the SIG, Unteroffizier Bruckner and Feldwebel Essner had been put through the grinder at Camp 020, one of Britain's most secretive and least known – but vital – initiatives in the war. Camp 020 always gave cover identities to those it had turned.

More formally known as the Combined Services Detailed Interrogation Centre (CSDIC), Camp 020 was a MI5 facility located within the most incongruous of settings – Latchmere House, a rambling Victorian-style mansion adjacent to Ham Common in the leafy London borough of Richmond. At Latchmere they specialized in inter-rogating German spies. Due to Ultra intercepts, British intelligence knew when and where German agents were being inserted into the UK. In all but one case they were captured, sent to Camp 020 and turned.

Camp 020 was run by a severe and uncompromising nonconformist, Lieutenant Colonel Robin Stephens, known as Tin Eye due to the steely gaze that peered out of his fierce face, his right eye sporting an ever-present wire-rimmed monocle. In many ways Stephens appeared like the archetypal Gestapo interrogator, yet he could not have been more different. Any form of physical abuse or torture was banned at Latchmere.

'Never strike a man,' Stephens exhorted. 'In the first place it is an act of cowardice. In the second place, it is not intelligent. A prisoner will lie to avoid further punishment, and everything he says thereafter will be based upon a false premise.' In other words, torture only produced what the torturer wished the prisoner to say. 'Violence is taboo, for not only does it produce answers to please, but it lowers the standard of information.'

The interrogators at Camp 020 relied instead upon the full gamut of psychological measures developed there – the stool pigeon, the cross-ruff and sympathy men – to break prisoners. Such methods proved remarkably effective: of the 400 enemy agents who passed through its portals, few held out for more than forty-eight hours once they faced their interrogators.

The tales revealed at Latchmere were sensational. They involved intrigue, fraud, blackmail, theft, drugs, perverts, playboys, prostitutes, violence and sabotage. But no matter what an enemy agent's story might be, Stephens sought only one outcome from any interrogation. It was at Camp 020 that the so-called Double-Cross System was perfected. Rather than imprisoning or executing the German spies, they were turned to work for the Allied cause, feeding back carefully crafted misinformation to Berlin via their radio sets.

Stephens nursed a burning hatred of cowards, turncoats and liars. It drove everything that he did at Latchmere. Camp 020 maintained files on all who were guests there. They were chillingly detailed, including photographs, letters, tape-recorded conversations, lists of associates, interrogation reports and confessions. A 'yellow peril' was compiled for particularly reviled agents – a file summarising the worst aspects of that individual's nature.

In the spring of 1942 Unteroffizier Bruckner and Feldwebel Essner were flown to Britain and supposedly broken at Latchmere. It was an extraordinary achievement, even for a place like Camp 020. This was no normal double-cross. Radioing back doctored intelligence was one thing, but Bruckner and Essner's mission was quite another. These former Afrika Korps sergeants were to train a unit whose express mission was to deceive, confound and kill their former brothers-in-arms.

Bruckner and Essner arrived at Buck's Bitter Lakes camp in late May 1942. Neither was Jewish, but at Camp 020 they had declared themselves passionately anti-Nazi. Their French Foreign Legion bona fides – they had fought on the side of France in the war's first months – lent credibility to their claims, and they were sent to Buck with a clean bill of health.

At first the SIG recruits were deeply suspicious of the newcomers, but as the weeks passed and Bruckner and Essner threw themselves into the training such suspicions began to subside. By mid-May the former POWs were largely accepted. The recruits were able to curse in an Afrika Korps soldier's typically colourful language, and Buck declared their training complete

The time for preparations was over; the great deception needed to be tested in action.

CHAPTER 8

The SIG's first operation was designed to test the waters gently. In early June 1942 Buck, Tiffin, Chunky Hillman and Opprower navigated their German vehicles around the enemy lines, heading for the coastal town of Bardia on Libya's border with Egypt. Dressed in the uniform of the German military police, the *Feldgendarmerie*, they set up a roadblock on the main coastal route, stopping convoys and checking their papers.

Such checkpoints were part and parcel of life in the Afrika Korps, and few suspicions seemed to be aroused. This was a DIY version of the LRDG's road watch: by noting the types of vehicles and reinforcements using the road, the SIG gathered valuable intelligence on enemy troop movements at first hand. It was a bold beginning.

They graduated to mingling with the German troops in their camps. The SIG operators milled around the canteens, buying cigarettes and chocolate and keeping their ears tuned to the rank and file's gossip. Tiffin, Hillman and Opprower even had the nerve to queue for wages from an Axis

121

quartermaster, using their forged pay books. Meanwhile, Buck and Russell were dining in the officers' mess, gathering intelligence on the status of Rommel's war.

This was just the kind of bluff and chutzpah that thrilled Churchill.

By now the SIG recruits had learned a towering respect and affection for their visionary commander, Captain Buck. 'Buck was a person to be trusted,' remarked Tiffin. 'A person you could talk to. A person . . . who speaks man-to-man, and highly intelligent.' Such sentiments were mutual: Buck had a high regard for his men. This was fortunate because the close-knit unit was about to be given its first major combat operation.

In late May 1942 Isaac Levy, a Jewish British army chaplain, was told about a somewhat 'unusual outfit' that was to be found at a remote map reference out by the Bitter Lakes, and tasked to pay them a visit to administer to their spiritual needs. Levy discovered the SIG in 'a shed crammed full of German uniforms and German army equipment . . . I learned to my surprise and profound admiration that this unit was destined to be dropped behind the lines for special commando operations . . .'

A hugely impressed Levy went about his duties, but while speaking to the men he learned of a 'painfully distressing' matter that was unsettling them. One of their number was distrusted, but Captain Buck had insisted that he accompany them on the coming mission. Bruckner, the brash, blond-haired former Afrika Korps sergeant, might well have made a decent trainer, but few in the SIG wanted him to accompany them deep behind enemy lines.

'Essner and Bruckner were very good instructors,' Tiffin remarked, 'but when we were told we were very soon going into action and that the two German soldiers would go with us, I protested. I said it was too dangerous.'

Despite such concerns, Buck had remained insistent: both Bruckner and Essner were entirely trustworthy, and they would join the SIG on the first of their forays with sabotage in mind. Chaplain Levy raised the men's concerns with Captain Buck. 'He disregarded the information,' Levy remarked of the encounter, 'and assured me that the doubts expressed were unfounded.'

As far as Buck was concerned, the two former POWs had been vouched for by Colonel 'Tin Eye' Stephens and CSDIC. Buck argued it was a 'necessary risk for training purposes and initial operations to have men who had recently been in the German army and knew the ropes'. Bruckner and Essner had already yielded 'intelligence with very valuable information about German dispositions, and had extracted information from many POWs on behalf of CSDIC'. They would be going with the SIG, no matter what, and the stakes could hardly have been higher.

In late May 1942 David Stirling had been

approached by Cairo high command with a most urgent request. Two Allied convoys packed full of war materiel and supplies were about to steam for Malta, the Mediterranean island long under siege by Axis forces. Suffering a round-the-clock pounding from the Luftwaffe, the population of the beleaguered island was on the brink of starvation.

Holding Malta was vital to the British war effort, but the convoys would be forced to run the gauntlet of German air attacks the entire length of their voyage. If Stirling's SAS could hit the Axis airfields from where the Malta sorties were being flown, it would greatly enhance the chances of the ships making it through. Seven airfields were identified as key targets, and the SAS prepared to raid them in a series of lightning hit-and-run sorties.

But Stirling had a problem. The most important airfields – those closest to Malta – were located around the eastern Libyan town of Derna, and these were also the most challenging targets. They were situated amid rough, hilly terrain, where there was a high concentration of enemy supply depots, workshops and infantry encampments. Any attempt to attack them from open ground was bound to end in failure, as the SAS's approach would be spotted.

Stirling figured that some kind of subterfuge was required to get his raiders into the area undetected. Racking his brains, he finally turned to the SIG. Stirling radioed Buck at his Bitter Lakes base, requesting a meeting in Cairo. There the SAS commander outlined a daring proposition: he wanted Buck's 'Germans' in the vanguard, driving Afrika Korps vehicles and escorting several truck-loads of SAS posing as POWs. In that way they could bluff their way through the German lines and strike the Derna airfields by total surprise.

Buck thrilled to the idea. This was just the sort of mission for which the SIG had been formed. The two commanders agreed that a unit of the Free French SAS would rendezvous with the SIG at the Siwa oasis. The raids on the airfields were scheduled for the night of 13 June – just prior to the Malta convoys setting sail – which meant that the SIG–SAS force would have to depart Siwa by 8 June latest.

Free French Lieutenant Augustine Jordain and his fourteen-strong party of SAS were flown into Siwa to link up with the SIG. A LRDG patrol was tasked to guide the unusual convoy across the initial stages of their desert journey, from where they would approach the enemy lines. Buck selected an eight-man unit for the mission: along with Tiffin, Chunky Hillman and Opprower, both Bruckner and Essner, the two Afrika Korps veterans, were in that number.

Buck assembled a convoy of four Afrika Korps vehicles. In the lead, carrying himself, Essner and Bruckner – with whom the British captain seemed to have established an unusual bond – would be a *Kubelwagen*, the open-topped military version of the Volkswagen, and the German's answer to the Willys Jeep. Though two-wheel drive, the Kubelwagen was light and manoeuvrable, and for Buck's purposes it very much looked the part. Behind the *Kubelwagen* came an Opel Blitz light army truck, followed by a heavier 3-ton German army lorry, with a 'captured' British military truck bringing up the rear. The rest of the SIG would ride in the trucks posing as guards for their SAS 'prisoners', who would be slumped in the canvas-covered rears, heads bowed as if cowed by defeat.

Prior to their departure Stirling flew into Siwa, bringing the latest intelligence and aerial photos. He wished the men bon voyage and good luck, and the convoy set out heading south-west out of Siwa.

So impressed had Stirling been by the SIG, that he'd recruited a handful of their operators to accompany his other airfield raids. One of those men, a German Jew called Karl Kahane, was a former soldier in the German army. On the coming raids he would help bluff Stirling's column through a hostile checkpoint, unleashing a volley of colourful curses on the German guards who tried to bar their way. In other locations on other airfield raids, the SIG would also prove its worth.

But the Derna mission would suffer more mixed fortunes. Unbeknown to Buck, Free French Lieutenant Jordain or David Stirling, fate was turning against them. Colonel Bonner F. Fellers, the US military attaché in Cairo, was a highly capable and dedicated man where the war effort was concerned. He'd sent an upbeat message to

126

Washington, giving details of the coming airfield raids. Unfortunately, the Germans had broken the US diplomatic Black Code and could read every signal sent.

The SIG and SAS set out, not knowing that the enemy had been forewarned that they were coming. For four days the LRDG led the convoy through barren, empty country, then they halted, and the SIG changed into their Afrika Korps uniforms. They were ready to cross the lines, except for one potentially crucial factor: the Germans' password for June had not yet been radioed through to them. They knew May's code – *fiume* (river) – but that was of little use now.

They radioed headquarters. The June password was still not known. Usually, it was easy enough to extract it from a hapless prisoner of war, but the interrogators in Cairo had had no such luck this month. The timescale for the raids brooked no delay. There was nothing for it but to proceed regardless.

Buck's *Kubelwagen* took the lead, as the other 'German' vehicles fell in behind. The convoy pushed north, the desert gradually becoming more broken and hilly, scattered with stunted trees and scrub. Though coated in a layer of dust, Buck, Essner and Bruckner looked crisp and smart in their Afrika Korps uniforms.

Atop each of the trucks perched a SIG operator, a Maschinenpistole 40 clutched in his hands. It was the habit of Afrika Korps convoys to post such lookouts, scouring the skies for Allied warplanes. The SIG operators were armed to the teeth: in addition to his main weapon, each carried a Luger on his belt, a bayonet sharpened on both sides to form a makeshift dagger, plus a 'potato masher' grenade. And beneath the tarpaulin of each of the trucks was hidden a pair of machine guns, with the ammo belts already in position. The SAS 'prisoners' had their weapons hidden beneath blankets, kitbags and the like, as they stared out morosely at the passing scenery, watching the Arab villagers who worked the fields to either side of the dirt road.

They first hit trouble in the early afternoon, when the British lorry broke down as it was crawling up a steep and winding incline. Buck couldn't afford to leave any men behind, so he took it in tow. An hour or so later Buck's *Kubelwagen* rounded a bend, only to find a red-and-white barrier barring the way. Buck was at the wheel and he barely altered his pace, only slowing at the last moment, as Bruckner and Essner signalled imperiously for the bar to be raised. The guards manning it were Italian, and Buck hoped their gestures of Teutonic impatience would do the trick.

For a moment the Italian guards went to do as bidden, but they must have thought better of it. One motioned the *Kubelwagen* to a halt, before stepping forward to demand the password. Bruckner leaped immediately into role. He'd been out on the front line for weeks, he explained. He had May's password, but not that for June. He was on a special mission, and digging out his papers he waved them impatiently in the face of the guard.

A second figure joined them. This was an Italian officer, and he suggested the *Kubelwagen*'s occupants join him in the guardhouse for a glass of wine, over which the issue could be straightened out. The officer explained that he had strict orders not to allow anyone through without the current password. The wine was drunk but he remained adamant. Bruckner decided to get angry: he became abusive, threatening to ring his superior and explain that the Italian guards were obstructing a German patrol in the business of war. Finally the Italian officer relented. He ordered the barrier raised, and Buck and party were able to mount up their *Kubelwagen* and lead the convoy through.

They pushed on towards Derna. At dusk a portly German corporal came charging out and waved the convoy to a halt at a roadblock. At first Buck was worried, but it turned out the man only sought to offer some friendly advice: British saboteurs were reported to be in the area, he explained, and they often ambushed convoys after dark. They should pull over at the next camp and spend the night there.

To allay suspicion, Buck did as advised. The enemy camp was a hive of activity. Buck, Bruckner, Essner and the rest of the SIG queued for lentils and dumplings, mess tins in hand, joining the mixture of Afrika Korps and Luftwaffe troops making up the camp. Meanwhile, the Free French

SAS spied on the goings-on through the slats in the rear of the trucks, wondering at the SIG's brazenness, yet fearful of discovery at the same time.

After an hour of such theatre, Buck decided it was safe to depart. The vehicles pulled out, passing groups of men bedding down for the night or playing cards and chatting, none of whom paid them so much as a passing glance. For now at least the deception seemed to be holding up. They pushed on for a few miles, before pulling off the road into a hidden campsite all of their own.

The following morning, 13 June, heralded the day of the raids. Buck talked things through with Lieutenant Jordain, and they decided it was crucial to get the current password. They might be challenged as they drove on to the target aerodromes, the attacks foiled at the last minute. Buck typed a letter on 'official' paper, asking the recipient to furnish the password to the bearer and explaining why he wasn't in possession of it.

Two of the SIG drove back to the checkpoint where the larger-than-life German corporal had warned them the previous evening about British saboteurs. He'd seemed like a jolly fellow and there appeared to be little risk in trying the ruse. They reached the checkpoint and produced their letter with a flourish. The hulking great corporal, who recognized them from the previous evening, laughed good-naturedly.

'You want to know the password?' he boomed. 'I don't believe I know it myself.'

He invited them into his hut. He asked his Italian comrade, who was sitting at a desk, if he knew June's password. The Italian was none the wiser. But after thumbing through the codebook on his desk, he declared triumphantly, 'Here it is! Eldorado.' The SIG operators saluted smartly, gave voice to their gratitude and departed forthwith.

Armed with the proper password, Buck moved his convoy up to a position five miles south-east of the airfields. This would be the rendezvous point, for there were two aerodromes to attack and the party would need to split up in order to do so. One would hit Derna airfield itself, the other Martuba airfield lying on the far side.

That afternoon Lieutenant Jordain and his Free French SAS were driven to Derna airfield to carry out a reconnaissance, peering from the rear of one of the trucks. They counted a squadron of Messerschmitt Bf 110s and a dozen Stuka dive-bombers. Martuba airfield was too inaccessible to risk a recce: they would simply have to hit it by surprise and see what targets of opportunity were present on the runway.

Buck and Lieutenant Jordain decided on the final plan of attack. Come nightfall, Buck and Essner would take Free French Corporal Tourneret plus three fellow SAS to hit Martuba. They would travel in a single lorry, with Buck and his SIG men posing as guards. Lieutenant Jordain, mean-while, would lead a team of ten SAS to attack Derna, targeting the Messerschmitt Bf 110s and the Stukas. They would travel in one truck, with Bruckner and two SIG operators acting as escort.

Once they'd destroyed the aircraft, the two patrols would circle back to the rendezvous point, where Tiffin would remain with the spare vehicles in reserve.

The two attack forces set off for their targets at 9 o'clock that night. It was already dark. In the rear of the truck heading for Derna airfield time seemed to drag interminably for the SAS 'POWs'. Bruckner was driving, but he kept stopping the truck complaining of engine trouble. In this way it took over an hour to cover five miles, and Lieutenant Jordain found himself growing increasingly anxious.

Just on the outskirts of the airfield Bruckner again brought the truck to a grinding halt. *What on earth could it be now?* Lieutenant Jordain wondered. To one side he and his fellow SAS men could hear a movie being played in the aerodrome's cinema.

Bruckner dismounted and raised the bonnet. He shouted something about the engine over-heating and needing to seek help. With that Bruckner was gone, crunching across the gravel towards a guardhouse just a few dozen feet away. As the raiders crouched in the truck, the SIG men felt the cold claws of suspicion tearing at their minds: had their worst fears come to pass? Was former POW Bruckner about to betray them?

A figure wandered over from the guardhouse. One of the SIG explained about the breakdown and why they had stopped, but at the same time he was wondering, fearfully, about Bruckner. Moments later Lieutenant Jordain heard the sound of running footsteps. He risked peeking out of the truck. No sooner had he done so than German soldiers pounced upon him and dragged him out of the vehicle.

The truck was surrounded by Afrika Korps fighters, their weapons at the ready. 'All Frenchmen out!' barked a figure. 'Out of the truck! Now!'

The next moment all dissolved into a firestorm of confusion.

One of the Free French SAS hurled a grenade, as another unleashed a savage burst from the machine gun mounted in the rear of the truck. The German soldiers dived for cover and Lieutenant Jordain made a break for it. The grenade exploded behind him, showering the enemy in shrapnel. Moments later SAS and SIG fighters, screaming their defiance and hatred, were trading fire with the enemy at close quarters.

Flare rounds went up from positions around the airbase, illuminating the scene. For an instant Lieutenant Jordain took cover. To him, the truck and its occupants seemed doomed, as machine guns started to pour in fire. The SAS and SIG must have realized the same thing, for a sudden and cataclysmic explosion ripped apart the air. Its epicentre was the truck: one of its occupants must have hurled a grenade into the ammunition heaped in its rear, having decided to go down fighting, taking as many of the enemy with them rather than be captured alive.

Lieutenant Jordain turned and ran. For two hours he flitted through the night as the truck burned and sparked in the distance behind him. He felt a great sadness for those who had needlessly perished, but an even greater anger that one of the Germans, Bruckner, had betrayed them – for he had no doubt that was what had happened.

It was only when Jordain reached the rendezvous and began to blurt out his breathless story to Buck and the others that he realized he was badly injured. He'd been hit during the airfield melee, but adrenaline and fear had driven him onward. Now that he had reached the RV, blood loss had rendered him all but incoherent.

As for Buck, the commander of the SIG could barely believe what the Free French lieutenant had to say: *Bruckner a traitor? Surely it couldn't be?* But nothing else made any sense. The snail's-pace journey to the airfield; the repeated stops due to 'mechanical trouble'; the final halt, claiming an overheating engine. It was all a long act, designed to deliver the men into enemy hands. Indeed, by now Bruckner had doubtless told his German comrades all about the RV point, and to tarry here a moment longer would invite certain capture.

Shocked and stunned at the terrible turn of events, the survivors mounted the vehicles and prepared to move out. 'I will take it from here,' Tiffin announced to Buck. The SIG commander seemed to be in a state of paralysing disbelief. 'We must try to get back to our camp, but I will sit next to Essner.'

To the veteran SIG, Essner was now one of the enemy. Tiffin joined him in the rear of the *Kubelwagen*, his hand on his Luger. 'If you move, you're a dead man,' Tiffin warned the hapless German.

A dark cloud hung over the remnants of the patrol as they hurried through the fearful night. The fact that Buck's team had set explosive on twenty-seven warplanes at Martuba, blowing them to pieces, barely registered. The greatest deception had actually been executed by Bruckner, who had played them for fools. The double-cross had in fact been a triple-cross, and Buck had been naive in the extreme to take the man to war.

Buck should have listened to his men. He had refused to do so, and as a result fourteen Free French SAS and two SIG had either perished or – worse still – been taken into captivity. Buck's Great Idea for the SIG had not been found wanting – the bluff had worked perfectly – but they had been sunk by the very basest of human instincts: betrayal.

Had Lieutenant Colonel Robin 'Tin Eye' Stephens got it wrong in recruiting Bruckner? Had Camp 020 messed up? Not necessarily. Bruckner had been turned to be the SIG's *trainer*, and in that no one doubted that he had done a fine job. Stephens hadn't been asked to find an Afrika Korps officer willing to go to war against his former comrades.

If he had, he may well have considered Bruckner the wrong candidate for the job.

Whoever was at fault, word of the disaster and bloody betrayal was whispered far and wide, and especially amongst Allied elite forces. It had reached the ears of the SOE Commando, of course – hence their unease at being given a mission by Haselden that hinged on a deception spearheaded by the SIG.

Who could blame them? Reputations are hard won, and after a sterling start the SIG had crashed and burned spectacularly. They had done so simply because Buck was the kind of character inclined to trust too much. It was to counter this that Lieutenant Russell had been brought in as second in command. Russell was a far tougher nut to crack, and it was decided that none but genuine SIG volunteers would be going on any future combat missions.

But that did little to offset the greatest damage that Bruckner's treachery had wreaked: his tell-all betrayal had alerted the Germans to the unit's existence and exactly what the British intended to use it for. As the men at Kufra prepared to head for Tobruk, the enemy was hunting for the SIG with an unprecedented ferocity.

They were doing so on the personal orders of Adolf Hitler himself.

CHAPTER 9

By the time they reached the Siwa oasis, Buck's raiding force had been reduced to one vehicle. Buck reported that Bruckner had been killed at the Derna aerodrome, along with the others. Sadly, this was wishful thinking. The full story of the debacle and bloody betrayal was revealed a few weeks later by an entirely unexpected source.

In the first week of July two Messerschmitt Bf 109s were shot down near El Alamein and their pilots captured. Under interrogation, Leutnant Korner and Oberleutnant Klager told the extraordinary story of how the events at Derna had unfolded. Sure enough, the Germans had received prior warning of the raid, including that a group of British saboteurs dressed in Afrika Korps uniform would execute the attack. As a result, a general state of alarm had been declared at all aerodromes.

Bruckner's treachery on reaching Derna airfield had been very deliberate. He had sought out the German commanding officer, alerting him to the truck-load of fighters dressed as Germans, and urging him to assemble as many men as possible. They had surrounded the truck, and the firefight had ensued, which ended with the massive explosion.

One of the SIG had got away. He'd found his way to a local hospital, for he was badly wounded. He claimed to be a German soldier, but the medics became suspicious. He was finally unmasked as a German Jew fighting with the SIG and he was tortured and executed.

The SIG had given themselves a nickname in German, one replete with dark irony: the *Himmelfarhts* – the Heaven Platoon. At Derna it had been borne out, but for all the wrong reasons: several operators had been sent to their creator and all due to Bruckner's betrayal. Yet lessons had been learned. Essner was damned by association. Two members of the SIG were ordered to take him back to a POW camp. In truth, it was never intended that he should get there. En route he would be 'shot while trying to escape'.

Meanwhile Bruckner had triumphed: after he had told all that he knew, he was flown to Berlin, feted by the Nazis and awarded the Deutsch Kreuze in gold, one of the Third Reich's most prestigious decorations.

The fallout from Bruckner's betrayal was to be long-lived. While the men of the SOE Commando knew precious little about the SIG, the enemy had learned practically everything courtesy of Bruckner. Buck's Great Idea – his platoon-sized deception force – had come to Hitler's personal attention. The very concept of Germans fighting *against* the Reich proved incendiary to the Nazi leader.

Again, the details of Hitler's reaction came to the Allies' attention via Ultra intercepts. On 13 June 1942 a 'Most Secret' message was sent from Hitler to the supreme command of the Panzerarmee Afrika, Field Marshal Rommel and his closest deputies. The intercepted and decoded signal was stamped by the British: 'To Be Kept Under Lock And Key And Never Removed From This Office.' It read:

> According to reports to hand there are said to be numerous German political refugees with the Free French units in Africa. The Führer has ordered that the severest measures are to be taken against those concerned. They are therefore to be mercilessly wiped out in battle, and in cases where they escape being killed in battle a military sentence is to be pronounced immediately by the nearest German officer and they are to be shot out of hand.
>
> These orders, being specially secret, are being passed verbally to commanding officers.

The message had been sent on the night of Bruckner's bloody betrayal at Derna. This was his lasting legacy: there would be no mercy shown and no quarter given to the SIG.

The insistence that Hitler's order must not be forwarded in writing, but was only to be circulated verbally, reflected the sensitivity of such instructions, which amounted to extrajudicial murder without any form of a trial. The Führer's order constituted a war crime, hence the extraordinary levels of secrecy surrounding it.

On 19 June Stirling wrote to Haselden, outlining the misfortune that had befallen the SIG. 'Buck is in having lost 14 Frenchmen and 3 Germans. Jourdain is the one Frenchman who got back. They got up to Derna and Martuba . . . all right and made a recce, but when the Derna party went in . . . for the attack they were betrayed by one of Buck's Germans . . . Hope this is plain. I have a fever.'

But planning for the Tobruk raid was already well under way. Nothing, not even the betrayal of the SIG, could be allowed to impede its progress. The various teams of raiders would be going in regardless.

Bruckner's betrayal would have one other unforeseen consequence for the desert war: it would inspire Rommel to launch his own imitation of the British special forces. Bruckner, of course, was acquainted with the wider operations of the SAS and the LRDG. He had knowledge of the desert raiders gained at first hand, which would prove invaluable to the enemy.

Prior to this, Rommel hadn't really understood what he was up against with the desert raiders.

Many of their operations were put down to local 'Arab saboteurs' trained and armed by the British. Even when it was obvious that Allied soldiers were in the vanguard, rarely would German or Italian forces pursue the raiders into the desert. The main reason for this was that the Axis forces disliked and even feared the vast, waterless wastes of the Sahara.

Extracts from a captured German report reflected their growing fear of such sorties. It described an attack by desert raiders hurling hand grenades into the German headquarters at Beda Littoria, a town in eastern Libya. That same night telephone lines were blown up and vehicles ambushed. The raiders wore plain clothes or nondescript uniforms, and when they were challenged they replied in German that they were German soldiers.

The report concluded:

(a) That the British were attempting by acts of sabotage to draw troops from the front and spread panic among the people.

(b) This sabotage was brought about by means of . . . long-range raids by motor vehicles . . . carried out by the famous Commandos instructed and directed by the Intelligence Service.

(c) That natives helped the British with shelter and information.

(d) That the British were going about populated centres in civilian clothes or a vague sort of uniform such as shorts and shirts with badges hardly visible, which would foil police, who mistook them for Germans.

In the spring and summer of 1942 Rommel decided that he needed to respond to such reports by fighting fire with fire. Yet again, it was Ultra intercepts that revealed to the Allies the German commander's intentions. Rommel ordered a singular individual, Ladislas Edouard, Count de Almaszy, to join him in North Africa.

Known as von Almaszy to the Germans, this Hungarian aristocrat was a World War One fighter ace, an amateur archaeologist and a fellow desert explorer of Bagnold and Prendergast's from the inter-war years. He'd been kept under close watch by British intelligence, and in the spring of 1942 decrypts of coded enemy transmissions revealed that he'd been attached to Rommel's staff for some special purpose. Given his desert experience it seemed a reasonable guess that Rommel was looking towards a new type of warfare.

Almaszy was about to be dispatched deep into the Sahara, ahead of Rommel's next great offensive: a massive thrust to smash his way through the Allied lines and on to Cairo. For that he needed accurate and up-to-date intelligence on Allied positions. Almaszy's mission – code-named Operation Condor – was to insert German spies into the Egyptian capital itself, via the 'back door' of the desert.

While traversing the Sahara, Almaszy would scope out opportunities for the Germans to counter the British raiding forces and to mount their own behind-the-lines operations. Rommel needed his spies in place because of fears that his primary source of intelligence – US Colonel Feller's Black Code messages – was somehow compromised. Rommel was starting to fear that he was being fed disinformation, and he was keen for human sources to verify things on the ground.

Rommel had been listening in on Colonel Feller's communications ever since September 1941, and he was privy to every dispatch sent from the US embassy in Cairo. The Black Code had been broken by means of an audacious piece of espionage, perpetrated in Rome. Italian agents had broken into the safe of the American embassy and copied every page of the top-secret codebook, before escaping undetected. The Italians had shared the prize with their German allies.

The well-connected and hugely respected Colonel Fellers was privy to detailed information on British military operations, information he then passed on to Washington. Unbeknown to Fellers, Rommel was reading his every message, and he had deemed them to be of 'sensational value'. Using a play on words, Rommel called those signals intercepts his 'little fellers'.

Unwittingly, Colonel Fellers had yielded Rommel 'the broadest and clearest picture of . . . [Allied] forces and intentions available to any Axis commander throughout the war'. But in recent months Rommel had grown fearful that the Black Code intercepts were perhaps too good to be true, which is where Almaszy came in.

To execute Operation Condor Almaszy was given a handful of men from the elite Brandenburger Brigade, a special operations unit attached to the German intelligence service, the Abwehr. Almaszy assembled five captured British vehicles, which he had fitted with sun compasses, sand rails and other LRDG-esque equipment. This bespoke unit – Sonderkommando (Special Command) Almaszy – consisted of eight Brandenburgers accompanied by two Abwehr spies.

Those Abwehr agents were old Africa hands. One, Johan Eppler, was a German Jew schooled in Egypt who had converted to Islam. The other, Peter Sanstede, was a well-built blond German who had worked on east African oil rigs prior to the war. On reaching Cairo, Eppler was to pose as a native Egyptian and Sanstede as an Irish-American. Each carried with him false papers, portable radios, plus £50,000 in crisp new sterling notes – a fortune at the time.

Once Sonderkommando Almaszy departed into the Sahara, Count Almaszy proved to have lost little of his desert expertise. His daily radio reports to Rommel's headquarters charted his steady progress south and then east into Egypt – tracing a route that was to be Lloyd Owen and the SOE Commando's in reverse. Almaszy reached the pass at Gilf Kebir – the towering red sandstone cliffs decorated by cave art – and found the track leading east to the Nile.

From there Sonderkommando Almaszy skirted the Kharga oasis and hit the first roadblock. Putting on his best English accent, Almaszy told the Egyptian policemen manning the post that the remainder of the 'English column' would be along soon. The barrier was duly raised and Sonderkommando Almaszy was allowed through.

Almaszy called a final halt just outside Asyut, the town where Lloyd Owen would steer his convoy of vehicles west into the desert. In the distance Almaszy could see the glistening waters of the Nile. Agents Eppler and Sanstede quickly changed into civilian clothes, gathered up their suitcases and with a swift goodbye set off on foot for the station, from where they would catch the train to Cairo.

As Almaszy's unit did an about-turn and prepared to retrace its steps, the Abwehr agents headed into town. They passed through two more check-points, their forged papers apparently standing up to scrutiny, and boarded the train. They steamed north to Cairo, where they rented a modest apartment, setting up their radios for making contact with Rommel's headquarters.

Operation Condor seemed to have succeeded absolutely.

In truth, the opposite was the case. Almaszy's diligent radio reports had doomed it from the start. The British D/F stations had picked up nearly all of his signals, and while many proved difficult to decrypt, they were enough to track his progress through the desert. Operation Condor's every step had been watched.

For a short while agents Eppler and Sanstede were allowed to go about their business. Eppler contacted one of Cairo's most famed belly dancers and seductresses, Hakmet Fahmi, who had recently taken a British major as her lover. While the major was kept entertained in the bedroom of her Nile houseboat, Eppler would sift through the contents of his briefcase. The papers he copied included what appeared to be priceless details of Allied troops movements, information that Eppler promptly radioed to Rommel.

Eventually, the British counter-espionage teams struck. Agents Eppler and Sanstede, along with their belly-dancing associate, were arrested. In the interrogations that followed the truth about the Germans having broken the Black Code was revealed. The two Abwehr agents had keyed their own coded radio messages to the pages of Daphne du Maurier's novel, *Rebecca*. They were persuaded to keep sending such encrypted reports, only now at the behest of the British.

Colonel Fellers was understandably upset when his role in providing intelligence to the enemy was revealed. But he was persuaded to stay on in Cairo and to keep sending his Black Code reports. From now on every aspect of his, and agents Eppler and Sanstede's communications, would be carefully crafted to fool Field Marshal Rommel.

Operation Condor had achieved exactly the opposite of what the German commander had intended. Count Almaszy couldn't know this, of course. He flitted back through the desert, unaware that Prendergast was under strict orders to allow him to slip through the LRDG's clutches. En route, Almaszy erected cairns in the desert, intended to act as markers for the Luftwaffe, when they flew missions to drop supplies. They would become the caches of water, fuel and ammo that a greatly expanded Sonderkommando Almaszy would use as it proceeded to sweep south to attack Kufra – for Almaszy didn't doubt the success of Operation Condor would win him Rommel's unreserved backing.

Sure enough, upon his triumphant return to Panzerarmee Afrika's headquarters, Almaszy received an on-the-spot promotion by Rommel to major. That August Rommel declared the Condor agents the greatest heroes of the Reich. The intelligence sent via their *Rebecca* codes – 'corroborated' by the Black Code intercepts – suggested that the Allied positions south of El Alamein, at Alam Halfa, were pitifully weak.

Attempting to punch through the lines and take Cairo, Rommel instead walked into a carefully prepared trap. His Panzerarmee was repulsed by the massed ranks of the Eighth Army. Rommel lost fifty tanks and many troops in his first major defeat of the war. That left him desperate for reinforcements, and the 13 September 1942 raids – in which Tobruk was the key target – were aimed at compounding that defeat.

Yet at the Kufra oasis Haselden was secretly worried. He couldn't reveal such concerns before the men, of course – he had to keep his disquiet utterly private – but with his good friend Lloyd Owen he felt differently. On their last day at Kufra the two men sat long into the evening, ruminating on the mission that lay before them.

Preparations at Kufra could not have been more exhaustive. Buck had kept his SIG busy. The Bristol Bombay that had flown them in hadn't just carried men and war supplies; it had also brought the materials necessary for the coming great deception. Buck carried the stencils down to the Kufra vehicle pound, while Chunky Hillman clutched the cans of paint that were required.

Rommel had captured hundreds of Allied trucks at Tobruk and they had been turned to serve their new masters. Buck intended to use this to his advantage. The SIG proceeded to give the vehicles chosen for the coming mission an Axis makeover, painting out the British markings and replacing them with the emblem of the Afrika Korps – a swastika superimposed over a stylized black palm tree.

Across the bonnet they painted the recognition symbol for *Beutezeichen* – booty – a foot-wide white stripe. That way, any German aircraft overflying the column would indentify them as Afrika Korps vehicles. To complete the deception, the trucks were painted with the insignia of a division of the Afrika Korps that really did exist, one that was positioned near El Alamein. It was a nice touch of authenticity.

Shaking off their reluctance, the commandos also got in on the act. They rehearsed mounting the freshly painted trucks and squatting in the rear looking suitably cowed. They trundled around the oasis with the SIG guards lording it over them, crying out German orders and threats. Such behaviour didn't come naturally to the commandos, but they figured they could swallow it for a short while, given it offered their only route into Tobruk.

Before them lay an epic journey north across 800 miles of desert, which for the most part was menaced by the enemy. Sand seas would need to be crossed and enemy strongholds circumnavigated, and Haselden was happy to leave route-planning to the LRDG. His mind was focused on the dazzling complexities of the coming attack, and Lloyd Owen shared some of his unease.

'John, you know security's been the worst ever for this trip,' Lloyd Owen ventured.

Haselden shrugged. 'I know. But there's nothing I can do about that. We're committed. We have to proceed as if security's been perfect.'

Although the Condor and Black Code pipelines were pumping Rommel misinformation, getting a dozen separate raiding forces onto their targets created its own inevitable 'noise'. Whether it was the flurry of radio messages or careless talk in Cairo bars, the enemy was bound to know something was afoot. But the real concern was Bruckner. Haselden and Lloyd Owen shared Buck's fear that the traitorous German had passed news of at least some of the coming raids to the enemy.

'It seems impossible by now that the enemy won't have every detail,' Lloyd Owen remarked darkly.

'You think they might be waiting for us when we drive into Tobruk?' Haselden forced a laugh. 'You know something, David, I have other worries . . .' He gestured, a wave of the hand encompassing the night-dark oasis and the sleeping men of the Commando. 'All this . . . This wasn't my idea at all. I never planned anything so . . . ambitious as all this. My suggestion was a simple act of sabotage. The thing's grown out of all sense and proportion.'

Haselden's initial plan had been a swift in-and-out operation designed to blow up the Tobruk fuel depot and ammo dump, and to free the Allied POWs. It relied upon speed, aggression and surprise, as had all the best LRDG and SAS operations. But others had got hold of the idea and inflated it grotesquely. It had mutated into a tri-service operation, combining a massive airborne bombing mission, amphibious assaults, landings by warships and the desert-borne raids. With such complexity, there was clearly so much more that could go wrong.

The genius of Haselden's plan had been to strike with maximum surprise. Tobruk was a port, and typically the defenders of ports expect to be attacked from the sea. The enemy would never have believed that raiders could cross approaching 2,000 miles of desert undetected to launch such a lightning raid, or that they planned to free thousands of POWs in the process. By aiming for the unexpected the original concept had held good. But the massive RAF air raid took away the element of surprise, for it would put the defenders at action stations. Rather than striking from the dark and silent desert, Haselden's men would be going into Tobruk during a veritable firestorm.

Yet like it or not, they were saddled with the plan. Haselden and Lloyd Owen had raised their objections repeatedly in Cairo, but the die was cast. The entire proposition had been hijacked by those of greater rank and influence.

Haselden betrayed little rancour or bitterness. His was just a matter-of-fact expression of concern shared with a trusted friend. Neither he nor Lloyd Owen would ever risk showing the slightest hint of doubt in front of the men, or of giving the impression that they were anything less than utterly convinced of securing victory in Tobruk.

In any case, they were halfway to their intended destination, they were soldiers and they had their orders. Plus they knew that Churchill was watching. 'Rommel. Rommel. What matters but to beat him!' the prime minister had chided.

For better or worse, there was no turning back now.

CHAPTER 10

Some 375 miles north of Kufra a long column of vehicles nosed its way out of the sun-scorched, jumbled mass of the Great Sand Sea. Instantly recognizable in their Chevys and Willys Jeeps, this was the LRDG patrol that had spent torturous days crawling over 'impassable' dunes, even as Lloyd Owen's convoy had guided the SOE Commando in a long loop south.

The patrol was made up mostly of New Zealand troopers and it was commanded by the inimitable Major John 'Jake' Easonsmith. Unlike many of his fellow commanders, Easonsmith – bearded, tousle-headed, his eyes seemingly fixed upon some distant horizon – had come up through the ranks. The son of a printer hailing from Bristol and a graduate of Bristol's Clifton College, Easonsmith had been a wine salesman prior to the war. He'd signed up as a private, but gained rapid promotion, serving as a sergeant in the Royal Tank Regiment.

In July 1940 Easonsmith had been commissioned as a lieutenant and won a MC. Volunteering for the LRDG in December of that year, he had, like Haselden, earned wide renown among the desert Arabs, who had come to call this softly spoken Englishman the Hero of the Desert. As with Haselden, Easonsmith also had the easy air of a natural-born leader, and was blessed with an innate ability to earn the respect and amity of his fellow warriors.

Easonsmith's firm, deliberate speech was warmed by a gentle smile, reflecting an inner peace that inspired all those he served with. He never seemed assailed by doubt, and he had an almost magical gift for putting other men's minds at ease. Another of the LRDG commanders, Bill Kennedy-Shaw, would describe Easonsmith thus: 'Brave, wise and with an uprightness that shamed lesser men, he was, I think, the finest man we ever had in the LRDG.'

But the passage over the great *erg* had tested even his equanimity. Growing frustrated at their progress through the unending sea of sand, Captain Alastair Timpson, a young Guards officer, had decided to push ahead in his Willys Jeep. He'd shot over the sharp crest of a dune, whereupon his vehicle dropped twenty feet and rolled, in the process injuring himself and his gunner, Guardsman Wann.

Captain Timpson suffered a fractured skull and he'd knocked out his front teeth. Even so he managed to scramble back up the dune to prevent the remainder of the patrol from shooting over the same drop and likewise coming to grief. Guardsman Wann was found to have a broken back and was paralysed from the waist down: if he was to be saved, he would need to be evacuated to hospital as quickly as possible.

Easonsmith knew there was no turning back with the wounded man. Operation Caravan was far too important to countenance any delay. It was also, arguably, one of the most difficult of all the raids that were slated for the night of 13 September. Once through the desert he needed to steer his patrol across 125 miles of terrain thick with the enemy to hit the airfield at Barce in the far west of Libya.

To make matters worse, this was in the very same area where Buck's SIG and the Free French SAS had been in action just three months earlier. Or maybe that was Easonsmith's greatest advantage: perhaps no German commander would expect the desert raiders to strike again and so soon in an area in which they had suffered so much death and betrayal. Either way Operation Caravan was a key element of the wider plan, being a decoy to draw the enemy's attention away from Tobruk.

Easonsmith decided to press on across the Great Sand Sea with his two wounded men. On the far western fringes there was a landmark known to all as Big Cairn. The five-foot-tall heap of rocks was a waypoint for RAF pilots flying into the desert on resupply missions. He decided to risk calling in a medevac flight to collect the two injured men. With Captain Timpson and Guardsman Wann lying in the rear of a Chevy beneath an awning to shield them from the sun, the convoy waited in the breathless, blistering heat.

Locating such a tiny landmark in the midst of a vast, featureless plain was no easy undertaking, and the first aircraft, a Lockheed Hudson bomber, failed to show. Leaving his superlative medic, Richard 'Doc' Lawson to tend to the injured, Easonsmith pressed on with the main body of men to the next major landmark. A convoy of the LRDG's heavy section – their resupply trucks – was supposed to be arriving at Howard's Cairn, carrying stores of fuel and water that had been driven out from Kufra. With the immense distances and the terrain they had to traverse, Easonsmith's patrol wouldn't be able to hit Barce and make it back again without taking on extra supplies.

At Big Cairn Doc Lawson gazed into the burning sky straining his ears for the distant drone of an aircraft's engines. He hailed from the Royal Army Medical Corps, but medical orderlies (MOs) played a highly unusual role with the desert raiders. Normally a MO would never wear a gun into battle. With his pay book and Red Cross armband identifying him as a bona fide medic, it was a chargeable offence to carry a weapon. But any who volunteered for the LRDG needed to be a little more flexible. They had to be happy combining their non-combatant role with that of a fighter.

The shortage of manpower meant they had to double up as gunners. Wearing a Red Cross satchel on the one shoulder and carrying a machine gun on the other was something that had never bothered Doc Lawson. It was an attitude that endeared him to his fellow desert raiders no end. Lawson was a highly respected and popular officer, and he was to play a crucial role on the coming mission.

But for now there were men's lives to be saved. The second aircraft, a Bristol Blenheim light bomber, found Big Cairn and landed successfully, but it was too small to accommodate the paralysed Wann on his stretcher. A further radio call was made, and the Lockheed Hudson that had failed to get in first time around was guided back to the landing ground. Finally, Captain Timpson and Guardsman Wann were loaded aboard and flown out to hospital in Cairo.

That left Easonsmith's patrol behind schedule and depleted by two, cutting its number from forty-seven to forty-five, riding in seventeen vehicles. The major wasn't desperately worried: no matter how testing the mission before them, he had every confidence in his New Zealand operators in particular, who worked well with the Guards.

His right-hand man was New Zealand Captain Nick Perry Wilder, a seasoned veteran of desert soldiering. Wilder would go on to win a Distinguished Service Order (DSO), discovering what became known as Wilder's Gap, an uncharted pass that would enable Allied forces to outflank Rommel's forces. Blessed with a dry but kindly sense of humour and a quiet fortitude, Wilder had a reputation for leading from the front, while always being ready with encouragement or advice.

Captain Wilder in turn relied upon his fellow countryman, the fiery Corporal Merlyn Haruru Craw, whenever the bullets started to fly. Half Maori, Craw was the explosives expert on the patrol. He'd learned his skills blowing up tree stumps on his father's farm in Linton, set on the southern tip of New Zealand's North Island. After volunteering for the LRDG Craw was sent on a formal demolitions course, where his tree-blasting skills were harnessed to the needs of desert raiding.

He had spent the few days prior to the patrol's departure building the charges needed for blowing up the warplanes at Barce. The make-up of the DIY incendiary devices had been arrived at by a process of trial and error. Half a kilo of Nobel 808 (a type of gelignite) was kneaded together with aluminium filings to form a ball. Empty beer cans were filled with petrol and attached to the charge, with a detonator and fuse inserted into the ball of explosives, the whole thing being parcelled up in an old draw-string ration bag.

When the detonator was triggered, the gelignite ignited the petrol, which burned, scattering the aluminium filings and spreading fire far and wide. Placed above an aircraft's fuel tank, the effect proved devastating: it would leave the target a burned-out hulk. But making the charges had its drawbacks: the 'nitro' was highly toxic, and a man could build no more than six bombs before developing a terribly debilitating headache. Craw had had a team of men working on the charges for the present mission.

So crammed were the patrol's vehicles with bombs, ammo and fuel that even a single hit with an incendiary bullet could transform them into a raging fireball. Indeed, Craw's Chevy was more laden than most. He'd had to make up some unusual charges for the coming raid. The plan of attack included blowing up the town's bank vault to liberate the millions of lire it was known to contain.

The money was to be used for some highly unusual purposes. Attached to Easonsmith's patrol was perhaps the most irregular of all the private armies that waged war in the desert – a unit known as Popski's Private Army (PPA). Its founder was Major Vladimir 'Popski' Peniakoff, and he commanded a force made up of local Arab fighters.

Portly, ageing, balding, Peniakoff was a character as colourful and eccentric as any. Russian by birth, he'd fought for the French in World War One, before settling in Egypt. When war was declared in 1939 he'd managed to secure a commission in the British military, and he'd specialized in raising Arab guerrilla armies to carry out freelance raiding operations against the Italian forces in North Africa.

As with Haselden's more intelligence-led ventures, Popski had teamed up with the LRDG on many an occasion, using them to taxi him to and from desert assignations. He had scored some notable successes, at one point blowing up 100,000 gallons of enemy fuel. He tended to pay his Arab raiders out of war booty, hence the need to dynamite the Barce bank vault and liberate the lire held there.

Indeed, there was something distinctly buccaneering about Easonsmith's patrol. The men tended to supplement their meagre rations with any wild game they could shoot. The animal's severed head – most often a gazelle – would be strapped to the grill of a Chevy, drying into a tight, grinning, fleshless death mask. Decorated with traditional Maori *tiki* symbols, stenciled with Maori names and bristling with weaponry, the Chevys were the pirate ships of the desert.

Woe betide any who got in their way.

Having rounded Howard's Cairn, Easonsmith led his patrol north almost 200 miles, driving fast on hard-packed flat *serir*, before they had to slow to an agonising crawl to complete a second crossing of the Great Sand Sea. The 600-mile-long mass of treacherous loose sand curled around to join the equally perilous Kalansho Sand Sea. The neck linking the two had to be crossed, and by the time they reached the far side they were eight days into their journey.

They paused just north of the dune sea at an area known to all simply as LG (Landing Ground) 125. A rough dirt airstrip hewn out of the desert, LG 125 was marked by the carcasses of burned-out Hurricanes and other warplanes. When the fortunes of the Allies had been higher, this had been a busy airbase serving the special forces on their secret desert missions. Now, it was derelict and unused, the nearest enemy positions being just a few hours away.

LG 125 was the point at which the path of Easonsmith's patrol and that of Lloyd Owen and the SOE Commando would cross. Easonsmith and his men were now well behind schedule. They'd been delayed in the treacherous sands, plus they'd lost time evacuating their wounded. Indeed, as the fresh tracks in the sand betrayed, Lloyd Owen's vehicles had already passed this way several days previously, heading north towards the coast.

Six days earlier Lloyd Owen's convoy had set out from Kufra, the most advanced British outpost in the desert war. Their final destination, Tobruk, lay over 600 miles due north, all of which was open, sun-blasted desert, and for the majority of which the convoy would be moving through territory held by the enemy.

Even so, it was a beautiful evening as the LRDG's Chevys led the column of Commando trucks north. Refreshed from their long rest, spirits were high and the commandos in particular were eager to be moving. Even their kilted commander, Major Campbell, seemed reinvigorated, although he'd been warned by Captain Gibson, the Commando's laconic Canadian medic, that once they returned to the rigours of the desert the dysentery might come back to haunt him.

The long column of vehicles wove its way among the palm trees, and around the bald-headed, humped forms of the bright red sand hills that dotted the landscape north of the oasis. Shadows were long, the air still and cool, and the desert felt remarkably pleasant and accommodating. They camped for the night twenty miles out of Kufra, ready for a dawn start on the morrow.

In the relaxed setting Buck waxed lyrical about the coming mission. In the company of the officers – Haselden, Lloyd Owen, Campbell, and his own second in command at the SIG, David Russell – he proved remarkably open and frank. He coolly outlined his ultimate aim: before they left Tobruk he was going to empty the city's bank vault.

There were enough present with an SOE affiliation to understand that theft, larceny, blackmail, burglary and assassinations were all part of the arsenal of the Ministry of Ungentlemanly Warfare. Even so, there were a few raised eyebrows. How did Buck intend to break into the vault? Buck explained that he'd been in touch with a marine who'd been a safe-breaker before the war. Once the port fortress was theirs, Buck and his partner in crime would join forces, blow the Tobruk vault wide open and make off with the booty. It was a nice thought, and something exceptionally cheering to ruminate on as the men bedded down on the sands for the night. But tomorrow was another day and who knew what it might bring.

On that the second day's driving the temperature

soared to around 48 degrees Celsius. Eyes smarted and throats burned. Memories of their earlier, nightmare journey came back to haunt the commandos: Lieutenant Graham Taylor, Campbell's second in command; Tommy Langton of sticky-bomb-throwing renown; Lieutenant 'Trolly' Trollope, who wilted under the desert sun; New Zealander 'Mac' MacDonald, who'd fought fascists in the Spanish Civil War; hulking great Hugh 'Bill' Barlow, of key-hurling fame; plus the severe, towering figure of Squadron Sergeant Major Arthur Swinburn, who had once looked down upon the scruffy, bearded LRDG as being an undisciplined, unruly rabble.

Not any more.

Both sides had learned a grudging respect for the other. The men of the Commando had witnessed the LRDG's mastery of the desert. In turn the LRDG had learned to respect the sheer guts and nerve displayed by the commandos. Despite returning to the furnace-like embrace of the desert, not a man among them was tempted to turn back. Haselden's enthusiasm for the coming operation had caught them all.

Their route took the convoy north-west towards the Zighen Gap, where the vast Kalansho and Rebiana Sand Seas intersect. A short stretch of *erg* maybe twenty miles across, the sun-scorched sea of soft, friable dunes still made for murderous going. Before venturing into the Zighen Gap, the entire convoy halted on firm ground to lower tyre

163

pressures to about half of what was recommended. Semi-inflated, the tyres would balloon out under their heavy loads, allowing the wheels to float over the soft sand. The LRDG had hit upon this trick to facilitate the crossing of dune seas through a process of trial and error.

But even the most experienced of desert wanderers could get caught out in such terrain, and Lloyd Owen's patrol had very nearly come to grief here. Months back they'd been on an extended raid and they'd long run out of water. Lloyd Owen had set a course for a feature known as the Motor Tyre Well. If they could find it, they were saved. If not, they'd almost certainly die of thirst. The feature was just as it sounded: a large truck tyre placed over the mouth of a deep desert well, to shield it from the shifting, blowing sand.

The Motor Tyre Well lay just to the west of the Zighen Gap. Their lives depended upon finding a tyre in the midst of the thousands of square miles of signless, trackless desert. Lloyd Owen had begun to notice symptoms of the dreaded *cafard* – the cockroach; desert madness – among his men. After hours in the Sahara with no water, men began to crack. He could see the wild staring eyes that betrayed the onset of *le cafard*, and he'd prayed that his calculations were correct.

Extreme thirst, the kind that kills, produces in the mind's eye incredible visions of great cool halls, complete with glistening white pillars and crystal pools of water. The more severe the thirst, the more fantastical the visions. Finally, when the mouth is too dry even to speak, the sufferer imagines diving into enormous lakes of water with jaws held wide, to gulp in the life-giving liquid. Hence the look of madness in the eyes.

Thankfully, Lloyd Owen's navigation had proved spot on. All of a sudden a tiny black spot had materialized seemingly from out of nowhere: the Motor Tyre Well. Figures crazed with thirst had climbed inside to scoop away the choking sand. Water began to flow. It was dirty and turbid, but to Lloyd Owen and his men it had signified life. They filled their bellies to bursting and refreshed their bone-dry jerry cans.

On the evening of their second day out from Kufra, Lloyd Owen led the commandos out of the sand sea directly to the Motor Tyre Well. After his sticky-bomb-throwing escapades, Lieutenant Tommy Langton figured clambering into the well had to be child's play. He dropped through the tyre to see what was what. It made for hot, claustrophobic work, but eventually enough of the sand was scrabbled away for water to begin to seep through. But it proved fouled by animal droppings. If they used the water to top up their jerry cans, it would only serve to pollute the rest.

They motored away from the well, camping some forty miles north. They were now spending their first night in what was considered to be truly hostile terrain, and the appropriate measures were taken. The vehicles were driven under the cover of whatever desert scrub could be found, before being sheeted over with camouflage netting. A round-the-clock sentry rotation was put in place, and there would be no merry cooking fires tonight. From here on in they could expect to come under attack at any moment and especially from the unfriendly skies.

Pushing due north the following day, Lloyd Owen prepared to steer the convoy past a coming choke point. If they were seen passing the fortress at the Jalo oasis – the most southerly position held by the enemy – they were done for. The Jalo garrison would radio in air strikes, and no ground patrol, no matter how well armed, could survive against German and Italian warplanes in so exposed a landscape.

From Zighen north to Jalo made for perfect desert driving, but it was the very worst kind of defensive terrain imaginable. Between the great shifting masses of the sand seas ran the Serir of Kalansho, a billiard-table-flat hard-baked mud plain stretching north 500 miles like a motorway. Over sixty miles wide in places, it offered perfect going but zero cover from marauding warplanes.

Oddly, no matter how fierce the desert winds, barely a grain of sand from the great *ergs* ever seemed to accumulate on the Serir of Kalansho. It was clear and firm all the way to Jalo. The Chevys and army trucks raced north, covering almost forty miles with each passing hour. At mid-morning a halt was called for the daily issue of fresh lime juice. Without it, on their restricted diet the men would fall victim to scurvy, a debilitating disease caused by Vitamin C deficiency.

At each stop Haselden made his rounds of the trucks, pausing for a brief chat and checking that all was good. That evening – their third out of Kufra – the vehicles were pulled into what was to be a temporary leaguer. They had stopped just short of Jalo, the enemy outpost. If they tried to sneak past during daylight they were bound to be spotted by the lookouts.

Lloyd Owen intended to press on after nightfall, sneaking past under cover of darkness, although pushing on at night would bring its own challenges, one of which was the cold. With sundown the heat seemed to be sucked from the desert air. A chill descended as rapid as it was surprising. The LRDG men were long accustomed to this and carried thick sheepskin jackets. But the men of the Commando were dressed only in their thin, tropical uniforms.

Haselden urged the commandos to wrap up in their army blankets for the coming leg of the journey. He also warned the drivers to keep absolutely alert and focused, fatigued though they might be from a long day on the move. They would attempt to crawl past Jalo without showing any lights, but with that came more danger. There was a risk of losing vehicles in the darkness or of trucks crashing into each other.

At dusk the wearied men clambered back aboard

their charges. They moved off in strict line astern, a snake of trucks and Chevys each sticking spitting-distance-close to the one in front, for fear of losing their way. The night was coal dark. Good for sneaking through undetected; bad for keeping a convoy of thirteen vehicles on the move. For hours they nosed ahead at dead slow, every man among them trying to avoid doing anything that might make the slightest unexpected noise. In the chill stillness of the desert night sound would carry for incredible distances, and the Jalo defenders would be listening.

All of a sudden, a word of warning was hissed down the line of vehicles: 'Tanks ahead!'

The column ground to a halt. The commandos gripped their weapons tighter, as tired eyes stared into the empty blackness, searching in vain for the shadowy silhouettes of enemy armour. As they strained their ears, they could hear the beat of engines thudding in the darkness. Taut, silent, alert, they awaited whatever was coming, poised to unleash merry hell.

Not that tommy guns would be much use against Rommel's panzers.

CHAPTER 11

The motors of the Chevys roared, as Lloyd Owen led his men in to investigate. Silhouettes had been spotted up ahead where there wasn't supposed to be anything but dead flat *serir*. If these were Rommel's battle tanks, the LRDG would have little option but to turn tail and run, taking the rest of the convoy with them. Even the Breda gun trucks would face a one-sided battle against heavy armour.

With each turn of the Chevys' wheels the silhouettes drew closer, melting out of the night, gradually gaining form and substance. Finally the truth became clear. These were no panzers; they were clumps of thorn scrub, appearing blocky and predatory in the blackness. Word was passed back down the lines. Nerves taught with tension relaxed. Figures laughed quietly into the dark.

A few miles east the enemy garrison at Jalo slept, and a handful of sentries kept watch even as an Allied force was secretly turning their flank. It had taken a punishing journey across 1,400 miles of desert to get here, but bit by bit and with agonising slowness the Tobruk raiders were slipping into Axis-held territory.

The vehicles pressed on into the night. Just to the north of Jalo the Commando suffered its first casualty. Pilot Officer Aubrey 'Scotty' Scott was attached to their number. His role was to liaise with the RAF, and to help signal the Royal Navy ships in to the landings in Sciausc Bay. He'd nodded off while squatting on the side of his truck, and tumbled into the darkness.

A sharp cry of alarm split the night. Scott had landed on his shoulders on the hard-packed *serir*, the blow waking him instantly. His truck scrunched to a stop. The errant RAF officer emerged from the darkness, shaken and breathless. Hands reached down to haul him back aboard.

'If you'd fallen out of your plane, Scotty, you'd have ended up a lot more hurt,' one of the commandos needled him.

Scott gave a sheepish shrug. He was well aware that if he'd knocked himself out in the fall, he would have been left behind.

Twenty-five miles north of Jalo Lloyd Owen finally called a halt. The men had been on the go for approaching twenty-four hours, and they were exhausted. Driving through the night in open vehicles, the conditions had been close to arctic. The commandos in particular were chilled to the bone.

Scattered around Lloyd Owen's chosen camping ground were the finely crafted flint weapons – axes,

arrowheads, blades – of a bygone desert civilization. But most of the men were too cold and tired
to care. They crawled under their blankets and
were dead to the world almost before their heads
hit the sand.

Lloyd Owen could allow no more than four
hours' rest. The Jalo garrison was known to possess
an airstrip. At dawn and at dusk each day a spotter
plane would fly a regular patrol radius, scouring
the desert to either side of the fortress. They could
not risk getting caught.

At first light Lloyd Owen and Haselden chided
the men into action. The column sped on, eyes
scanning the sky at their backs for the speck of
an approaching aircraft. But none appeared. Each
mile that they pressed northwards took them
further into enemy territory, but as yet they
remained unseen and undetected. It seemed as if
they had slipped through safely.

With sun-up, the commandos noticed that the
character of the terrain before them had changed
markedly. They were now following a clear path,
signs of wheeled and tracked vehicles criss-crossing
a wide swathe of desert. Enemy convoys frequently
passed this way, running supplies into the fortress
at Jalo. They would need to keep their eyes peeled.

It was dark by the time Lloyd Owen called a more
permanent halt, just short of LG 125. He could
drive the men only so far. His greatest worry now,
shared by Haselden, was the hodden-kilted Scot
leading the SOE Commando. The commandos'

medic had seen his warning come to pass: Major Campbell's dysentery was back with a vengeance.

At every stop during the long day's drive Haselden had walked back from Lloyd Owen's Chevy – in which he rode wrapped in a keffiyeh like the LRDG men – to check on Campbell. Though he tried to hide it, the major was racked by agonising stomach cramps, and could keep little if any food in his guts. His strength was failing, and Haselden was worried about his ability to lead the Commando into action on the coming raid.

Haselden needed to knit the entire operation together, coordinating SIG, commandos, RAF warplanes and numerous Royal Navy landings, not to mention the freeing and arming of several thousand prisoners of war. He needed Campbell fit and well so he could lead from the front as the commandos seized Sciausc Bay, knocked out any opposition, cleared the gun emplacements and turned them on the enemy. Yet the London Scottish major was fading fast.

At sunrise the following morning the convoy set forth on the final, and most dangerous, leg of its epic desert journey. The terrain before the raiders was like an eerie moonscape in the dawn light: it was littered with shell and bomb craters, scattered war debris and the blackened hulks of trucks, field guns and armour. They were pressing north through terrain over which the desert war had raged, as the coastal strip had been wrestled from Axis into Allied hands, and back again. It was a silent, sobering and haunting scene, especially for the commandos, many of whom had fought here and lost comrades in the heat of battle.

On the evening of 10 September 1942 Lloyd Owen led the Commando to Hatiet Etla, their last communal camping ground. Here they would lie up and make their final preparations for the assault, scheduled for three days hence. To east and west along the coast further forces were moving into their final launch positions: Easonsmith's Barce raiders; Stirling's column of SAS; the airborne and seaborne elements. Right now all seemed to be going to plan, and the enemy appeared none the wiser that their territory had been so deeply penetrated.

To the commandos, Hatiet Etla looked like nothing more than a wide patch of low scrub scattered among dry, rocky hills. But to the LRDG desert warriors this was perfect cover, and a rare find amid the monotony of the Sahara. It lay a hundred miles due south of Tobruk. The final run-in to the target would be made the day of the assault. In the meantime it was vital that the force wasn't detected. Lloyd Owen personally selected the site at which each vehicle would be reversed into a ravine or gully, shaded by stunted thorn trees, over all of which would be thrown camo netting.

By the time he was done, the entire convoy was well dispersed, occupying an area some several acres across. This would lessen still further the risk of detection from the air. In his note in the LRDG war diary, Lloyd Owen recorded: 'Force moved to good cover at Long 23 49 30 – Lat 30 40 17. No aircraft or enemy movement seen . . . Remained under cover rearranging loads and making trial preparations.'

Those preparations centred around the SOE Commando and the SIG, ensuring they got the coming deception just right. Captain Buck's detailed knowledge of enemy procedures would be at the forefront of the bluff. The eighty commandos would be crowded into three lorries prior to making their way through the lines. This was because the Afrika Korps was painfully short of fuel, and the Germans would cram some forty POWs into each truck when on the move. Buck figured they could get away with just under thirty per vehicle, SIG guards included, which should allow the commandos room enough to hide their weaponry, explosives, radios and ammo.

But this had never been put to the test, and at Hatiet Etla they went about their final rehearsals. The only way to hide all the gear was to have the 'POWs' seated in the trucks' rears, with blankets covering their laps and weaponry concealed beneath. They would be driving into Tobruk at dusk, and the air should be chilly enough to justify the rugs, especially as they would be riding in open trucks and most only had thin tropical uniforms.

A number of the men had another, entirely genuine, reason to want to wrap themselves in blankets. A curious phenomenon had arisen among those gathered at Hatiet Etla: during the freezing night drive several had caught colds. Pilot Officer Aubrey Scott, the man who had fallen asleep and tumbled from his truck, was decidedly more snuffly than most. He did the obvious thing and went to visit Gibson, the MO. He explained what was what, after which the big, black-mustachioed Canadian medic seemed to ruminate for a while.

Eventually he volunteered his remedy: 'Go grab yourself a shovel and dig a bloody big hole. That should sweat it out of you!'

Scott snorted: Gibson and his celebrated cold cure! As far as he was concerned, he could go dig his own bloody holes.

There was one major problem facing the force gathered at Hatiet Etla: a lack of suitable 'Germans'. Once it was showtime and they were headed for the Tobruk perimeter, they would need to have three guards per truck, Buck explained. One would be seated behind the wheel, one would be next to him, navigating, and a third should stand on the middle seat, head and shoulders thrust out of the open top of the cab, his weapon trained on the 'POWs' in the rear.

That was how the Germans did things, and they were sticklers for routine. The trouble was, even with himself and Russell, his second in command, included, the SIG was three guards short. There was nothing for it but to call for volunteers from the Commando itself. Some of the would-be POWs would have to step forward to act as German guards instead.

Buck and Haselden gathered the men in the shade beneath the thorn scrub. 'I want three volunteers,' Buck announced. He glanced around the assembled men, a certain gleam in his eye. 'This is a non-speaking part, so no need to know any German. But you're all aware of the consequences if you are caught wearing German uniform.'

A forest of hands shot into the air. There was a mood of reckless abandon among the force now assembled at Hatiet Etla, resulting in part from the incredible high they felt at having pulled off such a seemingly impossible journey. If they had been told at the outset where they were headed, few would have imagined it possible. Yet somehow, unbelievably, they were here in the heart of enemy territory, and not an Afrika Korps soldier seemed to know about it.

Buck selected three bulky individuals as his honorary Teutonic guards, knowing how big-boned German soldiers tended to be. The first was Lieutenant Tommy Langton, the seasoned SBS operator. The second was Lieutenant Bill Barlow, an equally hardened warrior, who seemed by now to be well over his key-throwing episode. Lieutenant Harrison, a Royal Engineer, was a similarly imposing figure, and he was Buck's final stand-in.

Each was issued with a German army greatcoat and an Afrika Korps cap, and furnished with a German rifle and associated kit. Then they had to clamber up onto the central seat in the truck cabs, poke their heads through the roof and get into role. Buck rode in the front truck, dressed as a lieutenant in the Afrika Korps, while Russell, the Flying Scotsman, rode in the rear vehicle, similarly attired.

As a final flourish one of the commando officers, Lieutenant Mike Duffy, was persuaded to ride in the central truck cab with his hand thickly bandaged. Acting as if wounded, in reality the bandage could be slipped off in a flash, freeing a hand grasping a grenade, just in case of emergencies.

With Langton, Harrison and Barlow in place, Buck urged the 'prisoners' to act their parts. 'Remember, chaps, you've been captured in fighting around El Alamein. You're been defeated, overrun and taken prisoner. Come on! You've got to look suitably browned off, dispirited, worn out and weary.'

He and Haselden showed the commandos how they wanted them to appear: slumped on the floor of the trucks, heads bowed in a listless and forlorn acceptance of defeat. The entire effect was aided somewhat by the appearance of the commandos. After days in the desert without washing, they were dirty, unshaven and their uniforms grubby and stained. Though appearing cowed and beaten, the commandos had to remain poised for action should they run into any trouble.

Lloyd Owen described watching the rehearsals for this final piece of theatre. 'The dispirited British "prisoners" at once leaped into life, produced weapons, wiped out the guard and drove off. I was impressed.'

Buck had the SIG do a final run-through of their own. When they were stopped at the perimeter checkpoint, as they were bound to be, Buck would present his intricately forged papers. They included a letter from a commanding officer on the front, explaining why the three truck-loads of prisoners had to be hurried into the Tobruk cages right away. In theory, there should be no road movement at night, unless it was an emergency.

When everything seemed shipshape, there was an impromptu parade, with Haselden and Buck inspecting a drive-past of the 'Afrika Korps' vehicles. In spite of the incredible stakes they faced, both men couldn't help but find the situation hugely comical. It was the rough and tough commandos trying to act their parts that had them really tickled pink, and they fell about laughing.

Parade done, the vehicles were shunted back into hiding, whereupon the men were given the happy news: there was 'too much' rum remaining. It couldn't be taken with them to Tobruk, for the trucks were already stuffed to bursting. The only thing to do was to drink it. It was their last night at Hatiet Etla, and the extra rum ration should ensure that things went with a bang.

In their unshaven griminess the officers were barely distinguishable from the men: they sat together long into the night singing lustily, as if by doing so they could stave off the trials and tribulations that were doubtless to come. In the festive air even the men of the SIG were invited to join the party. Buck decided to break his golden rule: for this one night his 'German troopers' would be allowed to mingle with the British raiders.

Tiffin had been attached to another clandestine operation, and so he hadn't made the Tobruk raid, but Chunky Hillman the gourmand, and Opprower the serial absconder from rear-echelon duties, were there. They settled down with the men of the commandos and the LRDG. As they rubbed shoulders for the first time with their brothers-in-arms, the SIG operators were painfully aware of their otherness. It was deliberate – by design, Buck's exacting design. But it was still difficult to manage, and not least because they knew that every man would be aware of the previous betrayal, by Bruckner, from which so much bloodshed had resulted.

In spite of such misgivings, the rum was passed freely back and forth, as all drank a toast to the raid on Tobruk. For better or worse they were going in as one unit now, and their differences would have to be put behind them.

As Haselden's force downed the last of their rum, on land, at sea and in the air the wider elements of the coming raids were massing. Sixty miles west of Hatiet Etla, Jake Easonsmith's LRDG thundered onward, Barce-bound. But as the column of vehicles climbed towards the dense, rocky hills of the coast, so Easonsmith became gripped by a sense of unease. They stumbled onto fresh tracks. Dozens of vehicles had passed this way recently, and they could only be those of the enemy. From the tracks alone Easonsmith figured the force comprised both tanks and armoured cars.

He consulted with Major Peniakoff. Popski and his Arab forces had spied out this area not a few weeks back. There had been no sign of armour this far south of Barce, nor was there any obvious reason for the enemy to bring tanks into this backwater, over 500 miles from Rommel's front line. The two commanders were plagued by doubt: was this an enemy search party looking for them? Had their passage via the Great Sand Sea somehow been detected? Had it all been for nothing?

Easonsmith had his signaller send a message through to LRDG headquarters, in Cairo, with news of the worrying developments. 'Easonsmith reports 30 very fresh tanks and MT driving eastbound on Abiar Mechili track . . .' (MT was shorthand for motor transport – trucks and light armoured vehicles.)

Major Prendergast responded with mixed news: 'Tell Jake 18 Italian bombers on Barce LG today. Also that further information . . . from Arab source states five thousand Italians in tents situated to north, south-west and south-east of town.'

Barce aerodrome was going to present a rich set of targets, with 18 bombers to blow to smithereens, but between there and Easonsmith's patrol were camped some 5,000 Italian troops, and somehow he was going to have to find a way through. Easonsmith asked for his warning about enemy armour to be passed to Lloyd Owen, and especially to David Stirling.

Even now the SAS commander was leading his 200-strong force on a similar route to Easonsmith's, as they pushed ever closer to Benghazi, just a little further up the coast. Stirling remained hell-bent on making Operation Bigamy a reality, by launching a savage diversionary attack to spur the Tobruk raiders' fortunes. The last thing anyone wanted was that force stumbling into enemy armour.

At RAF airbases up and down the coast British bomber crews – aided by a few dozen US Air Force colleagues – studied aerial photos of Tobruk harbour and their individual targets. In less than twenty-four hours they would be airborne, forming up for a massive bombing raid employing scores of Allied warplanes. In a discreetly tucked away hangar dummy parachutists were stacked up, ready for the decoy airborne assaults that were also planned.

From the British port of Alexandria the seaborne armada had already set sail, destination Tobruk. Destroyers, a cruiser, numerous MTBs and landing craft; this was a force to be reckoned with. The ships were packed full of the Royal Marines, Fusiliers and other combat units who would be going ashore at Tobruk, on the landing grounds seized by Haselden and his SOE Commando.

Admiral Sir Henry Harwood, overall commander of the seaborne elements of the raid, would describe it as a 'desperate gamble'. There were others of a similar mind. Winston Churchill himself would telegraph a personal message of encouragement and blessing to the Tobruk assault force. It would be addressed to 'Forces A, D, X and Z', encompassing the sea- and land-borne elements of the coming attack. 'Prime Minister sends you all his best wishes.'

Whether foolhardy optimism or an inspired and courageous endeavour, the raiders were going in.

CHAPTER 12

At first light on 13 September 1942 the forces gathered at Hatiet Etla roused themselves for action. On one level this day was no different from so many that had gone before. The sun rose, a golden orb that scorched its way into the cloudless blue sky. Figures wrapped in blankets traipsed in from their sleeping positions, mess tins clutched in hand.

It was a day like any other . . . except. The tea ration was overgenerous. There were lashings of hot, sweet *chai* – as much as any man could drink. It put the heart into these desert warriors but underscored the truth: today was different. One way or the other the next twenty-four hours would prove decisive.

A growing tension thrummed back and forth across the warming air. A brisk purposefulness took over, as breakfast kit was packed away and the trucks loaded with gear. Lloyd Owen's men were already waiting in their Chevys as the commandos stowed the last of their kit. Haselden flitted from figure to figure, dispensing a few final pleasantries and encouraging words.

Only the medic, Gibson, was nowhere to be seen. In fact, he was ensconced with Major Campbell in the sick tent, trying to convince him of the obvious – that there was no way he could lead the Commando on the coming raid. The major was so weak and pain-racked that he could barely shake his head in protest, yet shake it he did. Nothing that the medic might say would hold Campbell back from the fight, not as long as he still had life in his veins.

Gibson gave up: there was no telling the stubborn Scot.

The SIG operators made one last vital check to ensure that several sets of British battledress had been safely hidden in the rear of one of the trucks. These were in case of emergency: if they were ever in danger of being captured they would endeavour to change into those uniforms, to emerge dressed as proper British soldiers.

The spare trucks were being left at Hatiet Etla. From each Lloyd Owen removed the distributor cap, and then – making sure that the entire force was watching – he buried it by the front outside wheel of the vehicle from which it had been taken. If things went awry at Tobruk and the men had to break out into the desert, at least they would know how to get the trucks moving again. Assuming, of course, they could make it back to Hatiet Etla.

The spare food, water, fuel and other kit was piled aboard those trucks: it was more than enough to get a force of men back to Kufra. With a last look around the camp Lloyd Owen climbed into the lead vehicle, Haselden jumped in beside him, and the LRDG commander signalled that they should move out.

Six Chevys crawled up the slope leading north out of their place of hiding. Four army trucks followed. One would be abandoned at the dividing of the ways, serving as a rallying point, should Haselden's force run into any unforeseen disaster.

As the trucks edged out of Hatiet Etla the commandos felt more cramped than they'd ever been so far on this journey. It was unusually silent aboard the vehicles. Ahead of them lay a few hours' drive, before the final parting of the ways, after which they would take the plunge towards the Tobruk perimeter.

The terrain was open scrubby bush. The concentration of burned and twisted war debris was even greater here, and many of the scorched and blackened vehicles were similar to their own. They moved slowly, so as not to raise a dust cloud that might attract enemy aircraft, but if one did come searching all they would need to do was halt, and with luck they would blend in with the abandoned vehicles.

Mid-morning the LRDG column pulled into a shallow depression. Lloyd Owen had made good progress and it was time for a feed and a kip. The temperature rose and the hours seemed to drag. Figures dozed fitfully, their minds on what was to come. By four that afternoon the camp was on the move, the men restless and febrile. Tea was brewed. A final meal was eaten.

When the two units mounted their vehicles once more, Haselden was no longer riding in Lloyd Owen's Chevy. Instead, he'd joined Buck in the cab of the leading truck. The parting of the ways had begun.

Vehicles lurched and bumped over the hot, uneven ground. The sun was high in the sky, the heat merciless. But only a few hours of daylight remained, and with sunset they would be heading into Tobruk. The LRDG steered the convoy with ever-greater caution. Eyes scanned the horizon for the first signs of the enemy.

Then they saw it: a lone aircraft dipping low over the horizon. Right ahead of them there had to be an aerodrome, doubtless the one at El Adem, set on the southern outskirts of Tobruk. Once they'd destroyed the enemy's radio station, Lloyd Owen's men were slated to raid that airport, taking out the Stuka dive-bombers stationed there.

A second aircraft came in to land. It seemed closer now.

A while later Haselden pointed ahead. 'The LRDG have stopped.' Everyone knew what that had to mean.

The lead truck closed in on the six stationary Chevys. Every head was turned in their direction. There was something about the expressions on those weather-beaten, bearded faces. What was it? the men of the Commando wondered. And then they had it: the desert raiders were watching their approach with looks they couldn't quite hide, ones of disquiet and unease.

The four trucks came to a halt. The men of the Commando could guess how the LRDG warriors were feeling. They weren't happy to be leaving the commandos to face the cauldron of Tobruk without them.

Bill Barlow jumped down from the rearmost vehicle. 'Everyone off. Into your positions on the other wagons.'

A chill wind blew, presaging the coming darkness. The commandos moved quickly, working warmth into stiff and cramped limbs. Weapons, ammo and blankets were passed down. They moved ahead, taking up their prearranged places on the trucks in front.

The rear vehicle was driven into some bushes and the distributor arm removed, before being buried next to the front offside wheel. The truck had thrown its fan belt in the last few miles, one of the few mechanical failures they had suffered across thousands of miles of desert. But it should still be good for a last-gasp escape, if the commandos had need of it, and all made a mental note of its location.

From the vantage point of the three remaining trucks, the commandos could see now why Lloyd Owen's patrol had come to a halt. They were parked just short of a low ridge, known as Ed Duda, and from there they were in sight of the main coastal road. Three or four miles ahead they could see clouds of dust rising in the distance, and tiny specks moving on the highway.

That was it: the road into Tobruk.

And those were enemy vehicles.

Lloyd Owen walked back from his Chevy. Figures converged: Haselden, a stooped Campbell, Russell, Buck and Langton. They stood together in the chill wind, shivering slightly. For a few moments they talked through the final arrangements – mostly radio communications between the two units – but all knew they were simply trying to put off the moment of parting.

Then Haselden said, 'Well, goodbye, David. Best of luck, and thanks for everything.'

He held out his hand. His eyes were twinkling almost with amusement, or maybe the bedevilment of the hour. There was not the slightest hint of doubt or fear in his gaze any more. The two figures shook hands, as the men of the Commando and the LRDG prepared to go their separate ways.

There were handshakes all round. What more was there to say? With that the figures turned and in silence returned to their vehicles. Haselden climbed into the rear of the lead truck, so he could be close to his men: a commander with his raiding party.

Lieutenant Tommy Langton clambered into the third truck, pulling on his greatcoat and German forage cap. He slid through the opening in the cab roof and trained his German rifle on the figures in the rear. Mostly, they appeared suitably cowed.

But one of them, an irrepressibly cheerful fellow, was singing away to himself softly. Langton strained to catch the words.

'If you go down to Tobruk tonight, you're sure of a big surprise . . .'

Langton told the man to cut it out. He needed them looking and sounding as much like downcast, dispirited POWs as possible. He could sense their inner strength and fortitude and that their spirits remained high, and if he could detect that, so too could a genuine German guard.

'Hogan, dishevel your hair a bit!' he commanded. 'And Lofty, take that grin off your face. You're a prisoner of war, you know! Blackman, I can see the butt of your tommy gun. Cover it up, won't you!'

As he readied for the off, trying to muster an appropriate level of hatred for the English *Schweinhunde* that he had under guard, Langton saw one of the commandos – a man called Riley – give him a slow wink, which completely nullified the feelings of antagonism and enmity that he was trying to muster.

The quiet was shattered by the roar of engines firing into life. Gears were engaged, accelerators depressed, and the trucks lurched into motion. The convoy crawled past the waiting LRDG vehicles, crested the ridge ahead of them and was gone.

Lloyd Owen's men watched until the last wisp of dust was caught by the wind. A quiet, brooding foreboding gripped them. They feared for those eighty brave souls who had just passed them by.

Some surely would never see another dawn. They regretted now their earlier gruffness and impatience, especially with the Commando's lumbering progress through the desert.

'I wish we'd been kinder to them,' Lloyd Owen reflected. 'They're fine, brave men.'

The men of the LRDG had their own work to do around Tobruk tonight, but they didn't have to penetrate to the very heart of the enemy fortress, employing a deception that would earn every last one of them an all-but-certain death, if caught. They'd been three weeks in each other's company; it was a hellish difficult way to say farewell.

'For a few minutes we stood and watched them go, feeling bare and huge on this naked, scrubby waste . . .' Lloyd Owen would write of this moment. 'We had made many friends among the Commando and I had become particularly attached to John Haselden . . . Leaving him alone and unsupported at the moment when he might most want our help . . . was the hardest decision I have ever had to take.'

The eyes of those left behind followed the three trucks as they crawled down the far side of the ridge. Soon they were mere specks on the darkening horizon. Dusk was fast approaching, and with nightfall the LRDG themselves would be going into action, their first objective being to shoot up the Tobruk D/F station.

But Lloyd Owen felt strangely cut off from the thrill of coming battle. He didn't even want to move. Instead, he sat with his men as the stiffening wind buffeted their vehicles, watching their former comrades drive into whatever fate might await.

'It was terribly sad,' he recalled. 'We were almost in tears . . . knowing that we would be bloody lucky to see any of them again.'

In time the cold became unbearable, and the LRDG commander stirred. He turned in his seat to survey the terrain to their rear. He needed to find an area of hidden ground, before hooking around again and hitting their first target. His eyes scanned the landscape. Suddenly, they caught something: movement, betrayed by a billowing cloud of dust. Vehicles were speeding north, heading straight for the convoy of trucks carrying the Commando.

Lloyd Owen gave a cry of warning. His arm shot out, indicating the direction of approaching danger. It seemed as if the enemy were on to them after all, and sending in a force to hit Haselden and his men from the rear.

The six Chevys roared into life. Tyres spun on the dirt as Lloyd Owen led them off, sand and gravel flying from their wheels as they executed a tearing U-turn. In an instant these desert warriors had shaken off their malaise, for their brothers-in-arms were in mortal danger.

Lloyd Owen led the crazed charge down the escarpment. The enemy was ahead of them in the race, but the speed of the Chevys proved decisive. As they began to catch the patrol, the howl of their straining engines must have drawn attention. Up ahead Lloyd Owen could see vehicles pulling to a stop. Figures dismounted. For a moment he wondered if they were setting up defensive positions, before some started waving, as if in recognition.

The bearded desert warriors crouched lower over their weapons, as they thundered ever closer. They had identified the enemy by now: this was an Italian patrol, consisting of captured Morris trucks accompanied by an outrider on a Norton motorcycle. By the time the Italian soldiers had realized their mistake and raced to remount their vehicles, it was too late.

The six Chevys opened up, twin Vickers Ks, Lewis guns and the heavier .5 calibre machine guns hammering in a storm of rounds. The Italian vehicles began to move, but they were taking heavy hits. The LRDG Chevys circled the enemy column, pouring in fire. Bullets shredded tyres and tore through the thin, unarmoured flanks of the Morris trucks with an unrelenting savagery.

Figures tumbled out, screaming. Others tried to get the guns going on their vehicles, but it was all too little too late. The circling Chevys silenced the enemy gunners long before they could bring their weapons to bear. In a matter of minutes the battle was over.

Seven Italian soldiers lay dead. Two more looked mortally wounded. The rest were captives. Lloyd Owen questioned one, a lieutenant. He was almost speechless with fear. Haltingly, he explained that his patrol had mistaken the speeding LRDG column for Germans, which was why they had stopped. They were on a mission to collect spare parts for damaged aircraft, and they knew nothing of Haselden's force.

The lieutenant and his men had arrived in Tobruk only that day. They were part of an Italian division that had been ordered into the port fortress to beef up its defences. He also believed that German reinforcements were being rushed into Tobruk. All of this had been ordered in the last forty-eight hours, he explained. Lloyd Owen found the news deeply disturbing. It spoke to him of foreknowledge on the part of the enemy, who seemed to know that the raiders were coming.

Lloyd Owen was assailed by dark visions of Haselden driving into a trap. The priority now had to be to search for a lying-up point and to radio through details of what he had discovered. He found cover and managed to raise LRDG headquarters. 'Most Immediate. For Prendergast,' his message read. 'Lloyd Owen reports destroyed 2 cars one motor cycle and few men . . .'

But try as he might, Lloyd Owen's radio operator was unable to raise a response from Haselden. There seemed to be no way to get a warning through to him. But what if they could? Would Haselden really pull back? With so many elements of the coming operation depending on him, he could hardly cry off now.

And that was the single biggest weakness of the

plan. The desert raiders' credo was to strike targets of opportunity by surprise; they didn't work to strict schedules. Yet the raid on Tobruk was predicated on split-second timing, which left Haselden no choice but to proceed with his part of the mission come what may.

If an Italian division – upwards of 10,000 men – supplemented by German troops was being rushed into Tobruk, the enemy must have prior warning. Was it all down to Bruckner and his betrayal? Surely he couldn't have known the exact timing of the coming raid?

Either way, all Lloyd Owen could do was try to raise Haselden via his radio, before proceeding with his part of the assault as planned.

Some 200 miles west of Lloyd Owen's position, Jake Easonsmith's LRDG patrol crept through the rough, hilly scrub that surrounded Barce town. They'd moved off at last light from their encampment, which was set some twelve miles south of the target, sneaking past Italian positions in the gathering darkness.

Earlier that day, Popski Peniakoff had sent in two of his Arab fighters to recce the town and gather intelligence. Worryingly, neither had returned. Come mid-afternoon, Easonsmith had gathered his men for a final briefing. He explained the layout of the town: Barce was built around two main streets, arranged in a T shape. At the juncture of the T was the main square, which held the railway station and the bank. Off the square ran a maze of narrow, twisting streets lined with mud-walled houses, while the aerodrome was set at the bottom of the vertical stroke of the T.

Easonsmith planned to split his force into two attacking units. Captain Wilder would lead one, to hit the aerodrome. The other would have been commanded by Captain Timpson, but he'd been flown out of the desert with his head injury. Instead, Guardsman Sergeant Jack Dennis would lead the force to hit the enemy barracks, to stop them from coming to the airfield defenders' aid.

Easonsmith would remain with two jeeps as a headquarters unit, charged with causing general mayhem and confusion. Remaining fast and mobile, his objective was to hit as many targets as possible around the town, to give the impression that the raiding force was far larger than it actually was. A fourth force would consist of Major Peniakoff, with one jeep, keeping the exit road from town clear of the enemy.

To the rear of their entry point, Doc Lawson would remain with the radio truck as a rallying point. All vehicles would rendezvous there at the end of the raid. As the area was crawling with the enemy, they needed as many hours of darkness as possible in which to make their getaway. They would have to be in and out swiftly, and well hidden in the desert come daybreak.

The key target was the airfield. Two Italian units were stationed there. One, the 35 Stormo

Bombardmento (35th Bombing Wing), was equipped with Cant. Z.1007 Alcione – Kingfisher – three-engined aircraft, widely regarded as the finest Italian bomber of the war. The Alcione could carry approaching 5,000 pounds of munitions. The 66 Gruppo Osservazione Aerea (66th Air Observation Group) was also based there, flying Caproni Ca. 311 reconnaissance aircraft.

Indeed, several of those twin-engined Caproni spotter planes had flown over Easonsmith's position earlier that day. Wilder had been in the midst of briefing his unit when the first aircraft droned into view. It was a worrying moment, as faces glanced skywards apprehensively. Even Merlyn Craw paused from prepping his DIY incendiary bombs, getting to his feet to gaze at the sky.

The aircraft passed by. 'You know, Merlyn, you look just like Moses standing there,' someone joked nervously.

Craw cracked a smile. 'And you know what – this could be your last supper.'

The soldiers turned back to their tasks: cleaning weapons and prepping charges. It was less than an hour to sundown, the shadows were long and the vehicles well hidden: they had to presume they'd not been seen.

They were mistaken. The Barce sector commander, Brigadier General Umberto Piatti dal Pozzo, received several reports of sightings, including one of fifteen British trucks on the approach to Barce. One of the orbiting Caproni aircraft flew north from there and managed to drop a message alerting the nearest Italian force, the 7th Savari Cavalry, to the presence of the British vehicles.

The brigadier general took immediate action. He ordered a reconnaissance patrol from the 7th Savari to comb the area where the British force had been seen, and he dispatched eight Italian tanks to defend the Barce aerodrome, sending six more to block the streets giving access into the town. Pozzo also ordered all night traffic to be stopped and searched, and placed four armoured cars on the town square, to act as a mobile reserve.

Unaware of all this, Easonsmith led his column out of their place of concealment. With lights off, the seventeen vehicles moved north through the darkness, cutting any telephone wires they encountered along the route. If any enemy forces were alerted to their presence, they would have less chance of calling in reinforcements now that those lines had been severed. But Brigadier General Umberto Piatti dal Pozzo's troops didn't need any telephone warnings.

They knew already that the *pattagulia fanatasma* – the ghost patrol – was coming.

CHAPTER 13

The first unexpected challenge faced by Haselden and his commandos was the terrain. In the flat dusk light none had realized just how steep and treacherous was the descent from the ridgeline. Search as they might there was no obvious track, and with no LRDG patrol to guide them the lead truck had to steer the best course it could.

As the three vehicles bumped, skidded and slithered their way down the dry, rocky surface, no one could believe that they hadn't yet been heard or spotted from the road below. So slow was their descent that by the time the trucks were nearing the highway they were already a good thirty minutes behind schedule.

Suddenly, trouble seemed to be upon them: a pair of German light transport vehicles came barrelling along the highway. Unless the British convoy slowed, the two parties would surely collide as they converged, plus Haselden's convoy was bound to be spotted making its way through the rough bush and scrub.

Beneath their shielding blankets the commandos

gripped their weapons more tightly. All eyes were on the pair of German trucks, dreading the moment when they would slow to a stop on the road ahead. But they did nothing of the sort. Instead, they simply thundered past at top speed, seemingly finding nothing odd about a convoy of Afrika Korps vehicles crossing the scrub by the roadside.

Buck and Haselden knew they could afford no further delay. Their truck nosed its way up onto the road and turned left, accelerating onto the first proper stretch of Tarmac that any of them had driven on for three weeks or more. It might be potholed and sun-cracked, but to men in vehicles that had spent so long in the desert it felt as smooth as silk.

As the other trucks slotted in behind, Buck urged Chunky Hillman, his SIG driver, to put his foot down and steer hell for leather for Tobruk. The sun was already slipping below the horizon and no vehicles were supposed to be out after dark.

At first there was nothing but open scrub to either side of the road, but as they thundered west the first tents hove into view, marking the enemy encampments that sprawled outside the Tobruk wire. Moments later the speeding convoy was in among them, scattered ranks of grey, sun-bleached canvas stretching off to either side. In the rear truck Langton kept his gun trained on his 'captives', but even so his gaze strayed to left and right. He could see cookhouses, orderly rooms, sleeping quarters, medical tents and messes – with every-where figures hurrying to their duties.

It struck him as appearing like any typical British military encampment, and he had to remind himself that they were in reality on the outskirts of one of the enemy's most heavily defended strongholds. Occasionally, figures glanced up at their passing. Langton couldn't help but wonder if any were suspicious as to the identity of those in the speeding vehicles.

He tried to imagine himself in their shoes. The very idea that the enemy might drive into a camp set so far behind the front line would be incon-ceivable to the average soldier, especially if that enemy force was disguised as friendly troops. The realization reassured Langton, and he firmed up his hold on his rifle, hardening the gaze with which he kept watch on his charges.

But the surge in confidence was to be painfully short lived.

They'd been motoring for no more than twenty minutes when a lone spotter plane seemed to melt out of the fabric of the ridgeline above and come swooping down towards them. It rushed in at no more than 300 feet, and as the aircraft roared above the trucks the black dots of the pilot's head plus that of his navigator were clearly visible, gazing down at the vehicles.

Twice the aircraft circled the convoy. Langton studied the red fuselage and the ugly black crosses picked out against a white background. Then, as abruptly as it had arrived, it banked south and slipped into the gathering darkness, heading in the direction of El Adem airfield. Even though the watchers in the skies were gone, the anxiety lingered: had the spotter plane been waiting for them? Had their mission been betrayed? Were they driving into a trap?

Langton could picture a German operations room set somewhere inside the approaching wire. He could imagine reports being radioed in from the spotter plane, plus watchers on the road, as an Afrika Korps officer plotted the convoy's progress on a map. He could see the German commander rubbing his hands with glee, ordering those manning the ambush positions to hold their fire until they could see the whites of the British raiders' eyes.

The perimeter defences were fast approaching, and after the spotter plane's unwelcome scrutiny the atmosphere in the trucks had darkened. The men of the Commando could deal with everything but the possibility of betrayal. If treachery were afoot, their mission would be over before it had even begun.

Beneath the blankets hands fingered safety catches. The commandos felt increasingly certain that those manning the perimeter had been forewarned of their impeding arrival and of their true identities. Well, if that were the case they would just have to smash their way through in a storm of fire, they told themselves grimly. They had made it thus far and no one was about to keep them out of Tobruk.

A wall of tangled fortifications reared out of the gathering darkness. In the lead vehicle Buck grabbed his papers and leaned out of the window. The Punjabi Regiment captain was possessed of a remarkable, icy calm. He'd talked his way through enemy checkpoints on numerous occasions before, and never once had he felt as exhaustively prepared as he did now.

He straightened his cap and dusted down the epaulettes that marked him out as a lieutenant in Rommel's Afrika Korps. He stared ahead, the warped, rusting barbed wire of the perimeter defences and guard towers stark before him. He could see the break in the wire where the road passed through, with sandbagged bunkers set to either side, and in the gap itself a group of soldiers milling about.

Buck recognized them as Italians, which was mighty good news. Generally speaking, Italian troops tended to defer to their German 'superiors'. He waved his papers imperiously. The truck slowed a little, before the guards stood aside, lifted the barrier and waved the first vehicle on. The tension in the cab was palpable as they drew level with the sandbagged gun emplacements. It was all too easy. Not even a cursory glance at their papers.

Buck, plus Barlow in his standing position and Chunky Hillman at the truck's wheel, braced themselves for the storm of machine-gun fire they felt sure was coming. But nothing happened. They sailed through unmolested. The guards called out greetings to their German comrades. Remembering his part, Hillman yelled back the kind of coarse responses the Italians seemed to expect from their Teutonic brothers-in-arms, making suitable hand gestures.

'Dummkopf! Schweinhund! Flachwichser!'

The Italians waved and laughed and yelled back what had to be milder expletives in Italian, such was the relationship between the two allies.

The banter seemed to do the trick. Moments later all three vehicles were through. The SIG operators had played their parts to perfection. Buck's inflexible regime – the forced isolation, the deep immersion in Afrika Korps military culture, the POW trainers even – had proved its worth. After twenty-one days of merciless desert driving, the SOE Commando and the SIG were inside the wire of Tobruk.

The trucks pulled away from the perimeter. All around stretched the camps and fortifications of the enemy. For an instant the sheer stunning bravado of the moment had Haselden's force utterly gripped. The bluff had held good, and armed to the teeth they were prowling unnoticed through Rommel's prized stronghold. Few had actually believed it possible, yet here they were. The ruse had succeeded beyond all possible expectations, or so it seemed.

And then the convoy met oncoming vehicles. A German column was approaching in the opposite direction, at speed, no doubt bound for the front.

There was an almighty crash from the second of Haselden's trucks, and it all but veered off the road. It had cannoned into a speeding vehicle, striking it a glancing blow.

Behind them the enemy column halted. Figures crowded into the road. In the lead truck Buck urged more speed. No way was he about to stop and get embroiled in an argument over a road traffic accident. Angry shouts and curses chased after the vehicles. The SIG operators yelled back in equally brusque fashion, and the trucks sped on their way.

The moment of high tension passed. The road opened before them, and as they drew closer to Tobruk it grew busy with traffic. Faster vehicles – jeeps and light trucks – overtook the convoy, paying them little attention, and the men began to feel as if they were in the midst of the enemy's war machine, a part of it even. It was amazing how they just seemed to blend in.

Everywhere the roadside was busy with figures: German and Italian soldiers, slogging their way on foot to and from their evening meal, mess tins swinging in their hands. Now and then they stared at the dirty, unkempt prisoners visible in the rear of the trucks, signaling their approval to the guards. Facing an enemy such as this – dishevelled, broken and bowed – was it any wonder that Rommel's forces had scored such mighty victories.

What could possibly stop them now? the commandos wondered.

But in the see-saw roller coaster emotions of the moment, hope was about to veer towards fear once again. As if from nowhere, three motorcycles sped out of a side road. Two were combinations, a begoggled German soldier crammed into each sidecar. They pulled in close to the rear truck, sticking right on its tail and eyeing those riding in it with undisguised hostility.

The 'POWs' found themselves gazing into the inquisitorial faces of German military policemen. The motorcycles pulled ahead, each matching the speed of the truck it was now shadowing. Hostile faces peered in at the 'prisoners', and to a man the commandos felt as if they had been rumbled. Nothing else would explain the German MPs' behaviour.

Major Campbell was propped up in the back of the last truck, leaning against the rear ramp. He glanced at the nearest of his men. 'Get your gun, Glynn,' he hissed. 'Looks like the game is up.'

Private Glynn fingered the tommy gun under his blanket. The safety was off and at the slightest hint of danger from the motorcycling MPs he was going to let rip. Then, just as mysteriously as they had appeared, the motorcyclists were gone again, drawing ahead and disappearing in a cloud of dust.

Before those in the rear truck had time to recover their composure, another drama was upon them, and this time caused by one of their own. The big Irish Guardsman Hogan rose from his squatting position, unbuttoned himself and began to pee over the side of the speeding vehicle.

For a moment Tommy Langton was at a complete loss as to what he should do. What was appropriate behaviour in such a situation? Surely a genuine German guard wouldn't allow a British prisoner to pee in the faces of the Afrika Korps and their Italian comrades? Surely not? But if not, then what? What was he supposed to do?

He could hardly yell threats and curses in German – which he felt sure was the right thing to do – for he could speak barely a word. All he could think of was to raise his rifle and wave it menacingly in Hogan's direction. But even as he did so, Langton could hear the commandos giggling. Hogan's actions and Langton's confusion had them tickled pink.

They were passing through a thickly tented area, and Langton could see enemy soldiers gesturing at Hogan disgustedly. Hogan stared stonily back at them. Langton just had to hope the semi-darkness would hide the worst of his indiscretions. Finally Hogan adjusted himself, turned back to the truck and sat down, seemingly relishing the angst that he had caused.

They sped onward into the beckoning night. Not a minute or so later a brilliant light split the darkness. It soared into the sky, the fluorescent glow illuminating a large swathe of the enemy encampment from which it had been fired. Another Very light was unleashed, followed shortly by a third.

Each seemed to mirror the progress of the trucks, as if signalling their position on the road.

'Looks like someone's charting our progress into Tobruk,' someone growled.

Langton nodded. 'Sure looks that way.'

To Langton, each Very light seemed like a signal to the hidden ambush party that must be lurking up ahead. Every 200 yards or so one shot up in a graceful arc, turning night into near-daylight. The convoy was nearing Tobruk town, and if there was to be an attack this was surely where it would be sprung.

It would be any minute now.

The tension mounted.

They hit a second escarpment, which descended into Tobruk itself. The trucks shifted into low gear to negotiate the steep and winding descent that overlooked the dark harbour: ideal ambush territory.

As the lead vehicle crawled downwards, Haselden pointed into the gloom. A high rock face was silhouetted against the dying light of the sky. 'That's the bomb-proof fuel storage depot,' he announced, 'the one we have to destroy later tonight.' He didn't mention it, but that fuel dump hollowed into the rock face had been the chief target of his earliest plans to raid Tobruk, in a swift hit-and-run attack.

A figure swore softly at his side. It was Lieutenant Graham Taylor, Major Campbell's second in command. A true commando, he was never one to pass up the chance to hit such a juicy target.

He eyed the fuel depot hungrily. 'We could have blown it as we passed! We're so close. A few grenades might even have done the trick.'

Taylor was right, and Haselden knew it. But the present plan called for the SIG deception to hold right until they reached Sciausc Bay – the bridge-head for the coming seaborne landings. Only once they'd got those reinforcements landed would the Commando be free to bust open the POW cages, and fight their way back to this position to hit that vital fuel depot.

The road flattened out. Still no ambush had been sprung. The commandos were starting to believe that they had got away with it, when the lead truck ground to an unexpected halt. The assault plan called for the convoy to keep moving, turning right off the main route, taking a dirt track that threaded east along the harbour, leading to Sciausc Bay itself. So why the sudden halt?

Voices could be heard in front yelling in German. Russell jumped down from his position in the rear vehicle and hurried into the darkness. After a few seconds' indecision, Langton decided to risk leaving his place, to check out what was happening. Whatever was going on, it couldn't be good news.

He found Russell, Buck, Hillman and Opprower gathered around the lead vehicle and jabbering away in German. Langton couldn't understand much, but the gist soon became clear. A fence had been built along the right-hand side of the road, which barred the route that the commandos needed to take – the turn-off to Sciausc Bay itself. The fence certainly hadn't been there when the British had held Tobruk.

Paranoid minds began to wonder if it had been put there specifically to stop *them*. Maybe this was the moment of their death or capture? In the rear of the trucks the blankets were off now: guns were up and charged, ready to unleash hell. Buck led Hillman and Opprower to scout the route ahead. Maybe they had missed the turning?

Russell whispered to Langton that they would have to make a U-turn and go back, searching for an alternative route. Langton felt as if he had at least to act like the German soldier he was supposed to be.

He saluted smartly. '*Jawohl, Jawohl, mein Kapitan,*' he cried in his best schoolboy German, before turning back to his vehicle.

'Shut up, you bloody fool!' Russell hissed after him. 'Shut up!'

Nerves were strained to breaking point. Even so, Langton couldn't help but find the situation bizarrely amusing. He climbed back into his guard position, giggling to himself a little crazily.

Buck emerged from the darkness. The fence ended a few hundred yards ahead, he reported, and there a new track had been constructed leading down to the water. Word was passed along the line of vehicles. Buck, Russell, Hillman and Opprower were about to mount up when three powerful shots split the night. They had come from a big gun, and were evenly spaced: *boom, boom, boom.*

For an instant Buck feared that this was it – the signal to trigger the ambush. But then he remembered. 'That's the air-raid warning,' he cried. 'Time to get moving!'

The massed RAF warplanes had to be inbound to Tobruk. They clambered into the trucks and the column lurched into motion once more. It was just after nine o'clock. They'd been on the move for a little under three hours and they were falling behind schedule, but with a free run to Sciausc Bay it should all still be doable.

The road ahead took the convoy past a scattering of buildings on the outskirts of Tobruk town. It was almost pitch dark, but still figures were milling about at the roadside, mostly drifting towards the harbour area. Enemy soldiers, no doubt intent on a night out on the town.

Buck's truck slowed to a crawl and swung right, tyres crunching onto the uneven surface of the newly made track. Changing down through the gears, the others followed. Moments later the main route was behind them, as the convoy began to rumble the last few miles to the landing beach itself. Sciausc Bay lay some three miles east of the turning point. *They were so close.*

The tension began to dissipate. It was replaced instead by the adrenaline rush of imminent action. The blankets were thrown aside, though their weapons were still held down and out of sight.

The trucks trundled past groups of Italian soldiers heading out for good time. They stared curiously at the passengers and the 'German guards' before calling enquiringly, '*Prizione? Prizione?*'

'*Si, si,*' Langton called back in reply. '*Prizione!*' His bad Italian didn't matter; he was a German guard, after all.

'*Viva il Duce!*' the Italian soldiers cried lustily. To which the commandos replied under their breaths with a suitable string of curses.

Spirits soared. Now they were deep inside the enemy fortress, who was ever going to suspect them? The entire situation had become somewhat surreal. Unreal even. And then the first, plaintive wail of an air-raid siren cut the night. Moments later more sirens had taken up the warning, and an intense beam of light fingered into the heavens. Another and another joined it: searchlights.

The air raid was about to commence, which underscored how delayed the commandos were: the plan had them in position at Sciausc Bay well before the bombing was scheduled to start.

The beams of light fingered across the sky, being reflected in the still basin of Tobruk harbour. Now the commandos could make out the entire port and its key landmarks. What had been known as Admiralty House under the British was silhouetted against the water, plus the jetties and the wrecks of war-damaged ships that littered the bay.

The heavens began to reverberate with the distant roar of engines. The crash of anti-aircraft

211

fire split the night. Langton was amazed to see how near some of the gun emplacements were. In the muzzle flashes of the weapons firing he could make out individual members of the gun crews.

He was seized by an overpowering sense of unreality. They were so close to men they were soon going to have to kill, for these were the very weapons that they were supposed to turn on the enemy. Yet here they were, utterly unsuspected, believed by all to be friendly. He could only imagine the shock those gunners would feel when they were hit by total surprise and seemingly from their own side.

The track plunged lower, bringing the trucks to within a stone's throw of the sea. They'd been driving for fifteen minutes – surely they were nearing Sciausc Bay? Suddenly a guttural cry of challenge rang out from the front. The convoy ground to a halt. Dust filled the air, lit by the beams of the trucks' headlights.

In the harsh, sweeping glare of a searchlight reflecting off the water a German sentry could be seen up ahead, rifle ready and barring the way. There was a checkpoint blocking the route into Sciausc Bay. Russell jumped down from the rear vehicle. The tall Scotsman strode purposefully forward.

No one was about to halt the Commando or the SIG this close to their objective.

CHAPTER 14

Lloyd Owen had failed. Not that it would have likely made much difference, but still he was plagued by a crushing sense of failure. For the last hour or so he'd been trying to raise Haselden, but there had been not a sniff of a response on the radio.

His wireless operator was equally frustrated. 'Blast them!' he railed. 'Why won't they answer?'

Lloyd Owen didn't give voice to the obvious response, the one that was foremost in his mind. To do so would be to court disaster, he feared. To him there was only one possible explanation as to why Haselden might have gone quiet: deprived of any warning, he'd very likely driven into a trap.

But Lloyd Owen's fears, and those of his radio operator, were about to be swept away in the coming conflagration.

The air-raid sirens shrieked, spears of light pierced the skies above Tobruk and the airborne armada swept in to assail the harbour fortress, bang on schedule. Approaching one hundred aircraft were involved in tonight's raid, mostly RAF Vickers Wellingtons and Halifaxes, but it also included a squadron of United States Air Force B-17 Flying Fortress bombers only recently arrived in theatre.

They thundered across Tobruk in deafening waves. The first aircraft dropped blinding flares suspended under parachutes – light by which the bomb aimers could identify their targets. Moments later the leading warplanes unleashed their tons of high explosives, which crashed down around the harbour. Somewhere in that boiling cauldron were Haselden and his commandos, but Lloyd Owen had no time to worry about them now.

Under the cover of the air raid, his patrol had their own mission to execute.

'Pack up,' he ordered. 'Let's get moving.'

The men mounted their trucks and set off, heading down the escarpment directly towards the Tobruk perimeter. The night was black, the wind whistling up-slope bitingly cold, and the mood dark. It was the not-knowing that was so unsettling.

They'd chosen to drop down from the ridgeline at a place called Sidi Resegh, some twelve miles south-east of Tobruk. Few but madmen would attempt such an undertaking in the pitch darkness, and the going proved incredibly tough. In places the men were forced to walk ahead of the Chevys, removing boulders and clearing a track down which the trucks could crawl. The slope was precipitous, rocky and craggy, and there were moments when it seemed as if the vehicles must tumble over, those riding in them clinging on for dear life.

The one advantage of this route was that no one would expect to be attacked from such a direction and certainly not at night. Finally the gradient eased and they reached the level plain. Ahead, Tobruk was lit up in one long continuous blast, the flashes of the explosions bleeding into one another. Four-thousand-pound bombs were being dropped tonight, and Lloyd Owen and his men could see them erupting among the buildings of the harbour.

It had to be sheer hell right now to be in Tobruk under such an assault. The watchers hoped and prayed that none of the deadly payloads were about to be unleashed on Sciausc Bay – that was if Haselden's force had even made it in there.

Lloyd Owen led his six vehicles in line astern across the open ground. Flashes of explosions rippled across the plain, revealing a blocky silhouette just ahead of them. A pillbox – it had to mark the outer perimeter. He heard voices calling out a challenge.

His only response was to yell to his driver, 'Step on it!'

Within seconds they had crashed through, but behind there was the sharp eruption of gunfire. There were a series of deafening blasts in response, which told Lloyd Owen that his men were in action, their vehicle-mounted weapons hammering rounds out into the night. Several hundred feet beyond the perimeter Lloyd Owen pulled to a halt. He and his men paused, hunched over their guns, eyes scanning the terrain to their rear.

No vehicle emerged, so Lloyd Owen got down from the Chevy and started signalling with his torch. As no one opened fire on him, he began to shout, calling for the vehicles to converge on his position. Suddenly, a voice answered from the darkness, and the first Chevy nosed out of the shadows to join them.

Lloyd Owen counted the Chevys as they came in. Five, his own included. As luck would have it the missing vehicle was the wireless truck. Whatever might have happened they needed to recover it. Deprived of their radio they would be operating blind and would be useless to headquarters. Just as worryingly, the LRDG's codes and ciphers were stored in that vehicle. There was no way they could be allowed to fall into enemy hands.

Breathless figures emerged from the darkness. They turned out to be the crew of the wireless truck, moving on foot. Smashing through the perimeter their vehicle had been caught in a blast of enemy fire. They'd stalled and been unable to get it started again.

Lloyd Owen gathered a dozen men and with tommy guns at the ready they headed back through the dark bush towards the pillbox. Worried that he was behind schedule, Lloyd Owen hurried ahead, but the missing truck couldn't be located.

It was time to throw caution to the wind. He fired a Very pistol, the light erupting like a tiny fluorescent sun suspended in the sky. His men went down on their stomachs. Their commander remained resolutely vertical: *Where was that damned wireless truck?*

In the eerie white glow Lloyd Owen thought he could see it. He pushed forward, only to discover the silhouette of what was an abandoned horse-drawn cart. Lloyd Owen cursed. So did his men. The last thing they needed to be doing right now was blundering about inside the enemy's lines searching for a lost Chevy.

Lloyd Owen fired off Very lights in all directions. For an instant he was reminded of when they had girdled the Great Pyramid in lights – happier days. They were right back on the perimeter now, but amazingly there was still no incoming fire.

Lloyd Owen nodded towards the pillbox. 'Bastards seem remarkably uninterested,' he growled.

Suddenly someone spied the missing radio truck. It was just a few dozen yards to the side of the enemy bunker. Lloyd Owen decided that the outpost had most definitely had its day. He sent forward half a dozen men. The raiders' tommy guns barked, the shots sounding muffled amid the pillbox's thick walls. There was silence, more bursts of gunfire, and then a long beat of quiet.

His attack force returned, minus those who had gone forward to try to get the truck moving. Lloyd Owen heard an engine cough into life. Moments later the radio truck was on the move. A short distance from the pillbox it halted. The rear tyres had been shot out. Working as fast as they could, the truck's crew proceeded to change both wheels, while Lloyd Owen and the others stood guard.

Still no enemy fire came.

Lloyd Owen got all six vehicles on the move again. He now had to navigate them to their target – the enemy's D/F radio station. His mind was assailed by doubts. The plan called for their target to be hit at midnight, but they were running well behind schedule now. He worried whether the Sciausc Bay landing ground had been taken sucessfully. His greatest fear was that Haselden and his men had been lured to their deaths.

He forced the Chevys on at breakneck speed. They careered over earthworks, dodged around slit trenches, and tore their way through strands of barbed wire. Battered, dented but unbowed, the six trucks emerged onto the main coastal highway, the same road that Haselden and his Commando had driven along just an hour or so earlier.

Lloyd Owen's patrol headed towards the glow of explosions hanging over the port. The enemy's D/F station lay just a few miles ahead. They pressed onward at top speed, passing through encampments similar to those that the Commando had penetrated earlier, but unlike them Lloyd Owen's force was blessed with no deception or disguise. They were a British patrol driving through fortress Tobruk in full view of the enemy, with only the night as their cloak and their protector.

Their route offered a grandstand view of the air raid: the heavens were a mass of exploding flak, rent by fiery streams of tracer plus the jabbing beams of searchlights. The stark outline of a bomber was pinned by a cone of illumination, crucifix-like. Trapped within its brilliance, gunfire converged on the hapless plane. It plummeted earthwards trailing a fiery comet in its wake.

Up ahead Lloyd Owen spotted headlights. Some one else was moving through the firestorm. He pulled the trucks off the road, before sprinting back up the embankment, tommy gun held at the ready and a phalanx of raiders at his back. The lead vehicle's lights pinned him in their glare. The driver seemed to gun his engine, heading right for where Lloyd Owen was standing. Perhaps he'd recognized the LRDG commander for an enemy.

Lloyd Owen raised his weapon and pulled the trigger. Nothing happened. The bloody gun had jammed! Luckily, those on his shoulder opened fire a split second later, the night erupting to their punching percussions. Tommy gun rounds shattered glass. The lead vehicle skidded to a halt.

Bearded figures swarmed out of the darkness, surrounding the convoy completely, guns at the ready. Those riding in the vehicles were German soldiers, and they were clearly shocked and bewildered to have been set upon by these wild-looking British raiders this far inside the Tobruk perimeter.

One of the Germans was an officer. Lloyd Owen proceeded to question him. 'What's the big rush?' he demanded. 'Where are you going and why?'

The German officer jerked his head towards the firestorm that was the harbour. 'We're leaving Tobruk. There is nothing but chaos in the town. We saw no sense in staying there tonight, under your warplanes.'

There was little more of interest that the German officer was able to tell him. Lloyd Owen had his men disarm the Germans, after which they were forced at gunpoint to roll their own vehicles down the embankment that lined the side of the road to put them out of action.

Clearly, all was chaos and confusion in Tobruk, but that did little to assuage Lloyd Owen's worries about Haselden and his men. Either way, he needed to get his force on the move again before this small, impromptu action attracted more of the enemy.

At the approach of midnight Jake Easonsmith's patrol turned onto the main road leading into Barce town. The night so far had not been without incident. Although they'd navigated their way this far showing no lights, they'd still had to fight their way through several Italian checkpoints, unleashing machine-gun fire and hurling grenades.

They'd lost two vehicles en route, but suffered no casualties. They'd also captured a most helpful fighter. A local from the Senussi tribe – normally seen as being friendly to the British – Hamed had been press-ganged into service with the Italian forces. He'd seemed more than happy to swap sides and join the British raiders, and he was blessed with some juicy, if worrying, intelligence.

Earlier that day an Italian spotter plane had dropped a warning message to Hamed's encampment: 'British Motor Patrol has been spotted in the vicinity.' Presumably that aircraft had subsequently landed at Barce, where the aircrew had issued the same kind of a warning. Easonsmith now knew that the enemy was forewarned and forearmed, but that did little to alter his intentions: they would raid the Barce aerodrome come what may.

Just before hitting the main highway Easonsmith had ordered his wireless truck to take up a position hidden in some bush, adjacent to the tomb of a local sheikh. A grey-walled, flat-roofed building topped off by a spire resembling an obelisk, it was an easily recognizable landmark. This would be their immediate rally point, once the night's action was over. From there the wireless operator would maintain a radio link with David Stirling's SAS, who even now were going into action just to the west, at Benghazi.

Easonsmith ordered a reluctant Doc Lawson to remain with the wireless truck, which would also constitute their DIY medical station. He was convinced that tonight they would be taking casualties.

As they pulled onto the main drag, Easonsmith flicked the lights of his Willys Jeep to full. The fourteen Chevys and jeeps behind him followed suit. The impression he wanted to give was of an

221

Italian patrol returning to base, somewhat later than expected. Blinded by the glare of the incoming vehicles, no watchers would be able to identify the patrol, at least not before it was too late. Or so Easonsmith hoped.

He spotted the first obstacle: two Italian tanks, straddling the road. There was no doubt in his mind any more: their arrival was expected. He just had to hope that the lights-on ruse might hold, at least until the Italian armour came within range of his guns. These were Carro Veloce L3 light tanks, a far less threatening prospect than the heavy panzers of Rommel's Afrika Korps, but still more than a match for the LRDG's unarmoured, thin-skinned Chevys.

A 3.2-ton vehicle, the L3 had 13-millimetre armour and carried a crew of two, seated side-by-side in the turret. One was the driver, the other the gunner – most commonly operating twin 8-millimetre Breda machine guns. But there were also models equipped with heavier, 20-millimetre anti-tank weapons or even flame-throwers. Right now Easonsmith had no way of knowing which versions they were facing.

Easonsmith held his fire until they neared point-blank range. At such a close distance the .5-inch Brownings and Vickers might just be able to punch through the L3's armoured hides. When Easonsmith pulled the trigger of the twin Vickers K machine guns bolted to the dashboard of his jeep, the entire column opened up as one.

A barrage of rounds sparked and flashed along the flanks of the two tanks. The onslaught must have been devastating for those within; the crews would have been deafened by the sound of .303 and .5 rounds smacking into their hulls. Facing a blitz of some thirty weapons, the amount of incoming fire must have been utterly terrifying.

Even if the .5-inch rounds didn't penetrate the armour, their impact at such close quarters would cause slivers of steel to splinter off, turning the interior of the tanks into a whirlwind of shrapnel. Considering which, it was a miracle that the L3 gunners actually managed to return fire at all. Momentarily the tanks' weapons opened up, but that only made Easonsmith's gunners concentrate their fire on the L3s' slit windows.

As the LRDG column streamed past, guns blazing, razor-sharp shards of bullet fragments and splintered armour tore into the tanks' crew. By the time the last vehicle in Easonsmith's column had thundered by, the L3s' guns had fallen silent.

The column hit the first buildings on the outskirts of Barce town itself. Here the force divided. Riding in his command jeep, Captain Wilder led his New Zealand patrol straight on and then left, skirting Barce and heading directly for the airport. Guardsman Sergeant Jack Dennis turned hard left, aiming to cut the phone wires linking Barce with Benghazi and Tobruk, after which his patrol was to shoot up the enemy barracks.

Easonsmith had given them two hours to do

their work: by 0200 they should all be heading out to the rally point, at the sheikh's tomb. Popski Peniakoff's jeep would remain on the outskirts of town, to secure the patrol's exit point, while Easonsmith took two jeeps to tear around the streets shooting the hell out of anything that moved.

Lights blazing, Wilder's jeep led the convoy of four Chevys towards the airfield. As they approached he called a momentary halt and slipped behind the wheel of *Tutira III*, the Chevy he liked to ride into battle. The *III* denoted that its two predecessors had been lost in action with the LRDG. Beside him sat Trooper Derek Parker, manning the twin Vickers Ks, while in the rear stood Trooper Mick Holland, poised at the tripod-mounted .5 Vickers.

Pulses hammering, they approached the airfield. A turning led off right, disappearing into the gloom. Wilder spun the steering wheel and *Tutira III* thundered off the Tarmac onto the dirt road. From studying aerial photos of the aerodrome, he knew the airfield itself lay off to his left down a grassy track. But between there and here lay a checkpoint.

He swung the Chevy around a right-hand bend and the barrier hove into view. In his headlights Wilder could see sentries crowded around the gate. Arms were raised to halt their progress, and challenges shouted into the night. Wilder's gunner didn't hesitate: a long burst from the twin Vickers swept the checkpoint from right to left, cutting down the guards.

'We wiped them out without leaving our seats, but it was only the beginning of the battle,' Wilder remarked of the moment. 'We had to shoot our way onto the airfield.'

Wilder stamped on the brakes, skidding to a halt at the heavy metal barrier. He jumped down, as Trooper Parker kept him covered. The gate was closed, but no one had thought to lock it. The Italian commanders had presumed it impossible for any enemy force to approach the airfield from the direction of the main road, or from Barce town itself. Instead, they'd readied themselves for an attack by foot soldiers coming from the open scrub of the desert.

Wilder simply lent his weight on the gate and pushed it open.

Fire erupted from the trucks, tracer and incendiary rounds cutting through the air above his head. The gunners on the Chevys had spotted a group of Italian troops rushing from their positions to investigate the confusion at the front gate. Under withering fire they scattered.

Wilder leaped behind the wheel again and got *Tutira III* into motion. The five vehicles swept down the grassy track leading to the airstrip. Wilder knew from the aerial photos where the aircraft were likely to be: the big fat Alcione bombers would be parked up to left and right of their entry point, lined up neatly along two sides of the airfield, the smaller spotter planes dispersed among them.

To his left Wilder spotted a truck-and-trailer unit packed with drums of aviation fuel. A burst of fire from Parker's guns turned it into a raging inferno. As the flames popped and spat, sparks and thick black smoke erupting skywards, the intense light brought the entire scene into focus. To their immediate right lay a concrete block structure painted white, which housed the mess and the barracks.

As the Chevys passed the building, grenades were hurled through the windows. There was a series of hollow crumps as the high explosives detonated inside the building, blowing out glass and doors. Flames billowed from the shattered openings as those inside ran from the blasts, fire from the Chevys' machine guns chasing them through the smoke.

The patrol's guns were turned next on the main aircraft hangar, long bursts punching ragged holes in its corrugated tin flanks. Then Wilder spotted an altogether juicier target: the main fuel dump, 44-gallon drums piled high for all to see. Long bursts of the raiders' lethal cocktail of tracer, incendiary and explosive ammunition tore into them.

Moments later the first drums ruptured, gushing avgas and flame. As the fuel and heat spread, so the entire dump was transformed into a massive, seething ocean of fire. Wilder stamped on the gas. As his truck raced by he could feel the burning heat of the inferno hot on his exposed skin, the stench heavy in his nostrils.

Tutira III lurched and bucked over the uneven, grassy track, bursting through a hedge onto the airstrip. Wilder flicked his headlights to off. The ruse was definitely over, and he certainly didn't need the headlights to see by any more.

The exploding fuel dump lit up the first Alcione bomber, almost as if it were daylight.

CHAPTER 15

In Tobruk David Russell marched up to the German guard, gesticulating and crying out in his fluent German. With the deafening retorts of the anti-aircraft fire, and the crumps of powerful explosions from the port area, he had to yell to make himself heard. But the usual gambit of Teutonic impatience didn't seem to be working – not with this guard, at least.

The man remained stubbornly in place, rifle held at the ready barring their way. He eyed Russell suspiciously. What were they doing taking POWs further east, away from Tobruk? he demanded. All the POW cages were back along the harbour. And why were they on the move after dark? Didn't he know that all vehicle movement was forbidden come sundown?

Russell cursed the Germans and their discipline, their procedures, their rules. Tonight they would prove the death of this man. The tall, good-looking Guards officer steeled himself. He was not one for killing in cold blood, and especially not when his adversary hadn't been given a fair chance. But this was no time for gentlemanly conduct. After all, they'd been sent here to execute a most ungentlemanly kind of warfare, and in this brutal form of combat he who hesitated was very likely a dead man.

Russell killed the guard. Deed done, he took his rifle, dragged the body aside and strode back to the waiting trucks.

He threw the gun to the commandos. 'Hang on to this. He won't be needing it any more.'

He climbed aboard the truck and the convoy got under way again. Five hundred yards of driving and the three vehicles pulled to a final halt. They had made it into Sciausc Bay itself – where they would secure the beachhead, so the Royal Navy could land the main assault force. They parked in a wadi, on either side of which rose the steep headlands of the bay. It was almost as if they had driven into an extinct volcanic crater, the far edge of which had been worn open by the sea.

Haselden was there in a flash, moving down the trucks and urging everyone into action. All knew their roles. The Commando was splitting up now, one half to seize the western headland flanking the bay, the other the eastern spur – the heights from which they would safeguard the landing beach below. Figures began piling off as others passed down kit, weaponry and supplies. In spite of the intense blackness of the night, there was a glow of sorts emanating from the sea, particularly where it reflected the flash of exploding bombs from the harbour.

Pulses of light threw the terrain into ghostly relief. The wadi dropped away to what had to be a hidden cove – the landing ground. On a high point to the west lay a cluster of huts which served the gun emplacements looking out over the harbour. Those were some of the very first objectives of the Commando.

Relieved of his 'guard duties', Tommy Langton threw off his German disguise, dropping the clothes into a disused bunker. Lieutenants Barlow and Harrison were only too happy to do likewise. Their days in the Afrika Korps were over. Now they were back to doing what they did best: preparing to fight shoulder to shoulder with their fellow commandos.

Langton felt Haselden's grip on his arm. 'Tom, I want you to go with Colin's party. He's in a bad way, but he won't admit it. If you find his strength gives out, take over.'

Langton's mind raced. Before now his task had been simple and focused. With his SBS pedigree, he was to use an Aldis lamp – a Naval signal light – to guide the MTBs into Sciausc Bay. Once they were inbound, he was to act as a reception party for the landings on the beach. But now Haselden had tasked him with an extra, and altogether more onerous, undertaking. Should Major Campbell falter, he was to take over command on the eastern headland. But clearly he couldn't be in two places at once. Langton was about to give voice to his concerns, but Haselden moved swiftly away. Langton couldn't blame him; he had his hands more than full tonight.

Haselden had to lead the force seizing the western headland, where he would establish his headquarters, complete with radio communications. From there he was supposed to orchestrate the entire operation, pulling each and every element together at exactly the right place and time. Haselden had enough to worry about, Langton reasoned. Somehow, he would have to muddle through.

Major Campbell stepped out of the shadows. Still sporting his signature hodden kilt, he called his force together. Even though his voice sounded terribly strained, he was refusing to give in. He had survived twenty-one days of dysentery in the desert, and he remained determined to play his part now.

Campbell gathered his men in the darkness. He led off with Langton bringing up the rear. The column of men moved across the rocky floor of the wadi, their rubber-soled commando boots making barely a sound, and began to scale the eastern flank.

Meanwhile, Pilot Officer Aubrey Scott was climbing towards the opposite height, weighed down with his lights. Scott had agreed to carry both Aldis lamps to the headland from where he would start signalling. Langton's plan was to rendezvous with him there, once his mission with Campbell was complete. He'd retrieve his lamp, lug it across to the opposite headland and begin flashing away. With the lamp alone weighing five kilos it was going to be quite an undertaking, but Langton didn't see what alternative he had.

Up ahead he sensed the line of commandos come to a halt. Word was whispered from man-to-man. They'd hit barbed wire, very possibly delineating a minefield. Then, from just across the wire, a rifle shot rang out. One lone shot, the muzzle flash clearly visible against the dark, boulder-strewn slope. Had the men of the Commando been seen?

It hardly seemed likely. The night was dark in the way that only African nights seem able to be dark. Maybe a trigger-happy sentry? Or a misfire? In all the confusion of the air raid, had a nervous enemy soldier let rip accidentally? There was no way of knowing. Campbell sent a unit ahead to investigate the source of that lone shot and to drive the enemy onto the commandos' guns.

As they waited, Langton crept forward to the head of the snake. 'Sir, we need to keep moving,' he hissed. 'I'm supposed to start my signalling in a few minutes' time.'

'What d'you suggest, Tom?' Campbell replied. He sounded unutterably tired; by force of will alone he was holding up.

'I'd like to make a recce,' Langton suggested. 'See if the beach is clear – where the MTBs are supposed to land. If it is, we can pass by that way.'

Campbell nodded. 'Go scout the way ahead. Either way, we need a route through the wire.'

Langton did as ordered, weaving a path through

the barbed coils and braced for further rifle fire. No shots came. The path led to the beach itself. He flitted across smooth sand, still damp from the tide. Ahead, a wave rushed in, the sweep of a searchlight glinting off the water. In the open like this he felt horribly exposed, silhouetted as he was against the faint glow of the sea. He couldn't believe that he hadn't been seen.

He checked the beach from end to end: it was clear of the enemy. He glanced at the far headland: maybe there were gun emplacements up there, in which case they would be able to menace the MTBs as they came in, shooting up the soldiers as they waded onto the sands. The high ground would have to be cleared.

Langton turned and hurried back to Campbell. 'The beach is clear, sir,' he reported breathlessly. 'That's our quickest way across and up to the high ground.'

Campbell levered himself to his feet. 'Lead on, Tom. Show us the way.'

Langton retraced his steps to the beach, the commandos following – a long snake of stealthy warriors moving through the darkness. He led them across the deserted sands and up towards the heights, where they knew from the aerial photos that the first reinforced gun emplacements were situated. He found them, big sandbagged bunkers standing out stark and blocky against the sky.

Langton led the force to clear them, creeping silently through the first entrance, weapon primed and ready. It was empty. They all were. What the reconnaissance photos hadn't shown was that they'd been abandoned, their guns moved elsewhere. The question was where? Langton cursed the faulty intelligence. It wasn't the pilot's fault. It wasn't anyone's. These things happened in war.

Shots rang out from Langton's right flank. The first commandos were in action, clearing the position from which the lone rifle shot had been fired. Hidden among the rocks three Italians had sited an MG42 Mauser – a fearsome German machine gun often called a Spandau by British troops. It was capable of putting down 1,200 rounds per minute of fire. Fortunately, the Italians had barely got their hands on the weapon before the commandos were in among them, tommy guns blazing. The enemy were dead now, and the SOE Commando had drawn first blood.

Further shots rang out – a short, sharp burst of tommy-gun fire. Those clearing the trench had downed a fourth victim. It turned out to be one of their own. In the darkness, Hogan – the giant Guard who'd so enjoyed peeing from the speeding truck – had been challenged, and he'd failed to remember the password in time.

It was simple enough. Challenge: who goes there? Password: George Robey – Robey being a hugely popular music-hall comedian of the time. Hogan had failed to deliver the password. He'd taken a round in the thigh as a result.

While a party was tasked to help the injured

man back to Haselden's HQ, Langton pressed on. They followed a shallow ravine leading east, which widened out into a broad basin. Langton could just make out a hut ahead, with a large tent adjacent to it, half dug into the ground. Above it, two whip-thin wireless masts could be seen piercing the night.

Langton led the men to the entrance of the tent, creeping noiselessly across the open terrain. He flicked the flap aside, spying heaps of radio equipment and detecting the deep, regular breathing of sleeping men. He stepped back, holding the flap aside, as the commandos readied grenades. They tossed them in among the sleeping figures and dived for cover.

Ear-splitting detonations cut through the darkness. A storm of shrapnel tore through the tent's thin canvas sides. Commandos charged in, unleashing fire from their tommy guns. The hut received similar treatment to the tent. Their orders were crystal-clear for tonight's mission: Sciausc Bay had to be cleared of all enemy forces, to secure it for the coming landings. Not an enemy soldier was to be left at liberty or alive.

Meanwhile, on the opposite side of the bay Haselden's force were also in action. Lieutenant Graham Taylor, Haselden's second in command, was in charge of clearing the western headland. When he and his force of commandos had scaled the heights, Taylor ordered them into their positions.

'Form a line across the headland,' he hissed.

'Take cover as best you can, watch the skyline and don't let anyone pass. But don't fire, unless on orders of Colonel Haselden or myself.'

Haselden needed time to establish his headquarters. As things stood, their presence remained undetected. Long might that last. In an ideal world they'd get the MTBs in and the reinforcements landed before the assault went overt. Then they'd surge west, seizing this side of the harbour and freeing the POWs.

A natural-born commando, Taylor could hardly wait. His men spread out in a thin line. Down on their stomachs, they readied Sten guns, rifles and Brens, the bipod-supported light machine gun so favoured by British troops. The men of the SOE Commando had been free to bring whatever weapon they favoured.

Many had opted for the iconic Thompson sub-machine gun. Two decades old by now, it remained a favourite for various reasons, reflected in the weapon's nicknames: the Trench Sweeper, Trench Broom and Chopper. It was of rugged, reliable design, had a high rate of fire, and its .45-calibre cartridge delivered real stopping power. When fitted with a 30-round stick magazine, or a 50-round drum, it was possible to sweep an entire trench or bunker with bullets.

The commandos hunkered down, eyes scanning the ragged horizon for the enemy. Meanwhile, Haselden led a small group towards the one feature that dominated the horizon, a white-walled dwelling with a long veranda that had been nicknamed the Italian Villa.

This was Haselden's chosen headquarters – but first it had to be seized and cleared. No light seeped from the windows, nor was there any sign of movement inside, but still the advance party didn't take any chances. Haselden slipped into the shadows of the Italian villa's wall, crept along one side and gripped the door handle.

He twisted it and the door swung open. Haselden slipped inside. He moved without apparent hurry or fear, as if he were simply returning to his own villa after a day at the cotton mill. Three figures glanced up at him. Italian soldiers, they were seated at a table playing cards. Haselden could see the sweat glistening on their faces in the light of the candle burning on the table.

The nearest rose to his feet and went to salute an officer, not that he had ever seen one like this before – thickly bearded and with his hair all awry. He noted further similarly attired figures crowding in through the doorway. Buck and Russell had followed Haselden, and behind them loomed the giant form of the squadron sergeant major, Arthur Swinburn.

'*Tedeschi?*' the bewildered figure ventured. '*Tedeschi?*' Germans?

And then one of the seated Italians let out a strangled cry of alarm. As if from nowhere, a pistol had materialized in Haselden's grip. Suddenly all three of them understood. Somehow, unbelievably, this was an attack by the dreaded British raiders – the *pattagulia fanatasma;* the ghost patrol. Only that could explain their bearded, unwashed, wild countenances, not to mention the guns.

But how in the name of God had they penetrated 300 miles behind the front, and into the very heart of fortress Tobruk itself? It beggared belief, but the proof was before their eyes: they were staring down a commando officer's gun barrel.

Unceremoniously, the three terrified figures were thrust against one wall. Questions were fired at them by Haselden, who spoke excellent Italian. How many guns were sited on the headland? How large was the force that garrisoned them? And what unit did they hail from? Were they Italians or Germans? Where were their quarters? And where were the telephone wires that linked the villa with their headquarters in Tobruk?

The captives seemed almost too frightened to speak, although one, a NCO, was prevailed upon to start talking. Fifty gunners manned the positions on this side of the bay, he explained. They slept in four huts, but with the air raid most would have rushed to man their guns. Plus there was a command post, one to which he would happily guide the British raiders. As for the telephone cables, he wasn't entirely sure, but he vowed to help the British search for them. Anything, if his life might be spared.

Haselden ordered Graham Taylor to take the Italian corporal on a tour of their targets. He, meanwhile, would be busy in the villa, establishing his headquarters. Haselden sent a runner to fetch Doc Gibson, he of the celebrated cold cure fame: he needed the Canadian medic to establish a first aid post. He also ordered Captain Trollope to set up his radio kit and raise Cairo headquarters.

In spite of the Italian corporal's cowed demeanour, Taylor decided he would take no chances. He ordered one of his men to rope the Italian tight to his own wrist, before he flitted back across the terrain to the silent, watching commandos prone in their positions.

'On your feet and prepare to advance,' Taylor ordered. 'And remember, no one must be allowed to escape or give warning.'

The line of men rose, weapons at the ready. Taylor led them across to the villa, linking up with the Italian prisoner, their guide for the coming action. As they moved in silence across the hard ground, there was a momentary lull in the bombing raid. The skies appeared clear of any warplanes and the guns around the bay, deprived of targets, had fallen silent. The searchlights flickered out, awaiting the signal that the next wave of bombers was inbound.

In the comparative quiet New Zealander William MacDonald advanced in line with the section. Lieutenant David Sillito was a couple of steps behind him, an Argyll and Sutherland Highlander resplendent in his tartan. They moved slowly but purposefully, intent on making not the slightest sound that might raise the alarm among those they hunted.

A low rumble was heard out to sea: far off another wave of bombers was inbound. In the distance an enemy commander blew his whistle, the signal for his gunners to make ready. Breeches slammed shut on fresh anti-aircraft rounds, the noise carrying clearly on the cool night air.

Taking advantage of the momentary break in the bombardment, Buck called together his SIG. Their deception had served its purpose magnificently, and now he had a mind to some private marauding of his own. Before the alarm was raised, he and his men were going to bluff their way through to the nearest POW cages. There they would free and arm a force to come to the Commando's aid.

Looking for all the world like a squadron of Afrika Korps soldiers, Buck, Russell and their fellow SIG operators slipped quietly into the night.

There would be no stopping them now.

Meanwhile, Graham Taylor steered his line of men forward; according to their prisoner the first target was just ahead. But before they could reach it, the Italian soldier broke away. In the rush Taylor's man had failed to tie him securely, and the Italian had seized his chance. He sprinted into the darkness, only to stumble into a seeming giant.

SSM Swinburn didn't hesitate. Mindful of the need to kill silently, he drove his bayonet into the Italian's guts. There was a sharp scream, before the man crumpled onto the dirt. In the confusion someone fired at the dying prisoner. Surprise was doubtless lost. Taylor signalled his men forward at a run. They hammered into the first enemy positions – a series of reinforced gun emplacements.

Taylor flattened himself against a sandbagged wall. At around five feet tall, there was no way over it. He moved along, coming to an entrance. Camouflage netting hung over it, obscuring the way down into the dugout. Taylor, his pistol gripped in his hand, eased his way through the netting, treading silently on the first of the steps leading down into the pitch darkness.

Momentarily the buckles of the small pack that he carried snared in the netting. The figure to his rear worked feverishly to free him, all the time fearful of bullets snarling out from shadows within. The moment Taylor was released he slid down the remainder of the steps.

It was a gun emplacement all right. Two twenty-five pounders sat in the midst of the sandbagged position, but both seemed deserted. It was extra-ordinary. In the midst of such a fierce air raid, no one seemed to be manning the guns that defended the entrance into Tobruk harbour.

They cleared a second sandbagged bunker, this one harbouring a pair of searchlights. Again, they were deserted. Where were the enemy? Had they fled? It was unnerving. Unsettling.

The line of men surged onward. A small bunker of reinforced concrete materialized out of the gloom. It had the air of a lookout. Moving along one wall Taylor approached the door. He stood back, kicked it open and went to step inside. A rifle barked from within. Taylor felt the shock of a bullet striking him at close range, and passing clean through his body. A second rifle barked, this one tearing at the edge of his leg.

Hands reached for him and dragged him out of the line of fire. Then an imposing figure swung his arm, Swinburn lobbing in the first grenade. More followed. There were agonized screams from the darkness, as the blasts reverberated around the close confines of the bunker. No more shots would be fired in anger from there.

Taylor was sweating terribly from the pain and the shock of a chest wound, but he was still very much conscious. He was helped into nearby shelter. For now he would have to lie there and wait out the fight. As he surveyed the scene, searching for some kind of a memento, all he could find was a Chianti bottle. Empty, to boot. No doubt an Italian soldier had drunk himself silly here, not so long ago.

The anti-aircraft guns opened up again. Fire tore apart the heavens as the bombs started to rain down all around the harbour. The line of commandos pushed forward, now under David Sillito's kilted command. A row of huts appeared before them. Of wooden construction, each was built over a semi-basement dug into the ground. Somehow, men were sleeping inside, having dozed through the air raid and the gunfire.

The commandos kicked open doors and tossed grenades onto the comatose enemy. There were agonized screams and yells, which were met by further grenades. This was dreadful, murderous work, but the commandos told themselves that it had to be done. Unless they could clear the bay and hold it, the seaborne assault force would be unable to land: they would be blown out of the water by the enemy's guns.

Sillito reached the largest of the huts. Unbelievably, there were more men inside who had slept through the wild commotion. Thinking of the injured Graham Taylor, Sillito barged open the door, lobbing in a first grenade. The hut was packed with Italians who should have been manning the guns. Sillito called for more grenades. Eight went in, as half-naked figures crawled out of their bunks in terror.

Smoke and dust filled the bunkhouse. Sillito led the commandos in, guns spitting fire. Voices cried out in abject fear. By the time their work was done, Sillito figured as many as sixty Italians had died in that one hut alone.

Ahead of them, a second hut was under siege, as more commandos went into action. Twenty enemy died there. The Italian prisoner had told them there was a force of fifty manning the guns. It was many, many more. Either his had been a wild guess, or he had deliberately lied.

Figures ran for their lives now, scrambling down the cliff face at the very edge of the headland. The commandos followed. MacDonald found some ventilation shafts set into the top of the cliffs. He put his ear to the nearest. Above the crump and crash of the falling bombs he could hear voices. Italians, talking fearfully. *Fascists*, he reminded himself.

He rolled the first grenade down the shaft. The screaming was horrible. Fascists they might be, but they were still human. Around a dozen grenades were dropped down each of the openings. The screaming stopped for good.

The commandos fanned out, combing the entire expanse of high ground. Here and there a cowering figure was discovered, pleading for the mercy that could not be afforded him. And then, all of a sudden, the battleground of the western promontory fell silent.

The men stood staring into the night. It was lit by the flash of falling bombs and the glare of probing searchlights. Where was the enemy? they wondered. Surely it couldn't all be over? It had been too swift. Too easy. Only Taylor had been hit, and his injury was far from life-threatening.

They scanned the terrain suspiciously. Surely they could not have seized the western heights of Sciausc Bay so easily. They had been expecting so much more. They had been keyed up for a bloody struggle and for taking heavy casualties. But this seemed to be it. This was all it had taken to secured their objective.

In truth, no ambush had been waiting for them in Tobruk. Instead, they had routed the Italian defenders and this side of the bay at least was theirs. Of Campbell's force on the opposite headland there was no news, but they hoped he had encountered similarly light resistance.

In which case, Sciausc Bay – the much-coveted landing beach – was theirs.

Unbeknown to the commandos, *Generalmajor* – Major General – Otto Deindl, the overall commander of the Tobruk garrisons, had very different ideas. Already he'd received reports of an Allied air raid being pursued 'with great severity'. One of Deindl's trusted deputies, Major Liehr, warned him that the prolonged attack was very likely the prelude to a seaborne assault.

Deindl had a plan in place for just such an eventuality, code-named *Landealarm* – landing alarm. As soon as that code word was given the port's garrison would go into well-rehearsed defensive action. And Deindl had a good number of forces under his command: nearly 700 military police and *Wachbatl Afrika* – a guard battalion – troops, 1,400 men from various supply units, 300 Luftwaffe guards, plus the gunnery platoons. He also had the Italians to call upon, including a mobile reserve force and some 160 marines of the San Marco battalion. While Deindl didn't rate the majority of the Italian troops, those of the San Marco were decent and brave fighters.

At just past midnight, Deindl received his first warnings from his commanders that amphibious landings were under way, two miles to the east of Tobruk. In fact there had as yet been no seaborne landings, but Haselden's force was in the midst of clearing Sciausc Bay, that kind of distance to the east of the harbour.

At 0030 hours on 14 September, Deindl issued the code word *Landealarm* over the radio. In response, some 2,500 troops swung into action across the length and breadth of Tobruk, moving into their positions. Deindl ordered his commanders to resist 'the hostile landings with all . . . immediately available strength'.

It looked as if the commandos weren't going to have things entirely their own way, after all.

CHAPTER 16

At Barce, Captain Wilder led the column of Chevys onto the airstrip, moving at speed in single file and heading anticlockwise around the perimeter. The fat Alcione bombers glistened in the light thrown off by the funeral pyre of the airport's fuel dump. The raiders opened fire, streams of tracer rounds tearing into the nearest warplane, causing catastrophic damage.

The aircraft were parked facing the runway, which meant that Wilder and his men were unleashing their fire side-on and head-on into the warplanes as they sped past. Savage bursts tore into the flanks, then ripped into the open inlets of the Alciones' triple engines, stitching holes along the leading edges of the wings.

'We used tracer incendiary bullets,' remarked Wilder. 'If any of the aircraft had been guarded, the enemy must have withdrawn quickly in the face of our fire, for we opened up from a fair distance, and kept on firing until the time we were alongside.'

As the rounds punched into the aircrafts' fuel tanks, the aviation fuel inside started to flare and burn. Within seconds, the first aircraft was awash with flame, the scent of burning avgas thick and heady in the night air.

But the airstrip's defenders had started to fight back. The raiders' rearmost vehicles began taking hits, as a gun emplacement set atop the main hangar opened fire. From their vantage point, the Italian gunners would have a bird's-eye view of the action, and they began to pour down tracer onto the speeding vehicles.

From his vehicle at the rear, Chevy *Te Anau II*, Trooper Wally Rail unleashed an answering burst from his twin .303 Browning machine guns, raking the hangar roof from end to end. And from the tail-end Charlie itself – Merlyn Craw's *Te Paki III* – Keith Yealands hammered the hangar position with bursts from his .5 Vickers. Within seconds the enemy tracer started spurting directly upwards, as if a dead gunner had tumbled backwards, the claw of his hand still gripping the trigger.

But as soon as Rail and Yealands ceased fire the tracer flicked down again and re-engaged the patrol. It seemed as if the enemy gunner wasn't hit after all. He had to be taking cover from the onslaught, then returning to his weapon once he figured he could risk taking up the fight again. He was a brave and spirited adversary, and Wally Rail was about to learn just how accurate his rounds could prove.

A burst of tracer hammered in towards *Te Anau II*. Rail watched it grope for their vehicle, and then a round slammed directly into the pivot mount that held his twin Brownings. The bullet punctured the steel tube, shot up the inside vertically and emerged out the top in a shower of sparks. Rail almost had a heart attack on the spot: an inch or two to either side and he would have been dead.

'Jesus Christ! That was a close one, Wally!' the rear gunner piped up, as a long burst from his weapon sent the enemy running.

Rail swung his Brownings around, hammering a barrage of rounds along the left flank of the nearest Alcione, seeing chunks of the fuselage splinter and implode under the onslaught. Earlier in the war Rail had been on operations in Greece and Crete, where he'd been pinned down by the dive-bombers of the Luftwaffe. His unit had been decimated – now was the time for him to take his revenge.

To save weight and increase airspeed, the Alcione – like the superlative British Mosquito fighter-bomber – was mostly built out of wood. As with the Mosquito, it had a sleek, streamlined fuselage and it was fast, powerful and manoeuvrable. With its three Piaggio radial engines – one set in the nose and two on the wings – the Alcione could top 450 kph at full speed.

But as Rail was learning, the wooden airframe also meant that the Alcione burned very nicely. 'I'd suffered in Greece and Crete,' he would remark, ruefully. 'The spectacle of the blazing aircraft was the best sight I ever saw in the war.'

In the rear vehicle, *Te Paki III*, Merlyn Craw had

been ordered to put his explosive skills to good use. But this was no longer blowing up tree stumps on his dad's farm in New Zealand. Here at Barce, Craw was to deal with any aircraft that survived the machine-gun onslaught, and he had thirteen of his DIY incendiary bombs lined up for that very purpose.

He noticed that one of the smaller Caproni reconnaissance aircraft – distinctive, with its bulbous glass nose cone – had escaped the fire. *Te Paki III* slammed to a halt, Craw grabbed his first bomb, leaped down and sprinted for the target, Keith Yealands, his gunner, hot on his heels. Craw reached the aircraft, jumped up and placed the bomb where the wing met the fuselage, right above the fuel tanks. Yealands, meanwhile, covered him.

Charges in place, Craw triggered the ten-second fuse, whereupon both men dived for cover. A few seconds later the device exploded, showering the Caproni in a cloud of sparks of burning aluminium. The holed fuel tank started gushing flame, before the twin-engine aircraft was engulfed in the blaze. Job done, Craw and Yealands raced back towards *Te Paki III*. They reached the Chevy, leaped aboard and it tore off towards the row of burning warplanes up ahead.

Again and again Craw repeated this performance. By the time he was laying his sixth bomb there were burning and exploding aircraft to all sides. Ammunition in the Alciones' machine guns – two situated in an upper gun turret, one on the aircraft's belly, and one in each of two side turrets – was cooking off in the heat, heavy 12.7-millimetre rounds tearing through the air.

To add to the deathly confusion, Craw detected several enemy gun emplacements firing from positions set all around the airfield's perimeter. These had to be the aerodrome's anti-aircraft defences, and Craw could tell that the gunners were experiencing problems. The weapons had to be configured for shooting at Allied warplanes, not at vehicles tearing around the airstrip itself.

Streams of heavy tracer were hammering through the air, but it was as if the Italian gunners couldn't bring their weapons to bear low enough to engage their targets. 'The shells were going over our heads like round fiery balls, probably 20mm Breda,' Craw remarked. 'On the airfield we were all in a curve, with everything lit up by the fires . . . I can't understand why nobody got hit.'

In among the fiery chaos, Craw detected the crump of a mortar firing: the airport garrison was throwing everything they had at the raiders. But as the Chevys darted among the warplanes at speed, the Italian defenders had to be worried about hitting their own aircraft, and especially with a weapon like the mortar.

The roar of exploding shells cut through the night, but Craw didn't sense that the mortar fire was closing on them at all. The Chevys should make for easy targets, silhouetted as they were against the burning airframes, but the only way to take them on was to move in at close quarters, and none of the Italian garrison appeared to be overly keen to rush into that kind of battle.

Craw grabbed the next bomb. He'd spotted another aircraft that the leading Chevys' machine guns had missed. He signalled his driver to halt, then made a dash for the target. 'Despite what was going on around me,' he remarked, 'I was too busy doing my job to worry about fear.'

Five hundred yards to the south-east of the aerodrome, Jake Easonsmith led his two-jeep convoy into the heart of Barce. As the LRDG commander described it, they were going to 'proceed independently around the town area looking for custom'. Sure enough, Easonsmith spied a row of detached bungalows: officers' quarters.

Leaping out of his jeep, Easonsmith searched for a way of hurling grenades inside, but the windows were shuttered tight. Frustrated, he ran down the line of buildings, lobbing a grenade onto each of the flat roofs. As the first of the explosions echoed through the streets, Easonsmith knew they'd do little damage to the buildings or their occupants, but he consoled himself with thoughts of how they'd spread confusion and fear, which was exactly the object of the present exercise.

The two jeeps pressed on, breaking out into the town's central square. Crouched behind his twin Vickers Ks, Easonsmith opened fire instantly: he'd spied a pair of L3 tanks parked across the open plaza. He aimed for the thin slits of the windows. Rounds hammered off the armour, but some had to be finding their way inside, for the gunners didn't seem inclined to return fire.

Easonsmith's jeep was closing with the enemy armour when his guns jammed. A spent round was stuck in the extractor mechanism. His driver Lance Corporal Gutteridge didn't hesitate, slamming the Willys Jeep into a tight turn and slipping down a narrow side street before the Italian tank crews could recover and give pursuit. He parked up in some cover, so they could clear the stoppage.

Easonsmith, restless and hungry for action, decided to head off on foot while his men dealt with the jam. He crept up to what appeared to be a marketplace, set beneath a grand building of white arches and pillars. Spying a group of Italian soldiers milling about uncertainly, he pulled the pin on a grenade, let the lever fly and rolled it into their midst. Easonsmith turned and ran even as the grenade exploded, the Italians screaming and diving for cover behind the columns.

With the jeeps under way once more, weapons primed and ready, Gutteridge steered the small convoy into what had to be the Italian garrison's central vehicle pound. Behind some fencing they could see ten trucks, plus a fuel tanker and trailer. Easonsmith signalled his force to dismount. They got in among the vehicles, hurling grenades and unleashing bursts with their tommy guns.

By the time they were done, the fuel bowser was

spurting great gouts of flame, and each of the trucks had been torn apart by a grenade dropped inside the cab. As the jeeps roared away, fire lit up the streets of Barce town magnificently. This was just what Easonsmith had intended. The enemy garrison could be forgiven for thinking that an entire battalion of British raiders had set upon the place.

From the direction of the airport bursts of heavy anti-aircraft fire rolled across the town, interspersed with the hollow crump of explosions. It sounded as if an entire wing of RAF bombers was unloading on the place. Easonsmith knew differently.

That was Wilder's New Zealand patrol, unleashing merry hell.

Some 200 miles to the east of Barce, a massive RAF aid raid was pounding the enemy positions at Tobruk. Seventy tons of high explosive would be unleashed on the harbour area, and it was a tribute to the aircrew that very few, if any, stray bombs fell around the area of Sciausc Bay, where Haselden's force were engaged in bloody action.

For the first time since the fortress had fallen to Rommel's Panzerarmee Afrika, British troops now held ground inside the Tobruk perimeter. The western flank of Sciausc Bay lay in the Commando's hands.

A figure appeared at the doorway of the shelter in which the wounded Graham Taylor was nursing his chest wound. 'We're all good on this side,' the voice informed him. 'We've cleared the high ground.'

Taylor could tell that he'd suffered a punctured lung, and he felt weak from the loss of blood. Yet he was still very much conscious and in control of his faculties, and determined to remain in command of his unit. He called for Swinburn. The big SSM appeared at the doorway.

'Send up the success signal,' Taylor ordered, his voice tight with pain and exhaustion.

He handed Swinburn the Very pistol from his backpack. It should have been his job to signal the glorious news that they had seized their side of the landing bay bang on schedule, but he had every faith in the Commando's redoubtable sergeant.

It was a little after midnight when Swinburn sent up the red and green Very lights – the agreed code to telegraph success on the western headland. Perched on the furthest lip of the promontory, Pilot Officer Scott saw the lights go up. He readied his Aldis lamp for action. Glancing east, he awaited the signal from the opposite flank, indicating that side also lay in British hands. As soon as he saw it he would start flashing his regular beats of light over the ink-dark sea.

Even now the MTBs should be lurking offshore, awaiting the signals. Packed with machine-gun and mortar platoons plus infantry, they would be in silent-running mode. With very little armour, the comparatively light, petrol-engine craft could be throttled back to leave little wake and to create minimal noise.

As if to reinforce how imminent were those landings, the warplanes above Tobruk stopped releasing their flares. One moment the sky was awash with their glare, as if a hundred tiny suns were floating in the heavens. The next the last drifted to earth, and there were no more. The navy needed the waters of the harbour kept as dark as possible, to hide the armada that was converging on Tobruk.

At the Italian villa Haselden received Taylor's news with noticeable relief. He was seated at the table on which the three Italians had been playing cards not an hour previously. Runners kept arriving with updates, and in one corner Trollope and his signals section were busy with the radios. Just as soon as Major Campbell confirmed that the eastern flank was also taken, Haselden would radio through the news to Cairo headquarters.

From there wireless signals would wing their way through the ether to the commanders of the MTBs. They would then start to nose their craft into Sciausc Bay, using the two flashing Aldis lights as their guide. What could be easier? The only challenge now was time: it was well past midnight, and Haselden's cut-off point was 0200 hours. Ideally, the MTBs would be safely in long before then.

He asked Trollope, his signaller, to raise Major Campbell on the eastern side of the bay – or if not the kilted commander, then Lieutenant Tommy

Langton. But try as he might, Trollope could get no response from either of the men. Haselden was worried, but there was little he could do about it right now.

The injured Graham Taylor was brought into the villa, so Doc Gibson could treat his wounds. By some miracle the bullet had passed clean through his chest cavity without striking any ribs. The holed lung was Gibson's main concern. As he readied a syringe of morphine, Taylor noticed that there were a half a dozen other wounded gathered there.

Here on the western headland resistance was stiffening. From out of the darkness groups of enemy fighters had started launching probing attacks, seemingly designed to test the British lines. The commandos were holding firm, and they doubtless could do so until the reinforcements came ashore, but those MTBs and landing craft had better get a move on.

This was going to be a story to thrill the people back at home, the commandos told themselves. Rommel reeling from a shock defeat; struck by utter surprise where he least expected it, in fortress Tobruk; the Desert Fox hurt beyond measure on the eve of a decisive battle. After a string of defeats the British public needed the good news.

Further inland, Captain Buck and his SIG were also facing unexpectedly fierce fighting. Aiming to slip into Tobruk undetected, they'd stumbled instead upon an anti-aircraft gun emplacement, which was well manned. Judging it to be too close to Haselden's headquarters for comfort, they'd opened fire on the position. The Italian gunners had fled, leaving Buck and his men to occupy the guns. But not for long.

In short order the enemy were back, now wielding Maschinenpistole 40 submachine guns – the hated 'Schmeissers'. A vicious exchange of fire ensued. Four times the enemy rushed the gun emplacement, only for Buck and his SIG to hold their ground and to drive them off again. Finally, Buck and his men were able to roll grenades down the barrels of the AA guns, destroying each in turn.

But this didn't bode well for what Buck had in mind. The enemy had fought with spirit and determination, even if the suicidal bravery of the SIG operators had finally won the day. Yet the further into Tobruk they pressed, the more such forces they would doubtless encounter, and some were bound to be German troops, who held many of the central positions.

Buck just had to hope that their deception held, their Afrika Korps uniforms allowing them to slip through to the POW cages unmolested. Somehow, he had a sense that Haselden would be in dire need of the reinforcements those freed prisoners-of-war could provide.

The time reached 0115 hours. At Haselden's villa headquarters there was still no word from Major Campbell or Tommy Langton. Haselden hunched over the table, feeling the worry eating away at his guts. If no success signal – no Very lights – arced into the skies above the eastern headland, he would have no option but to cancel the entire operation. The fleet would be turned round – the troops they carried included – and sent back to port.

In which case, what was to become of the commandos, with no ships to pluck them off the coast and spirit them away to safety? Haselden wasn't about to risk the SIG ruse getting them out of Tobruk, for there was no way it would hold for a second time.

In the huts above the villa there were scores of Italian dead, many of whom had been cut down in their sleep; the commandos could expect little mercy if trapped here by the enemy. Haselden forced such worries to the back of his mind. Campbell simply *had* to fire his success signal. Any other option was utterly unthinkable right now.

At his headquarters, Generalmajor Deindl was equally determined that the British landings would be crushed. He was still trying to clarify exactly what was happening in and around the harbour, but the *Landealarm* had been issued, and shortly after 0100 hours he followed that up with a personal message to his commanders.

'Enemy Situation At Tobruk Is Confused. Set All Appropriate Units In Action In Order To Clarify . . . Fliegerführer Afrika And Fliegerkorps

X Will Carry Out Continuous Armed Recce Over And Around Tobruk.'

Deindl was mobilising his land forces, his anti-aircraft battalions first and foremost, to root out the British attackers wherever they might be. He also ordered all Luftwaffe aircraft to be ready to mount operations in support of those troops. He was soon to get his first concrete indication that Haselden's commandos were on the ground, and of their exact whereabouts.

In response to Deindl's message, Colonel Battaglia, the Italian commander in Tobruk, sent the following signal: 'Landing Of Enemy Forces In Unknown Strength At Marsa Umm Is Sciausc (Gulf East Of Tobruk Net Boom). Counter Attack By Abt. San Marco In Progress. Further Reports Will Follow As Received.'

This signified several things: one, the German and Italian high command knew by now that Sciausc Bay itself was the focus of the Allied action. They still presumed the assault to be a seaborne landing, so the SIG deception had clearly held good, but the unit sent in to clear the bay was none other than the marines of the San Marco battalion, the best offensive force that the Italians could muster.

The San Marco battalion had scored real success against the Allies. On 29 August – barely two weeks earlier – fourteen San Marco marines had been put ashore by an Italian destroyer behind the British lines. Their target was a railway and viaduct linking the British front to Alexandria and Cairo. They'd blown up the rail lines and escaped successfully at mission's end. They were fresh from that victory, and they outnumbered the men of the Commando two to one.

The thin khaki line around Sciausc Bay was about to be stretched to the limit . . . and beyond.

CHAPTER 17

By now, Captain Wilder's raiders had been shooting up Barce aerodrome for approaching an hour, and Merlyn Craw was on to charge number twelve. He noticed that his last bomb, number thirteen – unlucky for some – had a broken timer fuse, so he wired the two together, creating one larger device. Now to find a suitable target.

The Chevys pulled to a halt in a defensive position and surveyed the scene of devastation all around them. It was an awe-inspiring sight. Aircraft were in flames to all sides. Craw scuttled over to Wilder's Chevy for a quick natter. In the original plan he was supposed to hold back a charge or two for blowing the town's vault, but they agreed that the aircraft were just too enticing a target.

Craw spotted a Fieseler Fi 156 Storch – Stork – that looked completely untouched by the carnage. A German spotter plane, Craw hated the Storch with a vengeance. It had an incredibly short take-off and landing capability and could put down just about anywhere. For the men of the LRDG the

Storch was a veritable curse, able to hang in the air above them like a vulture, scouring the terrain.

On a previous patrol Craw and his fellow raiders had been forced to tangle with a Storch, and at very close quarters. The aircraft had been guiding in a unit of enemy ground troops hunting the desert raiders. Though the LRDG patrol was in good cover, the Storch had still been able to find them. The pilot had landed, intending to impart the news of the raiders' place of hiding to their hunters.

Instead, and under intense enemy fire the raiders had rushed the Storch and forced the pilot and co-pilot out at gunpoint. They'd proceeded to torch the aircraft, taking both of its hapless crew prisoner. Doubtless, Craw reasoned, if this Storch wasn't blown to smithereens it would take to the skies come first light, searching far and wide for the fleeing raiders.

Weighed down by the double charge, Craw scrambled across to the spindly-looking aircraft. It was painted in typical Italian desert camouflage – irregular splotches of green on a dull khaki background. Nearby lay the flaming wreckage of a Savoia Marchetti SM 79 Sparviero – Sparrowhawk – three-engine torpedo bomber. With its distinctive domed bulge behind the cockpit, housing a gunner's position, it had been nicknamed the Damned Hunchback and was instantly recognizable to Craw. A popular aircraft with the Italian air force, it was a bonus to have found one of those here. Already, Craw could see the aircraft's blackened ribs poking through the hungry flames.

Clambering up the wing strut of the Storch, he heaved the double charge onto the wing's upper side, triggered the fuse, jumped down and dashed away, yelling for the others to take cover. The explosion practically blew him off his feet. 'Because the charge was so big the others were warned to get out of the way,' he remarked. 'The small plane was blown to bits!'

Craw was out of bombs, few targets remained, and Wilder's patrol had turned Barce aerodrome into a veritable sea of fire. It was clear they needed to hightail it out of there. As Easonsmith had stressed, they needed to get well away from town and into the open desert come daybreak, when the hunt was sure to begin in earnest. Wilder led the column of five vehicles through the thick and choking smoke, heading back the way they had come, but there was no easy way to exit the airport.

'The only way out was the way we had come in and we made a dash for it,' remarked Wilder. 'The supply dumps near the barracks were still blazing, but the Italians now had machine guns posted there. For the first time since we had started some of the trucks were hit . . . somehow we had no casualties. But heavier opposition awaited us.'

The first sign of trouble was when Wilder's truck became bogged down in a soft-bottomed ditch – an anti-tank barrier lying adjacent to the barracks block and the main hangar. Suddenly, *Tutira III* was immobilized and all but defenceless. The Italians rained down a storm of rounds, as the vehicles that were still mobile encircled the stricken Chevy, hammering back return fire with every weapon in their arsenal.

There was no option but to manhandle the heavy vehicle free. As figures jumped down to do so, the airport garrison redoubled their efforts, pouring in machine-gun fire and mortar rounds. Somehow, miraculously, no one was hit, and while the Chevys took a pounding they were all able to speed away. The column formed up, throttles were floored and with screaming engines they raced for the exit, Wilders' Chevy in the lead.

'By the time we had destroyed all those planes, most of our magazines were empty,' Frank Jopling, Wilder's navigator, recalled. 'Knowing that before we could get away we would have a lot more shooting to do, the patrol set off for the rendezvous. However, it was not going to be quite as easy as it was coming in.'

As ever, Merlyn Craw's *Te Paki III* was the very last vehicle in line. 'The whole sky was now illumin-ated by a magnificent blaze of airfield fires that also lit up the town,' he recalled. 'The raiding party was well satisfied with its night's work and, having expended thousands of rounds of ammu-nition, needed to cool the guns and replenish magazines . . .'

They would have little opportunity to do either. Wilder presumed that the road by which they'd made their way into the airport would be blocked by now, so he opted to carry straight on, heading directly into the centre of Barce town. One of the vehicles in his convoy had a badly torn and dented mudguard, which bizarrely made a noise like a tank on the move, as the sagging metal dragged along the surface of the road. Nothing like telegraphing their position.

Wilder was approaching the railway station, when he spied two L3 tanks blocking the route ahead, with another pair positioned a way beyond them. Already the nearest had opened up with a storm of fire.

The L3s were armed with what looked like 20-millimetre cannons, and shell after shell whistled down the narrow street, which reverberated to the repeated echoes of the guns. It was 'heart-stopping stuff seeing this tracer coming boom, boom, boom off the road', recalled one of the drivers. 'We had no option but to charge at pace and hope for the best.'

Wilder's gunner, Parker, tried to return fire, but his twin Vickers had overheated and jammed. The rear gun was also out of action. In desperation, Parker grabbed a Very pistol and fired a flare directly at the two tanks, which seemed momentarily to blind the gunners. Even so, Wilder knew they were in desperate straits: they couldn't shoot their way out of this, the street was too narrow to turn round and the tanks blocked the way.

Acting on instinct, he gunned the engine of *Tutira III*. 'Get out of the way, you bastards!' he yelled.

He headed straight for the nearest tank at full speed, bracing his hands on the steering wheel as Parker held on for dear life. There was an almighty crash as the Chevy collided with the armoured vehicle, shunting it across the road, whereupon Wilder's truck cannoned into the opposite tank, finally bludgeoning a way through.

It was the driver's side that had taken the brunt of the impact, the curved wing being ripped clean away, the bonnet smashed inwards and the engine shunted back into the cab. But the solid bumper and bull bar had protected the front wheels, which managed to keep turning for a good few revolutions before the crippled Chevy finally gave up the ghost.

Wilder piled out. He was hurt: a gash to his right forehead was spurting blood, but it was only a flesh wound. He gathered Parker and together they rushed the two surviving tanks, quick as a flash rolling grenades beneath their hulls. They exploded with a flash and a roar, almost lifting each of the light armoured vehicles off the road.

Not content with that, Wilder and Parker tried to lever open the turret of the nearest tank, to lob a grenade inside, but the Italians had it firmly bolted. In any case, the grenades beneath the tracks seemed to have done the trick: the L3s' guns had fallen silent.

The next vehicle in line accelerated through the

gap that the lead Chevy had made. It was the lone Willys Jeep – Wilder's command vehicle. It skidded to a halt, Trooper Peter Burke, Wilder's driver, yelling for him and Parker to climb aboard. As they dashed for the vehicle, a burst of fire cut around their shoulders and Parker was hit.

The round entered the right side of his torso, tore through his body and exited from the left, spinning Parker round. He collapsed, the shock and the pain rendering him momentarily unconscious. He came to seconds later, only to see the jeep preparing to depart. No one seemed to realize that he'd been hit and wasn't aboard.

'Wait for me!' he cried. 'Wait for me!'

Despite his injury, he managed to drag himself to the jeep and throw himself aboard.

Ignoring his head wound, Wilder slid behind the Vickers machine guns, while Burke prepared to spirit him, and the injured Parker, to safety. As the jeep sped off, no one seemed to notice that two men were missing. Alan Nutt – Wilder's second in command on the jeep – had dismounted to help the others. In all the confusion, he'd been left behind. So too had Trooper Mick Holland, who'd been the rear gunner on *Tutira III*, the Chevy that had rammed the tanks.

For a few seconds Wilder's jeep weaved a crazy course along a street thick with Italian troops, but then they came upon the second brace of tanks. As Wilder opened up on the targets with the twin Vickers, the muzzle flashes momentarily blinded Burke, who was sitting beside him, driving furiously.

The jeep hit a roundabout at high speed, cannoned off it and overturned, skidding to a stop with its wheels in the air. Burke and Parker had been thrown clear, though the latter, with his injuries, was in utter agony. Of Wilder there was no sign.

Then, with a kick of dread to his guts, Burke spotted a figure sandwiched under the jeep. It was Captain Wilder.

Wilder was unconscious and suspended upside down in the stricken jeep. Petrol was leaking everywhere, spreading in a slick across the road. Burke grabbed the badly injured Parker, and urged him to help lift the upturned vehicle. The two men tried, but the effort proved too much for Parker. The pain in his guts felt like 'white-hot agony'. He collapsed in a pool of his own blood.

Parker needed medical help desperately.

Burke needed help freeing Wider.

He glanced up the street to see *Te Anau II* speeding towards them, with Wally Rail manning the guns. Burke ran into the middle of the road to flag it down. Fortunately, at that very moment the Chevy's driver decided to flick on his headlamps to see what lay ahead. Parker was pinned in the light, which was all that prevented Rail from nailing him with his twin Brownings.

'I said to myself, *There's somebody there; if he makes a false move I will spray him* . . .' recalled

Rail. 'I don't know why I didn't shoot him, as I shot at everything else that moved. Luckily I didn't fire, as there was petrol leaking all over the road and the smell was very strong. Firing a bullet into that would have ignited the fuel and they all may have been killed.'

The Chevy ground to a halt. Four men surrounded the upturned jeep, one on each corner. With a superhuman effort they managed to lift it onto its wheels, which was all the more difficult in that it was laden with jerry cans of fuel and water, plus cases of ammunition.

Wilder was dragged clear. He didn't seem badly injured; he'd just been overcome by the petrol fumes. He was also incredibly lucky. The jeep's hot exhaust pipe had been exposed to the air, and it was a miracle that it hadn't ignited the spilled fuel. Both he and Parker were unconscious by now.

They were loaded aboard *Te Anau II*, and the Chevy sped away, heading for the rendezvous point on the outskirts of town, at the tomb of the sheikh.

Back in Tobruk, Major Campbell's commandos had every reason to be late firing their success signal. In the thick darkness on the eastern headland of Sciausc Bay they had stumbled into a minefield. Laden down with heavy packs of explosives and mine clearance gear, the sappers of the Royal Engineers dashed forward to deal with the threat.

They got to work immediately opening a path across the field of death that barred their way. Every yard cost precious minutes. As the sappers inched ahead, using their detectors to locate the mines and then disabling them by hand, the commandos formed a line in single file, sticking rigidly to the safe path. But it was agonisingly slow and dangerous work. One wrong move by a sapper could spell sudden death and injury, especially since the commandos were bunched up in open ground. If they came under fire from a Spandau right now, they would be cut down in their droves. There was nowhere to run, or to take cover. To either side was terrain sewn with death.

Sweating, cursing silently and tortured by the delay, the first men made it to the far side. They spread out in defensive positions to cover the others as they hurried through. When the column was complete, Major Campbell ordered his men to race up the final slopes to seize the highest ground.

They split into sections now, clearing the terrain at a dash. Vicious little firefights erupted, then just as quickly petered out. Here and there small pockets of resistance were encountered, but a quick burst of tommy-gun fire or the blast of a grenade and the enemy was silenced. Groups of commandos kept running into each other. There were cries of 'Who goes there?' If the response was in startled Italian, a burst swept that position instantly.

Campbell's men pushed a good mile into the high ground above Sciausc Bay. After the superhuman efforts of the last few hours, the kilted major looked all in. He had to rest. Langton joined him, his eyes burning with anxiety. While they couldn't be absolutely sure the eastern headland was clear, no big guns menaced the landing beach, of that he was certain. And if they didn't send the signal now the whole operation would be in jeopardy.

'Sir, shall we put up the Very lights?' Langton ventured. 'There are no big guns left covering the bay.'

Campbell nodded exhaustedly, his features racked with pain. 'Yes, Tom. Send it. And thanks.'

Langton needed no second urging. He grabbed the Very pistol he had slung on his belt and fired the two signal lights high into the sky. They hung in the heavens, turning the night-dark terrain into near-daylight and throwing ghostly shadows across the jumbled, rocky landscape. Langton scanned all around: there was no sign of the enemy in any direction.

High above the eastern headland the two green Very lights traced a burning arc. It was nearing 0130 hours: late, but not too late for Haselden's purposes. When the glowing orbs were spotted, a wild cheer went up from the commandos ranged around his Italian Villa headquarters. That was the agreed code: Sciausc Bay was theirs. Figures thumped each other on the back, then grasped their tommy guns more tightly: *Let the enemy come.*

It didn't matter any more what forces they might be facing; with the bay in British hands, very shortly these slopes were going to be thronged with Argyll and Sutherland Highlanders and Royal Northumberland Fusiliers. These were crack infantry and machine-gun regiments, just what the Commando needed to reinforce and strengthen their lines.

Once they were in place, the commandos would break out and push into Tobruk, blowing up the port facilities and freeing the POWs. *Thousands of them.* Victory – it was still within their grasp.

Lieutenant Sillito dashed into the Italian villa to deliver the good news. Upon hearing it Haselden beamed with delight. The agonizing wait was over. He could call the seaborne raiders in. In his heart he had never really doubted that they would seize the bay, the crucial breakthrough for tonight's entire operation.

Haselden turned to Trollope, crouched over his radio transmitter. 'Send the success code word!' he announced cheerily. Haselden felt elated. The doubts that had assailed him had been swept away.

In the Signals Distributing Office, HQ Alexandria, a group of senior British military officers were awaiting Haselden's call. They chain-smoked and milled about nervously. If the code word wasn't received, the entire mission would be cancelled. The ships might be at the beaches themselves, but without the signal no one could be sure the troops were safe to land.

At just before 0200 hours – the cut-off point that would prompt the flotilla to turn round – a Wren was passed an incoming signal to type. She punched out the coded message. It was from Haselden. Officers crowded around excitedly, each grabbing a copy of the much-longed-for missive, before dashing away to their stations.

Word quickly spread: Sciausc Bay was in British hands. The first wave of MTBs could be sent in. Haselden's signal had arrived with just minutes to spare.

Rubber-soled boots flashed across the rocky terrain above Sciausc Bay as a figure made a mad dash for the beach. Langton had bade a hurried farewell to Major Campbell, for his duty lay in signalling the MTBs into land. He felt very much alone as he hurried through the deserted terrain. A gargantuan task faced him: he needed to get to the opposite side of the bay, retrieve his heavy Aldis lamp, then climb back to the eastern headland, to start signalling.

And already he was all but out of time. He charged up a ravine leading in the direction he reckoned he needed to go. He rounded a bend and suddenly he was in among a tented camp. A large canvas dome lay at the centre, surrounded by a cluster of smaller ones. Langton paused. He could hear voices, talking. A figure moved.

Langton realized that he was scared. He was alone in the pitch dark and surrounded by the enemy. It was easy enough to control one's fear when you only had to hide it from your brother warriors. Less easy when isolated and surrounded. Langton told himself to get a grip. There was no sign that the enemy was on to him. He needed to slip away quietly and get on with his task.

He veered left and scrambled his way up the side of the ravine. He felt breathless. Fatigue tugged at his steps. He wasn't as fit as he should be – the result of three weeks riding in the trucks through the desert. He reached the lip of the defile, gasping for breath and with his heart pounding fit to burst.

He dropped off the ridge, hurrying onward until he reached a cliff high above the sea. He realized that he was on the wrong headland. Somehow he'd circled back to the eastern promontory, to a point near to where he'd started. His Aldis lamp lay on the opposite side of the bay, in Pilot Officer Scott's safekeeping. As he glanced in that direction, he spotted the steady, rhythmic flashing of Scott's light.

What was he to do now?

It would take a good hour to cross the bay, climb to the heights, retrieve his lamp and make it back again. For a brief instant Langton cursed the fact that he'd been ordered to stick with Major Campbell. Then he felt a pang of guilt. The major – plagued by dysentery – had gone above and beyond what anyone could have expected of him. He'd commanded his men, scaled over a mile of rugged terrain, clearing it of the enemy, and he had not faltered until the very end.

But still Langton was in a proper fix. He shook his head to clear it. One thing was clear: Scott's Aldis lamp was signalling regular and bright. That would give the MTBs a line on the mouth of the cove. Langton had a torch in his backpack. If he used that, they were bound to pick it up as they approached the bay. It wasn't perfect, but Langton was running out of time.

Decision made, he headed for the furthest extent of the eastern promontory, where it overlooked the sea. As he picked his way through the darkened terrain, his mind turned back to Operation Flipper, the raid to kill Rommel. On Op Flipper Haselden had achieved a moment of perfection: as their submarine had surfaced Langton had spotted Haselden's signal light, blinking from exactly where it was supposed to be, bang on the landing beach.

But that was then and that was Haselden, and right now a flashing torch was the best that Langton figured he could manage.

He made his way along the cliff top, to where it dropped steep and precipitous to the sea below. He could just make out a shelf of rock jutting out into the water. If he could climb down to that he would at least get himself – and his torch – nearer to those watching from the decks of the MTBs.

The torch was infinitely weaker than an Aldis lamp, which meant he needed to get as close as possible.

Langton eased himself down the rock face, feeling in the dark for handholds. He reached a point where he was forced to discard his tommy gun and backpack, resting them against a deserted bunker built into the cliff face. Once the boats were safely in he'd retrace his steps and reclaim them. Using both hands, he lowered himself to the flat ledge of rock.

He sat, realizing suddenly how tired his legs were. He dug in his pocket, retrieved the torch, leaned back against a rock and began to signal out to sea. Scott's Aldis lamp was clearly visible to his left across the bay, tapping out the agreed recognition signal in Morse code: three Ts sent every two minutes. Langton did his best to synchronize his torch flashes with those of the Aldis.

His eyes wandered across the open expanse of Tobruk harbour, beyond the bay. The searchlights still lanced skywards, scouring the heavens for any further waves of warplanes. But the guns had fallen silent, and Langton could just make out the drone of the last of the bombers, heading home to their bases in Egypt.

He strained his eyes, hoping to spot the dark silhouette of an MTB nosing in towards the beach. On the far side of Tobruk harbour the destroyers HMS *Sikh* and *Zulu* should likewise be slipping in towards the shore, sleek and silent, their decks crowded with Royal Marines. But all he could detect was the lapping of the sea below him, and after the whirlwind of the air raids the settling calm.

A noise disturbed the quiet. It came from right behind him, on the route that he had just descended. He spun round. His eyes were straining and he opened his mouth wide – a trick he'd learned in the SBS that helped to boost your hearing. He held his breath, his right hand groping for the butt of his pistol as his left kept signalling with the torch.

No further sound came from the rocks above, and Langton told himself not to be so jumpy.

The column of six LRDG vehicles ground to a halt on the coastal road, as Lloyd Owen eyed the barrier that barred their way. His men were hyper-alert and hunched over their weapons. The route ahead was barred by a line of heavy barrels plus a decrepit-looking steamroller – cutting them off from their target, the enemy's D/F station.

Urging his men to stay alert, Lloyd Owen jumped out of his vehicle and approached the barrier. No sign of life anywhere. He yelled out the Italian password: '*Rosalia!*' Not the whisper of an answer. He checked out the terrain to either side of the road: ditches, with beyond those barbed-wire defences. There was no easy route through, either on or off the Tarmac.

The only obvious way to proceed would be on

foot, but Lloyd Owen wasn't about to abandon the vehicles. There was still the possibility that they would be called upon to ride to the rescue of some of Haselden's men, and the Chevys were both his unit's main firepower and the means to get them out of there.

The key thing now was to raise Haselden on the radio. If the mission was proceeding as planned, maybe they could still try to press on and hit the D/F station. And if things weren't going well, they might be needed to launch a desperate mission to link up with Haselden's force.

They pulled the vehicles off the road. Lloyd Owen ordered his signaller to break out his wireless and get to work raising Haselden. Meanwhile the rest of the force would set up a defensive cordon. As the radio operator kept calling for Haselden to answer, Lloyd Owen stomped about in the darkness, all thoughts of raiding Tobruk and of freeing POWs gone from his mind now.

All that mattered was knowing what fate had befallen Haselden and his commandos.

CHAPTER 18

At Barce the tail-end Charlie of Wilder's patrol, Merlyn Craw's *Te Paki III*, was in trouble. They'd stopped to check on Wilder's abandoned jeep, grabbing their tommy guns to investigate. It was then that their Chevy had come under heavy fire, the thudding beat of a 20mm Breda cannon – the very weapon that the LRDG's gun trucks carried – sounding horribly familiar to their ears.

The Breda was mounted on an Italian Autoblinda Ab 41 armoured car, an altogether more daunting adversary than their light tanks. More than twice the weight of an L3 and armed with the cannon in its turret, plus two 8mm machine guns, the Autoblinda was thickly armoured. With a top speed of some 80 kph, it was well capable of keeping up with the Chevys.

Craw and his fellows piled aboard *Te Paki III*, but as the truck sped away cannon rounds slammed into its backside, exploding among the jerry cans of fuel. An instant later the rear end of *Te Paki III* was billowing flames. The driver swerved in an effort to lose the armoured car, but caught a front wheel on some steps leading into an air raid shelter. The Chevy flipped onto its side and came to a skidding, grinding halt adjacent to the shelter. The sudden stop catapulted Craw the length of the vehicle. He landed with a crash at the bottom of the air-raid shelter's steps and promptly lost consciousness.

Te Paki III burned fiercely. Cans of petrol kept exploding, gouts of fire shooting across the street. Some of the spilled fuel found its way down the steps into the shelter, flowing across the floor and pulsing with flame. The heat became unbearable, and it was that which brought Craw to his senses.

He came to, only to discover that the shelter was crammed with Italian soldiers. No one seemed to have noticed him yet, but his escape route was blocked by a wall of fire. He edged further into the shadows. The Italians were praying, as the flames licked ever closer. Then, in the light of an exceptionally strong blast, Craw realized that he'd been recognized.

He drew his .38 revolver, only to see four Beretta pistols pointed in his direction. There was a brief fistfight, but in spite of Craw's raw strength he was finally subdued. He wasn't the only one of *Te Paki III*'s crew to be captured. The driver, Tom Milburn, plus the gunners, Ewan Hay and Keith Yealands, were also taken prisoner as they tried to escape from the burning vehicle.

Milburn managed to make it to the outskirts of town on foot, before he was jumped by bayonet-wielding guards. The Italians beat him with their rifle butts, smashed his head against a wall repeatedly and fired questions at him. The only response they received was that they could all go to hell.

Altogether, six of the airport raiders – Craw, Hay, Milburn, Yealands, plus Nutt and Holland – had been taken captive. Craw had lost his jacket, while Captain Wilder's had been discovered near the abandoned jeep. The Italian commander put two and two together and made six, presuming that Craw was the discarded jacket's owner, which meant that he had to be a captain and in command.

Craw was shown a map and ordered to indicate the route that the raiders would take to get them back to British lines. He feigned ignorance. The Italian commander lost his temper. He called for an armed guard and warned Craw that he would be shot if he didn't start talking.

Craw continued to act dumb and refused to salute any of the Italian officers. He received a beating with a rifle butt for his 'impertinence', but his stubborn silence – and that of his five fellows – bought those raiders still at large precious time.

The crew of Chevy *Te Aroha III* was the first to make the rendezvous with Easonsmith. En route they'd attacked one tank with incendiary bombs and grenades and rammed another off the road, in the process of which they'd ripped off a mudguard, a spare wheel and a sand tray. Trooper Dobson, *Te Aroha III*'s gunner, had taken grenade splinters in his back, but in the adrenaline rush of combat he'd failed to realize how badly he was injured.

On spying the sheikh's tomb with its unmistakable grey obelisk-like spire, the war-ravaged vehicle slewed to a halt. The wounded Dobson staggered off, mouthing, 'Water. Water.' Then he promptly collapsed. Doc Lawson examined him and pronounced him dead. Shortly after that the 'dead' man opened his eyes, gazed around himself confusedly, before declaring himself very much alive and still in need of water!

Only one other vehicle from the airport raid would make it to the RV: *Te Anau II*, carrying the injured Parker and Captain Wilder. It arrived there just after 0200 hours, meaning that the Barce airport raiders had executed their attack bang on schedule. The results spoke for themselves.

In the fresh air of the ride Wilder had recovered consciousness and seemed fully back in command of his much-depleted patrol. He reported in to Easonsmith that his force had hit fully thirty-two aircraft, and he reckoned that all were ablaze or damaged. Even from this distance, the aerodrome could be seen burning fiercely. The entire place looked to be awash with flame. For a moment Easonsmith studied the scene. As decoy raids went this was about as good as it got. What enemy would ever realize that the real target for tonight wasn't in fact Barce, but Rommel's stronghold – Tobruk?

The other raiding patrol reached the rendezvous shortly after Wilder, having spent their time shooting up the Barce barracks. They were missing one vehicle, a Chevrolet that had become detached from the column in the confusion of battle, but otherwise their casualties were minimal and their vehicles mostly undamaged.

All together, Easonsmith's force had lost nine men in action. But clearly, missing men or not, it was time to get the hell out of there. Doc Lawson slapped a bandage on Wilder's head injury, after which the column of vehicles formed up and moved out. It consisted of seven Chevys, with two further damaged trucks under tow, in addition to the three surviving jeeps.

The long line of vehicles pushed into a narrow valley called Got El Sas, lying to the east of the town. The roar of the Chevys' engines reverberated from the flanks of the defile, which were thickly wooded and cloaked in darkness. It struck the men as being the ideal kind of place to site an ambush.

The tension mounted as tired eyes – and freshly charged weapons – swept the dark, formless clumps of vegetation to either side. Suddenly, the night erupted with a burst of machine-gun fire. It spurted out of the bush, hammering in from the high ground. This was clearly the signal to trigger the main assault. Further machine guns opened up, amid a cacophony of rifle fire.

From the looks of the muzzle flashes, the patrol was facing a hundred troops, maybe more. Only speed – and sustained aggression – would get them out of this. At the front, Easonsmith's driver gunned the jeep's engine. Gears crunching and clutches screaming, the column of vehicles accelerated. And from all along the line of Chevys and jeeps the Vickers and Brownings belched fire.

In the darkness of the valley floor, the column appeared like a long snake spurting deadly flame. The gunners targeted the enemy's muzzle flashes wherever they could see them in the thick darkness beneath the trees. Exhausted, but wired on adrenaline, Wally Rail found it particularly hard to operate his twin Brownings: he had the badly wounded Parker lying at his feet on the truck bed.

Parker would just have to endure being showered with red-hot shell casings. They were fighting for their lives now.

As Jake Easonsmith's patrol headed into a well-set trap, Tommy Langton worried that the Royal Navy were about to do likewise, at Tobruk. As he perched on his rock shelf signalling with his torch into the empty night, he had the surprise of his life. All of a sudden a searchlight that had been probing the heavens swooped down through a forty-five degree arc, until it was pointing directly out to sea.

Moments later, the entire battery of searchlights seemed to do likewise. The shock hit Langton like a punch to the guts. He found that he was struggling to breathe. Before he could recover his wits, the shore guns opened fire once more, only now they were shooting into the sea and not the air.

'Before I had recovered from the surprise, pandemonium broke loose,' Langton remarked. 'This time it was the stuttering of machine guns and the heavier staccato note of pom-poms, and coloured tracer raced fantastically past me and out to sea.'

The tracer whipped past Langton's position in burning streams. His eyes followed the fantastical, fiery arcs, at the end of which he spied the wake of a MTB, lit up white by a searchlight. From his position low to the water the silhouette of the speeding vessel was clear, and he could see tracer cannoning off its hull and sparking high into the air.

'I heard the engines of the MTBs and occasionally saw them in the searchlight beams . . .' Langton recalled. 'There was extremely heavy fire from Tobruk Bay . . . the MTBs got caught in the searchlights and I could see their wake and tracer bouncing off . . .'

Another MTB was pinned in the deadly light, and nailed by a murderous concentration of fire.

'Why don't you come in?' Langton yelled across the sea, his voice tight with desperation. 'We're here! Come in! Come in!'

There was no answer but the sound of the waves just below the shelf of rock on which he perched.

A wave of anger swept over him. Here he was, futilely flashing his torch, while the landing boats were getting hosed down by enemy fire. None of this should be happening. How in the name of God had the enemy got wise to the flotilla of little boats in the dark waters off Tobruk? And why hadn't those boats already landed their troops on the beaches at Sciausc Bay? Couldn't they see his and Scott's lights?

Unbeknown to Langton, there had been delays getting the signals through to the ships, to clear them in to land. Delays that had kept the MTBs – twenty-odd boats and the hundreds of troops they carried – at sea. The ships' captains were under strict orders: if they didn't receive the coded radio signal they were to abort.

The MTBs' radio sets were notoriously unreliable. They were underpowered and prone to getting soaked in seawater as the boats ploughed through waves at speed. So it was that the flotilla had been weaving up and down the coast, their wireless operators hunched over their sets, headphones on, but hearing only an echoing void of static.

As the little ships dodged the probing beams of the searchlights, Generalmajor Deindl and his deputies were busy on shore in Tobruk. The German commander was suffering no such communications problems: detailed damage assessments were flooding in to his headquarters.

'Tobruk. Attack by 178 aircraft. 576 HE bombs. 6 men wounded. Several tents destroyed. 6 enemy aircraft shot down.'

There were reports that individual flak stations and gun emplacements were not responding on their radios, especially those to the west of Sciausc Bay. Deindl's commanders warned him that the British forces could only be in Tobruk with one purpose: 'the enemy will try to take possession of the fortress'.

That was like a red rag to a bull. Deindl issued his orders: as Sciausc Bay appeared to be the focus of the Allied landings, that would be the focus of his response.

'Luftgaustab Afrika Will Seek To Establish Contact By All Possible Means With The Flak Stations . . . It Will Also Organize The Holding Or Recapturing Of The Terrain . . . All Stations To Send Immediate Reports.'

Luftgaustab Afrika was Deindl's anti-aircraft ground defence command, the unit in charge of his flak guns and searchlight batteries. They were to track down their missing units and retake any areas seized by British forces, working in conjunction with the marines of the San Marco battalion.

Deindl also ordered the warships berthed in Tobruk harbour to go to action stations. The Italians had three destroyers docked there, and the Germans a mine-sweeping flotilla. They were to get up steam and start scouring the harbour for targets.

Tommy Langton noticed the volume of enemy fire increasing. Tracer sliced long golden-red knife-cuts through the darkness. If he kept his eyes still it flashed past quickly, but if he followed the passage of one glowing round, it seemed to grope its way across the water in a slow, ghostly arc. In spite of his frustration and rage, it was mesmerising.

Suddenly a searchlight whipped across the harbour, to pin Sciausc Bay itself in its glare. Langton was momentarily blinded. He went to take cover, before realizing that there was no way that he could be seen against the rocks at such a distance, for the light was coming from the opposite side of the harbour some two miles away.

Langton stayed where he was, staring down the beam of the searchlight. 'Bastards!' he yelled. 'Bastards!'

The only response was a most unwelcome one: the deep boom of heavier weapons began to echo across the water. With his heart in his mouth, Langton scanned the sea, searching for the big guns' target. On the opposite side of the harbour a searchlight probed directly out to sea. Momentarily, it glinted on the graceful, sleek lines of a British Tribal class destroyer: the *Sikh*.

As Langton watched aghast, a plume of white water erupted in the destroyer's wake. Another and another followed. The *Sikh* was taking fire, and Langton had no idea whether she'd yet to drop the first of her landing craft, packed full of Royal Marines. SBS canoeists in Folbots – collapsible canoes – should have gone ashore on the far side of Tobruk harbour, to mark the Marines' landing spot.

From there the marines were supposed to form up and fight their way inland, becoming one arm of the pincer designed to seize, and to wreck, Tobruk harbour. The other arm was to be formed by Haselden's Commando, but all this would only happen if the Royal Navy ships could get the troops in to land.

Taking a leaf out of the SIG's book, the *Sikh* had been given a makeover: she'd been painted in the distinctive colours of the Italian navy – grey, with a red-and-white diagonal stripe across the decks. But right now the disguise seemed to be having little effect, for *Sikh* was taking heavy fire.

There was nothing that Langton could do about the *Sikh*; his focus had to be on getting the MTBs in. A sea mist began to drift closer to the shore. He could hear the quiet throb of a petrol engine pulsing through the opaque mass, as a MTB nosed among the rocks – no doubt checking if they were in the right position. But still it didn't come in to land.

Langton felt so frustrated. Utterly impotent. How could it all be going so wrong? And then he was struck by a terrible thought: maybe they had been drawn into a trap after all? His mind went back to the road journey and the seemingly miraculous bluff pulled off by the SIG. He remembered the spotter plane that had swooped low over the convoy, and the Very lights fired as if to mark their progress. He thought of the motorcyclists who had ridden out to check on them at close quarters.

Now, as if on a single word of command, the searchlights had dropped down to scour the sea. Was it possible that the entire operation had been blown, every aspect of it known about and anticipated? A force of men – SIG and commandos – tricked into the heart of Tobruk, so as to lure the wider elements of the assault into a devastating trap, one expertly and cunningly laid?

There was no way of knowing, and right now Langton had to force all such worries from his mind, for below him a sleek dark shape was edging its silent way into Sciausc Bay. Langton had almost missed it. He'd all but given up hope of any of the MTBs getting in, but then his eye caught the flash of movement.

The lone craft was moving with barely a sound and causing little disturbance in the water. It was uncanny; ghostly almost. Langton felt his heart leap. He felt overcome with relief and exhilaration. He flashed his torch at it deliberately, sending a welcome signal. Maybe things weren't going so wrong after all.

If one little ship could get in, surely others could follow? Sure enough, Langton spied a second knife-sharp prow cutting through the dark sea, as MTB number two made towards the bay. For an instant he wondered how they had evaded the searchlights that were sweeping along this stretch of coast, blinding him each time they passed. It didn't matter. The little ships were coming in, and Langton was supposed to form their reception party.

He wedged his torch as best he could in a cleft in the rocks, the beam shining horizontally out to sea. Again, it was the best that he could do in the circumstances. He turned from the sea and began to scale the cliff, retracing his route. He reached the place where he had left his weapon and pack and groped around in the darkness. Odd, but there was nothing there.

He crept all about the bunker, but there was no sign of either his tommy gun or pack. He crouched, searching along the cliff face for the blocky silhouette of a bunker. Maybe this was the wrong one? But there was no other bunker. Then he remembered the noise that he thought he'd heard when signalling out to sea.

Fear welled up from the pit of his stomach. He told himself to keep calm and to keep his head. He searched around the bunker one last time. Both gun and pack were missing. Someone had been following him, it seemed, and they had deprived him of his main weapon, plus the grenades and other supplies that he carried in his pack.

Langton felt for his pistol holster, undoing the button. He flicked aside the flap. Then he stood up and set off, his legs feeling leaden with fatigue. He climbed, but the going seemed far tougher now. He crested a rise and stumbled into a ditch.

A voice rang out in challenge: '*Alt! Chi va la?*' – Halt! Who goes there?

It sounded high-pitched and youthful, and it was followed by fevered whispering. There was more than one enemy soldier. Langton levelled his pistol in the direction of the voices and fired two shots in quick succession. There was a cry – more of a whimper, like that of a panicky child. Langton hurried off, his legs suffused with a new energy, one fuelled by fear.

He reached the beach to find two MTBs close to the shore. The place was already crowded: a reception party of commandos thronged the sands. From the deck of the first boat a short, sturdy figure leaped down. He waded ashore and Langton heard him announce his arrival in the distinctive north-country tones of a Northumberland Fusilier.

'Sergeant Miller, sir, with two sections of Fusiliers and Vickers guns.'

The sergeant's voice was answered by the equally distinctive tones of New Zealander Second Lieutenant MacDonald, who was all businesslike efficiency.

'Good to see you, sergeant. Let's get your men and guns ashore.'

Mac was on the case, organizing the two machine-gun squads. Those on the MTBs' decks began passing down the Vickers, their tripods, ammo and associated kit. The water-cooled Vickers .303 was hugely popular with British troops due to its bulletproof reliability. Right now, the commandos could do with a few dozen Vickers sections to bolster their lines.

The cases of ammunition proved immensely heavy, and Mac sent a runner to fetch a truck. As he waited for the vehicle, the tough New Zealander hurried from one boat to the other, calling out instructions. Langton checked that all was in hand. Mac assured him that it was.

'Machine guns,' he announced breezily. 'Just the job, with the kind of trouble we've got brewing on the far side of the headquarters.'

Mac would get the guns moved to the high ground, he explained, set to cover the perimeter the Commando had thrown around the bay. It was the best he could manage, at least until more ships and men came in and the Commando could go on the offensive. And for sure more ships and men *had* to get in.

Langton caught the gist of what the New Zealander was driving at. Not even the SOE Commando could clear their side of Tobruk harbour with the force they had to hand, significantly depleted as it now was.

The priority had to be guide the MTBs in, and Langton was best employed doing so. But he'd enjoyed this short spell of contact with his fellow warriors, and he was loath to return to the solitude of his isolated shelf of rock, especially as the only weapon he had left was his pistol.

He accosted a figure standing by the water's edge, tommy gun cradled in his arms. It was one of the commandos, a man Langton knew only as Private Glynn.

Langton gestured with his pistol, indicating it was the only weapon he had. 'I need someone to accompany me to the eastern point. Will you come along as my escort?'

Private Glynn eyed the darkened headland that loomed above the beach. He looked less than keen, yet he had little choice but to agree. They set off, Langton retracing his steps and being mindful of the enemy that lurked in the shadows. They reached the cliff edge without incident.

Langton pointed into the void, crashing waves echoing up from the depths. 'This is where we climb down to the rocks.'

Private Glynn glanced over the edge. He eyed Langton apprehensively. 'If you don't mind, sir, I think I'll get back to the boys.'

Langton could hardly blame him. 'All right, Glynn,' he replied, trying to sound as if he meant it. He really would have preferred to have the company. 'Good luck.'

With that Private Glynn hurried into the night, and Langton turned to begin his descent into the darkness.

CHAPTER 19

At Sciausc beach, MacDonald heard a vehicle bumping down the wadi. In the glow from its headlights he could tell that it was the wireless truck. It pulled onto the beach and the men began to ferry the crates of ammo from boats to vehicle. Now and again the light from the truck caught the face of a fusilier. Mac could see how different they looked to the men of the Commando: they were fresh shaven, clean and smart.

After three weeks of rarely using a razor or washing, such neatness and cleanliness somehow appeared all wrong. In fact, Mac had grown to relish looking like a seasoned pirate, and particularly the effect it seemed to have upon the enemy. What was it about beards and wild, unkempt hair that seemed to strike such terror into their adversaries?

Curses rang out across the beach. He turned to the nearest boat. 'What is it? What's wrong?'

'We've piled the bloody thing onto the sand,' a voice replied. The MTB's crew had managed to ground her as they tried to edge closer to deliver the ammo.

'Can't you get her off?' Mac queried.

'Don't you think we're trying!' came back the exasperated response.

The MTB's engines roared as the skipper went to full power hard astern. The boat shook and throbbed, but it didn't budge. Mac stood to one side, so he could check for incoming craft. He surveyed the bay. Even if this one vessel remained stuck fast, there was plenty of room for the others to put ashore.

He felt his spirits lift. Two little ships had found the landing ground without any difficulty. More were bound to materialize. As Mac waited, eyes searching the dark waters beyond the bay, the free MTB threw a tow onto the beached vessel and began to try to pull her clear. Its powerful engines churned up the waters of the bay, but still the stubborn craft refused to budge.

Loaded with men and war materiel, the wireless truck began to crawl back up the wadi. After fifteen minutes it reached the high point, where Sergeant Miller gave his orders. One section was to scale the western flank of the bay, to set up their Vickers covering the beach, to safeguard the other boats as they came in. The other section would set up their gun facing west, into Tobruk – bolstering the Commando's thin khaki line.

Langton, meanwhile, dropped down onto his lonely ledge above the sea. He retrieved his lighted torch from the crevice in which he'd left it. That, at least, hadn't been filched by the enemy.

Far across the water he figured he could see the silhouettes of vessels. He counted seven: a squadron of MTBs moving in line astern towards Tobruk. He saw the little ships circle in towards the boom net that barred the entrance to the harbour, from where they picked up a bearing and turned due south, heading directly for the landing beach.

But as they crept closer, the searchlights playing across the entrance to Sciausc Bay found them. Like moths, the little ships seemed drawn to the lights, and then the shore guns opened up and the MTBs gunned their engines and leaped out of the line of fire. In a deadly game of cat and mouse, they raced to lose the enemy gunners.

Langton started flashing desperately, synchronising his signal with that of Pilot Officer Scott, whose light he could see blinking out from the opposite headland.

To Langton the twin pinpricks of illumination spoke most powerfully to those at sea: *Come in! Come in! Come in!*

At Haselden's headquarters the kilted figure of Lieutenant Sillito decided to go on the offensive. Attack was often the best form of defence, and the commandos were men of action. All this waiting – for the MTBs to drop their reinforcements; for the destroyers to do likewise on the opposite side of the harbour; for the combined force to seize the initiative – was getting to his men, and especially since the fire on their positions was growing heavier by the minute.

Sillito passed word to his deputies: to MacDonald, who'd just rejoined them from the beach; to Bill Barlow, the hulking great artillery officer who never felt more alive than when in combat; to SSM Swinburn, who towered over Barlow even and was a cold-eyed killer when faced with the enemy.

Hugging cover, groups of commandos formed up and advanced into the darkness, seeking contact with the enemy. Quick but savage firefights erupted. Tracer arced through the sky, as the commandos rooted out their adversaries with aggression and savagery. Already, they'd lost brother warriors to death or injury and no quarter would be given.

A searchlight swung across the bay, probing the battle-torn headland. Bigger guns began to fire, unleashing long streams of tracer that looped across the water, hammering into the blood-soaked ground. The commandos could see little rhyme or reason in the enemy's actions: at such a distance, they would have little chance of distinguishing friend from foe. But even so, this was fast becoming a decidedly unhealthy place to be.

A runner was sent to the villa headquarters, to warn Haselden. He received the news of the stiffening battle with stoical calm. They were under siege. The siege would be broken. They just needed to get the little ships in.

But beneath his unruffled exterior Haselden was worried, and mostly about Major Campbell.

He'd received not a single report from the sick and weary leader of the force clearing the eastern headland, apart from his Very light success signal. For approaching five hours now – only radio silence.

He glanced around the villa HQ. 'What's happened to Colin? All this time and not a word.'

No one volunteered an answer. The only man who might know something was Tommy Langton, and he was perched on the opposite cliff, flashing signals into the night. Haselden asked Sillito to lead a small force to investigate: he needed to know what had happened to Campbell and the missing half of his Commando.

Sillito led the redoubtable Swinburn plus a few good men east across the bay. They were forced to cross the minefield, following the path of disturbed ground that Campbell and his sappers had left. Then they began to climb.

Sillito halted abruptly. From out of the darkness up ahead a massive Breda cannon was pointing at his chest. The muzzle gaped darkly. A soldier was hunched behind it, eyeing Sillito's kilt suspiciously. Sillito stepped to one side, crying sharply to the figure right behind him, 'Yours!'

In one smooth motion Swinburn raised his tommy gun, sighted and fired. The burst swept the gun position. Sillito and his party raced ahead, clearing the emplacement of the last of the enemy.

As the final shots died away all became quiet again – spookily quiet. They searched high and low, but still there was no sign of Campbell and his men. With the fighting growing fiercer on the western side of the headland, Sillito figured they could afford to tarry no longer. They needed to get back to their positions and to lead their men in battle.

They turned and hurried away, this time skirting along the beach. One MTB was there, hard aground and seemingly abandoned. A silhouette loomed out of the darkness. The challenge was thrown out and answered. It was Tommy Langton, breathing hard. He and Sillito exchanged notes. Langton figured that Campbell's force must have run into heavy resistance somewhere to the east of the bay. Nothing else could explain their silence.

Langton had left his torch wedged in the cliffs, and Pilot Officer Scott remained in position, signalling with his Aldis lamp. He had come to check on the landing beach, hopeful of discovering that further craft had come ashore. Where there was light, and the MTBs still circled out at sea, there was hope, or so he reasoned.

Bursts of fire rang out above their heads: the familiar sound of Vickers machine guns. The Fusiliers appeared to be in action, which was both good news and bad news. Good, because there were no finer gunners in any regiment, and no finer weapon for them to be using. Bad, because it had to mean that the enemy had advanced to within reach of their guns.

★　　★　　★

The enemy was also closing in on Jake Easonsmith's patrol, as the column of Chevys tried to bludgeon its way out of Barce. The V-shaped defile of Got El Sas echoed to the continuous thunder of gunshots and the scream of tortured engines, as the speeding convoy ran the gauntlet of the ambush.

In among the rocks the Italian commander, Brigadier General Umberto Piatti dal Pozzo, had secreted a force of 150 troops from the 7th Savari Cavalry – the same unit that had been tasked with hunting for Easonsmith's patrol, when the spotter aircraft had found them on the previous evening. The 7th Savari had failed to stop the British raiders then. They had vowed to do so now.

From the rear of the speeding Chevys figures ramped their smoking machine guns to left and right, as they hammered rounds into the enemy's positions. Barrels were red hot and breeches spewed spent brass, which flew in all directions. The encounter was bitter and bloody and at close range, and inevitably the desert warriors started taking injuries.

From a vehicle there came cries of: 'Casualty! Casualty!'

The words were torn away by the slipstream and buried under the cacophony of noise: howling engines, the rasp of wheels spinning on loose gravel, men yelling hatred and aggression, thumping exhausts, and over it all the sharp crack of enemy rifle fire, plus the buzz-saw whirr of the convoys' machine guns.

The column had raced half the length of the defile when the first vehicle skidded to a halt. A front tyre had been blown out, struck by a hail of bullets. In the LRDG it was sacrosanct that if one vehicle were ever forced to a halt under hostile fire, all would stop to provide cover. The column did just that, as the occupants of the crippled vehicle leaped out and went about changing the wheel.

The stricken vehicle was none other than *Te Anau II*, the Chevy that had rescued Wilder and Parker when their jeep had overturned. As if the crew had not been through enough already, the driver, David Warbrick, was forced to hunker down by the punctured wheel, loosening nuts as the rounds tore past him. In the rear of the truck Wally Rail tried to provide answering fire, while yelling at the wounded Parker lying at his feet to keep his bloody head down.

Other Chevys circled the immobilized truck, like cowboys protecting a wagon train. Warbrick worked feverishly at the punctured wheel, as Jack Davis, *Te Anau II*'s commander, wrested a spare off its mount on the bonnet and rolled it across to him. All the time Warbrick was crouched in the dirt, shivers running up and down his spine, as he expected a bullet to rip into his back at any moment.

Small-arms fire pinged and sparked off the metal flanks of *Te Anau II*. A unit of the 7th Savari was pressing home an attack, racing in on foot and firing their Mannlicher-Carcano six-round carbines as they went. A long burst from Rail's twin Brownings cut them down, scattering the survivors into the darkness.

As Rail ceased fire, Warbrick slid back behind the wheel, gunned the Chevy into motion and accelerated away. *Te Anau II* bucked and kangarooed over some hidden obstruction: it turned out that in his haste to get moving Warbrick had forgotten to remove the jack. They'd driven over it as he'd pulled away. No one was about to turn back to fetch it.

The remainder of the column fell in behind *Te Anau II*, but in Popski Peniakoff's jeep all was not going well. Peniakoff could see the streams of tracer slicing through the trees. He found it somehow hypnotic, especially as he knew that many more invisible bullets – standard non-tracer rounds – were also cutting through the air.

He felt a sudden kick to his left hand, which was knocked off the side of the jeep. An instant later he sensed a similar blow to his left knee. He held up his hand. His little finger was dangling, held on by a sliver of skin. His knee had taken shrapnel splinters, while his driver, Pongo Reid, also seemed to have been hit in the leg. Popksi asked if he was all right.

Reid guffawed. 'Yeah. Jesus Christ, trust me to be the unlucky bloody bastard!' He didn't stop driving.

Popski felt a blind rage sweep over him. After

stirring up a hornets' nest in Barce, there had been neither time nor opportunity to rob the bank vault, and now his vehicle and his crew were being shot to shreds. He swivelled his twin Vickers and fired burst after burst at the flashes beneath the trees. Once he'd exhausted the circular pans of rounds – each packed with ninety-seven .303 bullets – a hand reached out from behind and slotted on full ones.

As Popski remarked, 'I went on firing with rage in my heart.'

At the end of the defile, the enemy had crept to within a few yards of the track. Sergeant Jack Dennis, who'd led the raid on the Barce barracks, was behind the wheel of his jeep, with Guardsman Roy Duncalfe alongside him, manning the twin Vickers. They'd already caused havoc in Barce, throwing a chain over the telephone lines and driving off to drag them down. After that Duncalfe had used a grenade-launcher to blow apart the barracks itself.

Neither felt like getting killed now, but the enemy had crawled in so close that Duncalfe couldn't depress his Vickers low enough to hit them. Instead, he was forced to snatch his neighbour's pistol and his own, as he proceeded to unload on the crouching Savari riflemen two-handed, doing a fine impression of John Wayne.

The mad dash down ambush alley had thrown up clouds of red dust, giving the men a wild, devilish appearance. But as the final vehicle emerged from the fire, Frank Jopling, Captain Wilder's navigator, was hit. 'About the last shot that was fired hit me in the leg,' he recorded later in his diary. 'I thought it was shattered; you would almost swear that it had broken the bone.'

As the tail end of the convoy broke through the ambush, the enemy guns fell silent. Easonsmith's patrol had successfully run the gauntlet, using a combination of speed, aggression and raw fire-power to do so. But dawn was not so far away, and with every halt and every battle the chances of making their getaway lessened, especially as they were carrying wounded.

Easonsmith pushed ahead for a further eight miles. They needed to pull off the road under good cover. Vehicles required attention; so too did the injured. The column nosed in under a thick stand of trees. Doc Lawson got down to treating the casualties. Jopling had to be carried from his truck to have his leg wound dressed. Reid could just about walk, but Peniakoff's finger had to be amputated.

As for Parker, Wilder's driver – shot through the guts – only evacuation to a fully functioning hospital would save him. While under attack in the valley, Doc Lawson had proved himself to be one of the quiet heroes of the patrol. Dodging gunshots, he'd dashed from truck to truck, checking on the wounded. He'd even carried Parker to the comparative safety of his own vehicle through a barrage of fire.

Three of the Chevys were found to have taken serious hits. Two were repairable, but one was finished. While some busied themselves in the half-light preparing a hurried meal, others unloaded all the stores and ammo from the stricken vehicles. Weapons were cleaned and recharged, although many hoped they had run the worst of the enemy gauntlet by now.

They'd been halted for maybe an hour when rifle fire ripped through the gloom beneath the trees. A line of foot soldiers was spotted creeping through the undergrowth towards the LRDG's position. Easonsmith mounted his jeep, and with Duncalfe manning the front guns set off to see what could be done about the enemy.

He drove in a wide loop, bringing the jeep onto a shallow ridge on the left flank of their adversaries. The line stretched out before them. Without warning they opened fire from the jeep. With each gun belting out 950 rounds a minute, a whirlwind of rounds ripped into the enemy formation. For a few seconds they tried to hold their position and return fire, but then the line faltered.

The jeep's gunners kept pouring in the fire. Those of the enemy who hadn't been hit broke and ran now, scattering into the bush. As the jeep hurried back to the leaguer beneath the trees, those aboard were well aware that, 'today, the enemy was not to be outdone'. The Italians and their Arab conscripts had fought with spirit and determin-ation, and they'd kept harrying the patrol.

There was no doubt about it: they would have to get moving again. Time bombs were set in the crippled trucks to deny them to the enemy. That done, the column set a course across country for Chedda Bu Maun, further to the east of Barce, where they were scheduled to link up with David Stirling's SAS, fresh out of the Benghazi raid.

But the terrain proved punishing. The rough driving took its toll, the rear axle on the wireless truck shearing its bolts and dropping out. Easonsmith could not afford to be without communications so they were forced to stop and fix it. The ends of the bolts would need to be drilled out by hand, making this a long job. As luck would have it, the immobilized truck had come to a halt on a bare hilltop, but there was little anyone could do about that.

The rest of the vehicles were hidden among the scrub in the shadows of the surrounding valleys as the mechanics got to work. The men lounged beneath the cover, trying to grab some much-needed rest, the first streaks of the coming dawn lighting the skies to the east. Daylight – it would soon be upon them, and it was no friend to hunted men.

Each man grabbed his personal 'bail-out' kit: a small pack containing emergency rations and water. These were always kept within easy reach, should they be forced to abandon the Chevys and go on the run. With the disabled wireless truck stuck on that exposed hilltop, there was a real risk that it might be seen from the air when the enemy started flying their dawn patrols.

In which case the men might need to grab their bail-out kits at any moment and run.

CHAPTER 20

In the makeshift sickbay at Haselden's villa headquarters, Lieutenant Graham Taylor had woken from a drugged sleep. The morphine had killed the pain but it had also sent him to la-la land, and he had no idea how much time he had lost. Despite the plugs inserted into his lungs and back by Captain Gibson of the Royal Army Medical Corps, he felt strangely fit and strong.

For someone who had been shot through the chest, he figured he was bearing up pretty well. More than anything he hated being trapped here and not being out on the headland commanding his men. He could hear the sharp crack of gunfire and the odd round or chunk of shrapnel rattling against the villa's thick walls.

He turned to Gibson: 'What's happening, John?'

Gibson gestured at the score of injured men littered around the room. It looked full to bursting. 'We're all but finished, Graham,' the Canadian drawled. 'There's a damn big force out there bottling us in.'

'What about the reinforcements?' Taylor could see the faint light of dawn filtering through the window, so the MTBs should have long ago disgorged their legions. Indeed, by dawn on the 14th the Commando should have linked up with infantry and marines landed by ship, and taken possession of Tobruk harbour, not to mention freeing the thousands of POWs.

Gibson shrugged. 'Only two boats got in. The rest are still out there, trying to run the gauntlet.'

Exhaustion was writ large across his features; the Commando's medic had had one hell of a night of it. He'd had to resort to far more than his celebrated cold cure – go dig a big hole – to treat the injuries that the commandos had suffered during their long night at Sciausc Bay.

Gibson glanced at the window. 'With the search-lights and the guns . . . the boats didn't make it in. And now it's almost light. We've had it, chum.'

Taylor got to his feet unsteadily. He felt shaken to the core. Only two boats had managed to land; the rest hadn't made it. Somehow, calamity had befallen the Commando, and all the while he had been pumped full of morphine and lost to the world. It felt all the more disastrous, hearing this from their easy-going, unflappable medic.

If the MTBs hadn't made it in, what of the rest of the Royal Navy flotilla? he wondered. What of the ships charged to pluck the commandos off the shores of Tobruk, come mission's end? Presumably there was going to be no nice comfortable ride back to Alexandria, from where the seaborne armada had first set sail. In which case, wounded or not Taylor needed to get back out there and fight.

He stumbled outside. He could only move with difficulty, but he was certain he could grasp a weapon and shoot straight. The first thing he saw was Captain Trollope, their signals officer, lying on the ground almost at his feet. Trollope had professed a hatred of the outdoors and an aversion to combat: neither was in evidence now. He had a rifle grasped to his shoulder and was firing directly across Sciausc Bay in what had to be the direction of the enemy.

Taylor slumped down beside him. They talked. Trollope explained that they were surrounded. The enemy had broken through Major Campbell's cordon in the east and were pressing in from all directions. Haselden was awaiting a signal from headquarters that would determine their next course of action here on the beleaguered headland.

If the destroyers had managed to drop the main force of Royal Marines, the Commando was to fight its way into Tobruk. Or what survived of the Commando, anyway. Even if the marines hadn't made it, as long as the ships remained just off Tobruk they were to hold this headland. Their orders were to prevent any enemy vessels from slipping out of the harbour and getting in among the MTBs. To that end they had men sited on the cliffs, manning the captured guns.

'And what about when we run clean out of ammo?' Taylor asked.

Trollope didn't take his eyes from his rifle. 'No one's got round to discussing that yet. I'm in favour of grabbing the wireless truck, loading a bunch of us aboard and charging through the lines.'

Taylor was impressed. 'Good on you, Trolly,' he declared, as Trollope went to reload.

This was so out of character, or at least the kind of character that Captain Trollope had affected for much of the mission. Here was a man apparently of dash and daring, demonstrating a casual, almost devil-may-care attitude. But Taylor knew that his own options were limited. Wounded as he was, would he survive a lurching ride at top speed over rough ground, to smash a way through the enemy cordon? Would his chest really stand it?

A call came from within the villa. Trollope was needed at the radio. He handed his rifle to Taylor, and with a glance at the enemy positions he crawled back towards the building.

Inside, the smack and slap of bullets was loud against the walls. A powerful engine revved in the distance: it sounded like that of a Stuka. It was most likely one of those based at the aerodrome on the far side of Tobruk, preparing to get airborne as soon as it was light.

Trollope made his way to the radio set. He grabbed the transcript from his radio operator: message just in. He read it thrice over as he tried to steel himself to deliver it to Haselden: 'Force A failed to land.' Force A meant the several hundred

313

marines riding on the destroyers. Lord only knew what had happened to them.

Trollope carried the fateful missive across to Haselden. He found him deep in conversation with one of his deputies, 'Old' John Poynton, a gunnery officer who'd blagged his way onto the present mission. In his thirties, Poynton was one of the oldest men in the Commando, hence the nickname. By rights he shouldn't have been there at all: he'd wounded his arm in training just a few weeks back, concealing his injury when volunteering for the present mission.

Poynton was explaining that he was worried about the coastal guns. All the effort expended in capturing them would be wasted if they were retaken by the enemy. Trollope interrupted, handling Haselden the signal. He watched the commander read it and his expression barely change. No doubt about it, Haselden had fortitude and grit beyond measure.

Haselden glanced up from the message. He ran his eye around the room. His demeanour alone was sufficient to grab the attention of all in that bullet-pocked room. 'I'm sorry, chaps, but this is the end now,' he announced. 'It's every man for himself.'

No one needed telling what the message said.

Haselden vacillated for a moment, before turning back to Poynton. 'Spike the guns, John,' he confirmed. 'Quick as you can now.' Poynton was to dynamite the coastal defences and blow them to smithereens.

The gunnery officer hurried off, dodging bursts of fire as he dashed for the cliff-edge emplacements.

The fateful message had been received at 0526 hours. It was way too late – dawn would soon be upon them. If they were to have any hope of escape it would have to be by the desert, linking up with Lloyd Owen's patrol, but daylight would reduce their chances massively. In the backs of their minds were images of blasted huts filled with the corpses of the Italians who'd died in their sleep. They could expect no mercy from those that had them surrounded.

Haselden had a young son, Gerald, who had already lost his mother; he would be orphaned if his father perished here in Tobruk. But Haselden barely hesitated. It might be 'every man for himself now', but he knew where his duty lay: it was with the most vulnerable, the wounded. If he were to attempt to break out he would be taking them with him. No man under his watch was to be left behind.

He gathered his commanders: 'Trolly' Trollope, the kilted David Sillito, the heavily bandaged Graham Taylor, nursing his chest wound.

'We'll need to try to save the wounded,' Haselden remarked matter-of-factly.

'We could try the wireless truck,' Trollope ventured. 'Run the enemy lines, that kind of thing.'

'What about the MTB in the bay?' Sillito suggested. 'We can't all get away, but maybe we can get the wounded down there and to safety?'

'The navy couldn't get the thing off, so what chance do we have?' someone objected. 'And how do we start the damned thing?'

'Well, it's no good staying here.' It was Taylor. In spite of his chest wound, he was desperate to break out. A commando through and through, he detested being bottled up under siege. 'Let's at least get the walking wounded down to the MTB and give it a try.'

Taylor's suggestion seemed to be the best, perhaps the only, option they had right now.

Two figures appeared in the villa's doorway. They looked utterly self-possessed and unruffled. They were also dressed in German uniform, which proved momentarily unsettling before they were recognized. It was Buck and Russell, and they appeared 100 per cent convinced that they would find a way out of the present impasse, just as they had squeezed out of many a tight corner in the past.

On one occasion when they were deep behind the lines with the SIG, Buck and Russell had strolled into a German officers' mess. There had come a moment when it had seemed they were about to be unmasked, so they'd grabbed their pistols and fought their way out, reuniting themselves with the column of vehicles and making their getaway. Doubtless they had something similar in mind now.

Haselden eyed the two new arrivals. 'Any news? We could do with something right now.' He was enquiring after Buck and Russell's mission to free the POWs. Was a force of liberated Allied prisoners about to ride to their rescue?

Buck shook his head. 'John, it just seemed impossible. To make it through. Place is crawling with the enemy.'

'Any news of Colin?' Haselden asked. By 'Colin' he meant Major Campbell, the leader of the force on the eastern headland.

Buck and Russell were as much in the dark as anyone. No one seemed to know what had happened to Major Campbell or his force of commandos.

'Well, we can't wait any longer for him,' Haselden announced. 'We'd better get on the move.'

'I'll lead the walking wounded down to the beach,' Taylor volunteered. He seemed to have forgotten that he was one of them, and one of the more seriously injured.

Haselden smiled. 'Good man. See if you can get that boat started.'

Aided by Doc Gibson, Taylor began to check on the wounded, to see who might be able to move under their under steam. With help, a dozen men clambered to their feet. Some looked white as sheets, but at least they were capable of standing. That still left a similar number who were stretcher cases, and had no way of making it down to the water.

'Let's put the rest of the wounded on the truck and smash our way through,' Trollope volunteered.

Haselden smiled again. 'Good idea, Trolly. Let's get started.'

The column of walking wounded formed up and Taylor led them out the rear entrance of the villa, which was a little more sheltered from the enemy fire. He steered the line of bandaged and bloodied men downhill, sticking to the cover of a path that picked its way along the side of a ravine. Over the rough ground their progress was painfully slow.

A figure hurried past in the opposite direction. Finally, a runner had made it through from Major Campbell's party, fighting his way past the enemy to do so. He reached the villa, to find a ring of grim-faced commandos manning sand-bagged positions. Two massive figures appeared to be spearheading this side of the defence: SSM Swinburn, steely-eyed and utterly undaunted, and big Bill Barlow, who gave every impression of relishing the fight.

The runner dashed inside. He delivered a breathless report to Haselden. Campbell's force of commandos had stumbled into a savage and bloody series of battles. They'd pushed east from Sciausc Bay, trying to seize the gun emplacements in the next cove, Marsa Said. But the thick concrete bunkers were dug into the cliff and shrouded in barbed-wire defences. Try as they might, the commandos had been unable to get near them.

Heavily outnumbered, they'd been shot to pieces. Campbell's headquarters section had been taking fire from a building they had previously cleared.

Major Campbell and Lieutenant Mike Duffy – the man who'd used his bandaged hand to conceal a grenade, as they'd posed as POWs in the trucks – had been forced to take cover behind a low wall.

After reloading his weapon, Duffy had raised himself to check on the source of the enemy fire. He'd been shot instantly in the head. In a typically selfless and heroic act, Campbell, the dysentery-stricken commander, had crouched over Duffy checking him for signs of life. Realizing the man was dead, Campbell had been retrieving his weapons and ammo when he was shot in the buttock.

Campbell's force had suffered many more wounded and dead. It was dark news indeed for Haselden, but not entirely unexpected. He'd feared Campbell and his men must have run into trouble, for nothing else would explain their silence.

One by one, the SOE Commando were being wiped out.

Deep in the guts of the valley below – the valley of the shadow of death, as they had come to think of it – Buck's SIG were also fighting for their lives. Privates Rohr and Opprower hunkered down in the half-light, as a volley of shells screamed across the water and slammed into the open terrain, showering deadly steel splinters and pulverized rock in all directions.

From Tobruk harbour itself the big guns had been turned on Sciausc Bay. With each salvo Rohr and Opprower hugged the cover of the rocks, as the earth shook and vibrated beneath them and the air whined and howled with shrapnel. A cloud of thick, acrid smoke drifted across the valley, obscuring the dark silhouettes of the slopes to either side, hanging heavy and biting in the nostrils and leaving a bitter taste in the mouth.

Indeed, the events of the last few hours had left a bitter taste for the SIG operators. They'd failed in their mission. Or perhaps that was too harsh: they'd succeeded spectacularly in bluffing the Commando into fortress Tobruk. But they'd failed to inveigle their way into the harbour itself, to reach the POW cages and unchain the prisoners. Had they succeeded it could have turned the fortunes of the battle, but Tobruk was crawling with enemy, and with the best will in the world there had been no way through.

Upon breaching the Tobruk perimeter perhaps they should have driven the convoy directly to the POW cages, as if delivering a consignment of fresh prisoners. The trucks could have been packed with extra weaponry, and they could have started the uprising from within. That way, no one would have needed to rely on the ill-fated seaborne landings. But this was no time for hindsight or what-ifs.

As another salvo howled in to pound Sciausc Bay, Rohr and Opprower saw one of their trucks, lovingly decked out in Afrika Korps colours, take a hit. The shell exploded right beneath it, rocking the vehicle savagely on its springs and raking it with red-hot shrapnel.

Moments later, it burst into flames. It took bare minutes for the truck to be reduced to a gutted skeleton. A figure emerged from the smoke, running at a half-crouch. It was another member of the SIG. He reached their position and dived, breathless, into the cover of the rocks.

The three men gathered close and talked together in German, the language that came most naturally to them. He'd come with word from Captain Buck. The game was up, and they should attempt to break out and evade the enemy while there was still a little cover provided by the half-light of dawn.

But before they did so they absolutely had to drop the German disguises, for their Afrika Korps uniforms would be a death sentence if they were caught. They also had to destroy all the carefully crafted paperwork that corroborated their identities: the love letters, photographs and pay books; it all had to go. And, in a final effort to annihilate all traces of the ruse that had got them thus far, they would have to torch the surviving vehicles.

The three men hurried to their tasks. A fresh salvo of fire tore into the wadi, throwing up fountains of earth and rock, thick clouds of dust drifting into the air. A second truck was hit and caught fire: one less for them to worry about. They headed for the last surviving vehicle, leaping aboard and searching it from end to end, but there were no hidden bundles of British battledress anywhere to be found.

The spare British uniforms had to be in one of the other trucks, which had been reduced to gutted, smoking ruins. Which meant they had nothing to change into. There was no time to ponder or lament the loss. They dumped all of their cherished SIG paperwork in the cab of the one intact vehicle, sloshed in some petrol and threw in a lighted match. It went up with a greedy, hollow whump.

They ran from the truck as the flames spread, ammo and fuel starting to cook off violently in the rear. With every minute the terrain all around them was brightening. They had to seize the moment to escape, and they absolutely could not do so dressed as they were. They bolted for the cover of a cave. Inside, they did the only thing they cold think of: they stripped.

They piled every item of Afrika Korps uniform they possessed in a heap, and set the whole lot on fire. They kicked and poked at the flames until every last stitch of clothing had been burned to ashes. But now they faced a new predicament. Buck had been so single-minded – so obsessive, you might argue – that everything down to their underclothes had been Afrika Korps issue. They were naked now, and surrounded by the enemy.

Better to be captured like this than in the uniform of the enemy, Rohr and Opprower told themselves, though it would take some explaining.

They needed clothing – something; anything – to cover themselves. They started to quarter the ground: surely, some of the men of the Commando must have fallen here. Before long they stumbled upon some corpses. Grotesquely twisted, they had been caught in a shell burst.

It was sickening work, but it had to be done: they began to strip the bodies. Between the dead, they managed to cobble together enough sets of uniform passably free of blood or shrapnel holes. Thus clothed, they turned away from the valley of death and began to climb, making for Haselden's headquarters.

Buck was there, and they needed his guidance. They had every faith in their commander. Only he could lead them out of such a seemingly impossible situation, where death seemed to stalk them on all sides.

Ahead of them at the Villa, Trollope, Doc Gibson and Haselden began to bring out the worst of the wounded, so they could be loaded aboard the wireless truck. The trouble was that it was parked a good distance from the villa, and the ground between was exposed and completely devoid of cover.

Russell – the Flying Scotsman – didn't hesitate. Chased by a hail of fire he dashed across the open space, slid behind the wheel, fired up the truck and drove it to the building. Soon the vehicle was full, its rear compartment crammed with bandaged, bloodied figures. Incredibly, some still had their weapons with them. They readied tommy guns for the coming battle, which they feared would prove their last.

On a word from someone, Russell got down from the truck. Neither he nor Buck was going with it. Something else was mooted for the two SIG commanders, still dressed in their Afrika Korps officers' uniforms. The imposing figure of Bill Barlow took Russell's place at the wheel. He grinned from ear to ear as he revved up the engine, ready for the off. Gibson, the medic, joined those in the rear.

Buck spied one of his SIG still dressed in German battledress. His face darkened. 'For God's sake, man, find some British uniform,' he yelled. 'And burn everything you've got on you. God help you if you get captured like that!'

For some reason Buck seemed completely oblivious to how he was dressed, or maybe it was entirely deliberate. Either way, the man that he'd been shouting at broke into a good-natured grin. It was the portly, cheery figure of Chunky Hillman. He'd been too busy fighting to worry about changing his damned clothes.

On the extreme tip of the war-torn headland Gunnery Officer 'Old' John Poynton busied himself with the task that Haselden had given him. With the sappers in tow he went from one captured gun emplacement to the next, laying charges. One after another they were detonated, the coastal defence guns being ripped asunder.

Job done, Poynton led the sappers and his gunnery section in a crazed dash across the headland, making for Haselden's headquarters. They ran in a fearful crouch, bent double in an effort to avoid the enemy fire. Silhouetted against the lightening sky, the enemy targeted them mercilessly. Long bursts of fire raked the ground across which they ran. A figured stumbled and went down. Another halted, ran back to the fallen man, checked, then dashed on again.

Poynton charged into the villa, eyes wide with adrenaline and gasping for breath. He'd seen Lieutenant Harrison, the gunnery commander, fall and had run back to check on him. Harrison was one of those who had volunteered to act as a German guard on the drive-in, along with Langton and Barlow. Now he'd been shot through the chest and was dead.

Poynton looked for an officer to report to. From the vantage point of the high ground he'd spotted armoured cars, plus tanks, moving in on the Commando's final redoubt. The only man of senior rank that he could see was SSM Swinburn, whose giant form seemed to have taken command of the battle.

He gave Swinburn the grim news. His only response was to direct Poynton and his men to where the villa's defences most needed shoring up.

They were commandos: there was fighting to be done.

CHAPTER 21

The sky was barely light when the first enemy aircraft circled low over Jake Easonsmith's broken-down wireless truck, marooned as it was on the bare, rocky hilltop. It dived over the position several times, before widening its orbit to encompass many of the vehicles hidden below. Eventually, it broke off the search, flying away in the direction of Barce.

There was little doubt that the patrol had been seen.

What made it worse was that the plane was a Caproni Ca. 311 reconnaissance aircraft, no doubt flying out of Barce aerodrome itself. Wilder could have kicked himself. He could have sworn they'd nailed all the Capronis parked at the airfield. They were distinctive, with their twin engines and bulbous glass nose cones, and he'd counted six that had been shot to pieces. But amid the confusion one must have got away.

Jake Easonsmith took immediate control of the situation. He raced up the hillside, slid behind the wheel of the wireless truck and released the handbrake. He wrenched the steering wheel around, pointing the nose of the truck down into the deepest ravine that he could see. Freewheeling, it began to gather speed, bucking and plunging as it thundered over boulders and crashed through bushes.

Eyes watched in fear as the Chevy careered over the ground, their commander crouched over the wheel. It skidded on loose stones, crashed over bushes and thundered onward, at every moment the watchers expecting it to flip onto its back, trapping their leader beneath its bulk. But somehow, miraculously, it did nothing of the sort. Instead, Easonsmith piloted it to the depths of the ravine and stepped out as if he'd just been parking on a street of his native Bristol.

In spite of the carnage caused at Barce aerodrome, the runway itself was still usable. As soon as there was enough light ten Fiat CR.42 Falco – Falcon – fighter-bombers of the Italian air force's 47th Gruppo Assalto flew in and landed. They'd come from a neighbouring airbase, at Benghazi. A biplane of solid construction, the CR.42 was the most numerous Italian warplane of the Second World War.

It might look outdated, but the RAF had praised the aircraft's exceptional manoeuvrability, plus its immense strength and robustness. On some fronts it had achieved a kill ratio of 12:1. It had a crew of one, boasted a top speed of approaching 450 kph, and packed a significant punch, carrying two 12.7-millimetre Breda machine guns and 440 pounds of bombs.

Shortly after the spotter plane had completed its overflight, a formation of six Falcons appeared in the dawn skies to the west of Easonsmith's patrol. The LRDG commander had considered getting his column on the move, but he'd figured they stood less chance of being spotted if they remained in their places of hiding, the Chevys roped over with camo netting. Movement tended to draw the eye, especially in broad daylight.

At first the flight of aircraft seemed to avoid their position, but it soon became clear why. The time bombs left on the stricken Chevys had just gone off, the burning trucks emitting thick black palls of smoke, and the Falcons had gone to investigate. They could be seen diving over the area and machine-gunning the thick clumps of vegetation that surrounded the burning trucks. But the pilots soon tired of such sport.

They flew east, arrived over the patrol's position and began their attack. Executing slow orbits, they dived one by one, raking the bush with 12.7mm rounds. On one vehicle a gunner tried to answer fire with fire, but he found his weapons were jammed. The intense combat of the past twelve hours, followed by the flight through the open bush, had taken its toll, dirt and grime clogging the mechanism.

Moments later the same gunner saw a Falcon diving straight at him. He jumped off and ran at the same moment as the warplane opened fire. It scored a direct hit on the heavily laden Chevy. The Falcons were firing explosive and incendiary ammunition, which wreaked havoc among the vehicle's ammunition and fuel.

Frank Jopling, Wilder's navigator, was also on that Chevy. 'Well, the worst certainly came,' he later wrote in his diary. 'Six CR.42s dived on us continually with their guns blazing . . . I never knew a fighter could carry so much ammunition. My truck was the first to go up in smoke and we were unable to salvage anything.'

That burning Chevy was none other than *Te Aroha III*, one of the two survivors of the airfield shoot-'em-up, which had escaped Barce town by ramming a tank out of its way. It was now more than done for, thanks to the circling warplanes.

Beneath another patch of scrub Doc Lawson was crouched over the wounded in the rear of his truck, trying to shield them from prying eyes. Quiet, unassuming, unflappable, he remained in position whispering reassurance as the first Falcon dived above them, raking the ground with exploratory fire. The gods seemed to be watching over them that morning: by a seeming miracle both the injured and the truck escaped being hit.

The Falcons moved on, assuming that stretch of bush to be free of targets. Doc Lawson continued to comfort and reassure the injured, as the aero engines snarled and roared in the skies above them. Those sheltering in an adjacent patch of bush weren't so lucky. Captain Wilder, already suffering from the gash to his head, was hit. This time it was far more serious: he'd been shot through both legs. He was rushed across to Doc Lawson's truck for treatment, the medic trying to staunch the bleeding amid a hail of enemy fire.

Finally, after two hours of unleashing hell, the six aircraft peeled away. No one doubted that they'd be back. It was only a short flight to the aerodrome to re-arm and refuel.

In the temporary lull, Popski Peniakoff and Easonsmith gathered at the wounded Wilder's position. Wilder and Peniakoff gave voice to their thoughts: wouldn't it be better to make a run for it, using the guns to hit back at the slow and low-flying biplanes? Easonsmith argued against this. They might be low and slow now, while the Chevys were in cover, but the Falcons could be fast and nimble when they had need to be. If the patrol showed themselves, the enemy pilots could lurk at altitude, beyond the reach of their vehicle-mounted machine guns, hunting down the Chevys one by one with their bombs. It was better to remain where they were, in the cover of the low-hanging trees, and to wait out the storm.

Twenty minutes after the first attack a second wave of Falcons arrived overhead. The murderous diving and strafing recommenced. Men dodged from truck to truck, desperately trying to salvage water and fuel from the onslaught. A truck trying to evade the fire pinned a trooper against a tree. He was able to yell out a warning before he was crushed, but his ribs suffered a bad bruising: more work for Doc Lawson.

There was a momentary respite when a pilot failed to pull of out his dive – perhaps he'd stalled, or suffered a mechanical failure – and slammed his Falcon into the unyielding terrain. The warplane disintegrated and burst into flames, a cloud of dark smoke fisting into the early-morning skies.

It was a moment of relief during an otherwise hellish morning. The unrelenting and tireless Doc Lawson managed to shift most of the wounded to the furthest truck, a good 500 yards or more from the circling Falcons. But with his severely lacerated stomach Parker, Wilder's gunner, couldn't be moved. Parker had to remain where he was, and Doc Lawson was determined to stick with him.

They were sheltered by a spreading olive tree, with a thick camo net slung over their vehicle. Incredibly, Parker was still conscious. He glanced up into the sky to see the faces of the enemy pilots gazing down at him through the branches, as they scoured the ground for targets. Parker felt Doc Lawson shift from side to side, as he used the bulk of his body to shield him from their gaze.

It was furnace hot and flies – damned flies – were everywhere, drawn to the scene of sweat and blood. It was mid-morning and already they'd lost several vehicles, as well as the fuel and water they carried. And they'd taken further casualties. Ahead lay the long and tortured journey across thousands of miles of hostile desert, and with every sortie by the Falcons their chances of making it were plummeting.

★   ★   ★

On the path above Sciausc beach, the injured Graham Taylor led the column of walking wounded towards the grounded MTB. It sat there like a stranded whale that had blundered onto the sands. Dawn was fully upon them now. Taylor glanced out to sea. In the gathering light the sight that met his eyes was chilling: a British destroyer was on fire, thick black smoke roiling into the sky.

One gun on the ship was still active, replying to the streams of cannon rounds that kept slamming into her superstructure. She looked crippled and helpless. Now the commandos had their answer as to what had happened to the marines of Force A – those whom the destroyers were supposed to land. Presumably they had been caught in a similarly murderous barrage of coastal fire.

Taylor turned and scanned the sea beyond Sciausc Bay itself. A few MTBs could be seen circling, stubbornly refusing to give in, but in the dawn light the shore gunners had their range now, and they were pounding the little ships.

A constant stream of warplanes was taking to the skies above Tobruk. They roared over Sciausc Bay heading directly out to sea, no doubt hunting the British warships. All at once a fighter with British markings came swooping in low over the headland. A ragged cheer went up from the commandos. Where there was one fighter there might be more.

But as the aircraft circled over their position, they realized what it really was: a captured British aircraft was being flown by a Luftwaffe pilot, and he had come to get a closer look at whatever force remained at large in Sciausc Bay. Clearly, it wasn't just the British who were fond of such deceptions. It roared away before the commandos could so much as unleash a single round in anger.

Taylor halted on a particularly steep stretch of the path. He needed to catch his breath; they all did. Some of the walking wounded seemed so utterly broken that he wondered if he could ever get them moving again. From above he heard a truck engine revving, as it prepared for departure. That had to be Trollope, putting into action his plan to charge the enemy lines with the worst of the wounded.

God bless the man.

Sure enough the wireless truck was loaded with the most seriously injured commandos and Bill Barlow was at the wheel, ready for the off. From the cab he cried out, 'Where's Trolly? And Colonel Haselden?'

Both the force commander and Trollope had made it clear they were coming with him. Someone said Haselden had gone to scout the route ahead. Then a figure appeared from the valley below. There was a force of enemy advancing along the track that Barlow intended to take, he warned. Unless they were dealt with, the truck would blunder right into them.

Buck and Russell called together the SIG. Chunky Hillman and Rohr responded instantly, dashing over from the positions where they'd been helping bolster the villa's defences. At Buck's command, the four men started a mad charge downhill towards the approaching enemy. It was growing lighter by the second, and the four tried to stick to the thickest shadows. But movement drew the enemy eye, and fire chased after them

Somehow, all four survived the charge unscathed. They spotted a lone figure ahead of them. It was Haselden, and he was taking the fight to the enemy single-handed. Facing him were ten Italian soldiers, with a machine gun that was spitting and spraying fire. Haselden was a few dozen yards away from them, replying with bursts from his tommy gun.

Buck, Russell, Hillman and Rohr took cover as the Italians turned the weapon on them. A hail of rounds kicked up dirt and rocks on all sides. Haselden used the momentary break to charge forward, his tommy gun blasting fire. Amazingly he drove the Italians back. Buck, Russell, Hillman and Rohr could hear him yelling for support. They broke cover, charging to his aid.

A figure stumbled and went down. It was Rohr. He was lying in the open, writhing with pain. Buck stopped, doubled back, grabbed Rohr and half carried and half dragged him into cover. From above he could hear Barlow revving the engine of the truck, preparing for his very own version of the Charge of the Light Brigade.

Haselden, still in the vanguard, drove the Italians

back still further. Buck yelled that they were running short on ammo. With barely a moment's hesitation Russell turned and sprinted back up the hill, aiming to fetch more rounds.

As Russell hammered uphill so the truck began to career down it, Barlow grinning maniacally at the wheel. It surged ahead on the uneven track, going at the kind of speed that such a vehicle had never been designed for over such terrain.

Up ahead Haselden saw the Italian machine-gun party swivel their weapon towards the oncoming vehicle. He broke cover, screaming his rage and with his gun spitting fire. The Italians began to break. Before the approach of this wild man the first had already started to turn and run. Their machine gun coughed once, twice, but it was too late: Barlow had forced his way through, the truck piled with wounded careering past triumphantly. Within moments it was lost to sight.

But Haselden was down.

Buck could see him lying on his front about ten yards in front of the enemy. Bullets swept over the area from all different directions. Buck wasn't even sure who it was that was firing, friend or foe. Hillman was ahead of him, crouching in some bare cover, his ammo exhausted. The portly little SIG had proved once again that he had more courage and bravery than most men could ever hope to muster.

'Colonel Haselden!' Hillman yelled. 'Colonel Haselden!'

They watched the fallen figure for any sign of

movement or response. There was none. All of a sudden, from out of nowhere the wiry figure of MacDonald came charging past. The New Zealander dashed ahead of Hillman and raced to their fallen commander. He bent to grab Haselden and throw his bloodied form over his shoulder.

As he did so a stick grenade sailed through the air. It landed on Haselden's back and exploded. MacDonald was hurled off his feet by the force of the blast. He scrabbled for some cover. His face was scorched black, yet otherwise he appeared to be unscathed.

He crawled back towards Hillman. They took one last glance in Haselden's direction. MacDonald didn't need to tell Hillman what he already knew to be true: not even Colonel Haselden, their legendary and inspirational leader, could have survived that.

Lloyd Owen felt desolate. As the pink blush of dawn illuminated the entire coastline before him, he was utterly torn. On the one hand he could see that all was not well in Tobruk: the coastal guns were laying down a fierce barrage, which meant that the best-laid plans had come to naught. By now the commandos and marines should have linked up to wreck those port defences. He could only imagine that the marines had failed to get ashore, and of Haselden's force he'd had not the slightest news.

He faced a stark choice, and in a sense he was

damned whatever he opted to do. They could press ahead with the six vehicles charged to attack the Tobruk D/F radio station, as part of a wider mission that appeared to have gone horribly wrong, but to do so would be tantamount to suicide. The hue and cry was up and his patrol would be hunted down in full daylight.

He could continue to lurk where he was, awaiting a call from Haselden, but with light was bound to come their discovery. Or he could retreat, sneaking out through the Tobruk cordon while they still had shadows in which to hide. If he returned to Sidi Rezegh – the heights from which they had first descended to the Tobruk perimeter – he might be able to raise Haselden from there.

The air above Tobruk was already thick with enemy warplanes, and Lloyd Owen reckoned it was only a matter of time before his patrol was discovered and shot to pieces. It was the most difficult decision of his life, but only he – as patrol commander – could make it. He ordered his men to withdraw.

They mounted the Chevys and moved fast, retracing their steps through enemy camps waking up to a new day. Here and there figures lit fires to brew their early morning tea. Occasionally a sentry stared at them curiously, but few if any cried out a challenge.

The patrol left the Tarmac and 'withdrew back along the same roads to Sidi Rezegh, having great difficulty in avoiding minefields and enemy posts',

Lloyd Owen would report of this dark moment. 'At Sidi Rezegh tried to contact HQ LRDG and also B Force . . .' B Force was Haselden's Commando.

At one stage an enemy fighter plane flew at fifty feet right across them. Somehow, it didn't detect anything out of the ordinary and flew on, leaving them unmolested. Despite the patrol slipping through the wire, a terrible choice had been forced on Lloyd Owen and he would be tormented by it. He had left the others to their fate, but it had been the right decision and a courageous one.

The worst thing was deserting his close friend, a man he respected and revered enormously. Since their parting the evening before he'd yet to glean any news of Colonel Haselden.

Lloyd Owen led his patrol to a position twenty miles south of Sidi Rezegh, where there was good cover. With the vehicles pulled in under thick scrub, his signaller got busy with his wireless. It seemed to take an age to raise a response and the news was far from encouraging. Indeed, Major Prendergast – the LRDG's commanding officer – seemed to know little more than Lloyd Owen.

From Cairo the Commander in Chief, Mediterranean, had sent Prendergast a desperate message, reflecting the confusion that gripped all in headquarters. It read: 'Report now time at which . . . patrols were last heard and report directly they are heard in future. This required to show us they are still alive.'

Cairo headquarters had no news of the fortunes of any of the special forces involved in tonight's mission: that included Stirling's SAS at Benghazi, Easonsmith's LRDG at Barce, Lloyd Owen's patrol, or the SOE Commando charged to take Tobruk. For all Allied high command knew, every one of those units had failed catastrophically – a fear reflected in the desperate phrase, 'show us they are still alive'.

Cairo headquarters knew that calamity had descended upon the Tobruk raiders – both land and seaborne forces. It was the full extent of that calamity that remained uncertain. A report received that morning read, 'Destroyer landings failed. Force B situation obscure. Took first objective but only 2 MTBs landed with reinforcing troops.' *Force B situation obscure*: on the morning of 14 September 1942 the fate of Haselden's Commando remained utterly unknown.

The first message received by Lloyd Owen's radio operator that morning was one of warning. Prendergast signalled: 'Inform Lloyd Owen Italian armoured cars and one Infantry Battalion leaving Bardia for Tobruk at 0900 hours today and that there are Italian Battalions in area . . . which may be moving on Mersa Sciausc. Tell him to tell Haselden.'

Of course the warning had come too late for Haselden and his Commando. In any case, no matter how hard he tried Lloyd Owen could not raise a response from the Tobruk raiders. No matter how many times they called, no one was answering.

A follow-up message from headquarters was equally disheartening. 'From Prendergast. Ask Lloyd Owen if he is in touch with Haselden and to send us a sitrep regarding his own activities and those of Force B. We have no news from Force B.'

It was a bitter irony. Prendergast was asking Lloyd Owen for news of the missing Commando, yet Lloyd Owen's entire purpose in contacting headquarters was to seek news from *them*. He sent his response. It told Prendergast the dark truth: he was 'out of touch with Force B and had withdrawn from perimeter to learn situation'.

Confusion reigned.

As the morning heat intensified and Lloyd Owen's exhausted men tried to snatch some rest, he could get no news whatsoever of his comrades' fortunes. He gazed north, tortured by his fears for the men that they had been forced to leave behind.

In the valley below the villa the two sections of Fusiliers were doing sterling work: it was their Vickers machine guns that were holding the enemy at bay.

A figure rushed up to speak to Sergeant Miller, the Fusiliers' commander. It was a red-faced and breathless Bill Barlow, and he'd been under fire all the way to their position. He'd navigated his truck into the depths of the valley, he explained, but it had finally come to grief on a treacherous stretch of track. He wanted the Fusiliers to re-site their guns so they could give cover to the wounded.

Barlow seemed resolutely cheerful. He intended to shift the wounded out of the truck with Trollope's help. Sergeant Miller knew his stuff. They were eight belts down on the Vickers, but they still had ammunition remaining. And while they had bullets they could help. He gave his orders. The teams worked feverishly, shifting guns and ammunition to cover the new objective. The Vickers roared and spat fire. The sustained barrage forced the enemy back. In the brief respite, Barlow and his fellow grabbed the wounded and came running.

A little further up the valley there was nothing more that Buck, Hillman or MacDonald could do for Haselden. He had sacrificed himself so the truck loaded with wounded could break out. The Spandau gunners were still in place, and enemy reinforcements were streaming in. Buck, Hillman and MacDonald grabbed the wounded Rohr and headed in the only direction left open to them, downhill towards the beach.

As they staggered along the path, they were glad of the bursts of covering fire coming up from the cove. Russell had made a dash for the MTB, and he'd got its deck-mounted twin Brownings working. The Flying Scotsman was raking the wadi where Haselden had fallen with long bursts of fire.

Down in the bowels of the ship Tommy Langton was also busy. There had been little point remaining

341

at his post, desperately signalling seawards. No more little ships were coming in, that much was clear. Russell had told him that Haselden was dead, and that the walking wounded were en route to the beach. Taylor had a mind now only to determine how they might all escape.

He'd collared a commando who wore a sailor's cap, in the hope that the man might have an idea how to get the MTB's engines running. They crouched over the gleaming twin motors.

The sailor fiddled with a few of the complicated-looking switches and dials. He scratched his head. 'I'm a mechanic, but I'm damned if I can fathom that lot out!'

Above them the Brownings ceased fire. Langton went to investigate. He found David Sillito and Russell deep in conversation. It seemed that Graham Taylor and the rest of the walking wounded were stranded on the path up above them, exhausted and unable to go on. It didn't matter a damn if they could get the boat moving; the wounded were never going to make it.

The situation appeared utterly dark.

Even Lieutenant Sillito – the recklessly brave Argyll and Sutherland Highlander – had realized how dire things had become. Knowing how much the enemy hated the kilted Scots – 'the ladies from hell' – he'd exchanged his Argyll kilt for a pair of shorts that he'd found somewhere.

He would fight to the bitter end, but there was little point in making himself a marked man.

CHAPTER 22

Generalmajor Deindl was suffering no such uncertainty and confusion as that which assailed the Allied high command. In fact, by now he knew *everything*: in the war-torn bays around Tobruk harbour his men had just made a truly remarkable discovery.

A few score marines had managed to make it off the destroyer *Sikh* before she started taking murderous fire. In flimsy lighters – barely seaworthy landing craft, which had been cobbled together in Alexandria – they had struggled bravely in towards the beaches. But their numbers, once mustered, were pitifully small.

Of the hundreds of marines scheduled to reach Tobruk, only a fraction had made landfall, losing much of their weaponry and supplies when their boats were swamped in the choppy seas or dashed to pieces on the rocks. The marines had nicknamed the lighters floating coffins. Sure enough, many had been forced to swim for it and some hadn't made it at all. But a few of the flimsy craft had been beached, and reports concerning the landings reached Generalmajor Deindl's ears.

Already, they were sounding a triumphant note. 'The attack by the English . . . has been shattered. Over 75 enemy troops and 5 landing craft destroyed, and with them the threat of invasion is lifted.'

Deindl was taking no chances, however. At 0743 he signalled: '*Landealarm* is still to be maintained.' A phalanx of German soldiers cut along the beaches, as the surviving marines tried to fight their way inland. Some of the landing craft were captured. One was found to contain a folder stuffed full of the entire Tobruk assault plans. The papers were rushed into Deindl's eager hands. Now he knew it all.

The captured papers even included an address that was supposed to be delivered to the Arab population of Tobruk once the British forces had seized it. How presumptuous that had been. But of more use to Deindl were the detailed outlines of the plan of attack: timings, numbers of assault craft, routes, positions, and the individual units involved. From this, he could direct his forces to pinpoint targets.

Deindl ordered his warplanes into action: they were to conduct aerial searches over the exact locations where the British forces were supposed to be, tracking down any who still had fight in them. Aircraft were also to scour the seas off Tobruk, searching for the Royal Navy armada that the papers revealed in all their exacting detail.

It was time to finish this: remorselessly, tirelessly, they would hunt the British enemy down.

★ ★ ★

Haselden may have given the order 'every man for himself', but you'd never have thought it with the battle now raging at the villa headquarters. Having seized their slice of Tobruk in an audacious and dashing bluff, the SOE commandos weren't about to give it up so easily. A small band had gathered, determined to hold out to the very last.

Meanwhile Pilot Officer Scott had finally abandoned his lonely position on the cliff face: there was no point in signalling with the Aldis any more. Only one place made any sense to head for: the villa headquarters, which resounded with the crack and thump of battle. He wished he'd abandoned his post earlier, for the headland was being swept with small arms and machine-gun fire.

He began his sprint towards the villa. As he ducked among the boulders and sparse cover, bullets ricocheted with spine-chilling screams from the rocks all around him. He kept pushing ahead, dodging from one patch of bush to another. It was terrifying, but he had to rejoin what was left of the Commando. It was fully light by now, and he regretted not having made a run when darkness still cloaked the terrain.

His had been a long and lonely vigil, one fraught with frustration and disappointment. All that signalling and only two MTBs had made it. He craved the companionship of fellow soldiers. If he was to die, he wanted to do so in the company of like-minded souls.

He paused for a moment as a sleek grey form

slid quietly into the bay below. It was an E-boat – the nearest German equivalent to the MTB. No sooner had it made the shelter of Sciausc cove than it opened up with its three 20-millimetre cannons, raking the eastern walls of the wadi with fire. Figures ran from the onslaught, and even from this distance Scott could tell that they were German troops. The E-boat had mistakenly opened fire on its own side. After a few sustained bursts, it withdrew again: presumably there was better hunting out to sea.

Scott spotted a group of commandos in a position between him and the villa. They seemed within his reach. He made a last, lung-bursting surge, bullets tearing at his heels. Gasping for breath he vaulted in beside the commandos without suffering a scratch.

A soldier turned towards him. 'Dunno how the devil you got across there,' he remarked incredulously. 'They were all firing at you, you know.'

Scott couldn't understand how he'd made it either. But he was among friends again, which was all that mattered now. He grabbed his weapon and began to search for the enemy. It was time to return some of that fire.

Lieutenant Mike Roberts had led an equally death-defying run for the villa headquarters from the eastern side of the bay. The force he was leading included the wounded Major Campbell. Still resplendent in his hodden tartan, the injured commander was ensconced in the villa's sickbay now.

Campbell's surviving commandos had brought with them sixteen Italian prisoners, who had been bundled into a shallow ditch on the north side of the villa. By rights, that should be the safest place right now, on the furthest side from the encircling German and Italian forces. Even so, they were lying on their faces in that ditch, trying to shelter from the bullets and grenades unleashed by their comrades.

Pilot Officer Scott ran his eye around his new position. The enemy were massing in a wide arc west-south-east. He could see their forms slipping from cover to cover as they crept ever closer. Fire pulsed in from their positions, pulverising the walls of the villa, from which chunks of masonry and rock flew in all directions.

They had brought up a mortar platoon. Shells tore into the dirt and scrub all around the building, as the enemy gunners began to find their range and their aim. But under SSM Swinburn's direction, the tommy guns of the Commando answered them, blazing away in glorious defiance.

John Poynton and Swinburn lay side by side behind one of the villa's sandbagged defences. They saw a mass of enemy troops rise as one and rush their position. Swinburn called for every gun to be brought to bear, and the wave of enemy soldiers faltered and broke under the onslaught. For a brief moment the fire slackened.

Poynton figured they couldn't survive many more such assaults. Part of the problem was their position. The enemy was getting around both their flanks, and they were being hit by machine-gun fire from all sides. What they needed was to fall back to a vantage point from which to pour down fire onto the enemy. Poynton cast about for such a position. He spied a ridge to the rear of the villa: that would do nicely.

Poynton told Swinburn what he intended. He'd take a party of troops and take the ridge. Swinburn and the main force would need to give them covering fire, after which they would swap roles – Poynton's men providing cover as Swinburn led the main force after. They'd regroup on the ridge and take things from there.

Poynton called to his men – his fellow gunners, those who had manned and then helped destroy the captured shore defences – to follow his lead. They signalled they were ready. As Poynton leaped to his feet to lead the charge, he could hear the heavy thump of tommy guns hammering out covering fire.

Quite by accident his route led him right over the trench in which the Italian prisoners were hiding. As one they broke and ran. All of a sudden Italians and British were charging up the hill, side by side. Incoming fire slackened as the Italian attackers realized they were shooting at their own men. Poynton seized the moment, running behind the prisoners, shouting and yelling and kicking them forward.

Up the hill and over the top they charged,

Poynton and his force diving into cover, not a man among them seeming to have been hit. As they readied their weapons, a savage burst of Breda cannon fire stitched an arc across the high ground, and Poynton saw the Italian prisoners take to their heels. He decided to let them go: quite possibly they'd saved the lives of all the British soldiers now manning that ridgeline.

Poynton managed to grab a glance downwards. He saw Swinburn, his giant frame crouched beside the villa's sandbagged defences, waving his arms above his head in an X. The meaning was clear: his force could not follow. A second wave would never make it across that open ground, especially without those Italian prisoners to shield them.

Mortar rounds slammed into the ridge, tearing apart the earth and hurling debris into the air. No way could Poynton and his force hold their position here for long.

'We've got to keep moving,' he yelled.

He glanced into the valley, along the path that the injured Graham Taylor had taken the walking wounded. He could just make out the form of the MTB. Maybe down there was some promise of respite. Yelling at his men to follow, he led a mad dash for the path leading to the beach below.

Fire swept the open ground. Two men among his party fell and didn't get up again. Several more were wounded. Poynton reached the path and began the scramble down. The MTB drew him to it. He saw troops milling about: more of the Commando heading for the beach.

He raced towards them. Too late he noticed the German helmets. There were scores of the enemy. Two dozen Schmeissers were levelled in his direction. The time to turn and run was long past. Low on ammunition, exhausted and burdened by wounded, he realized this was the end.

Poynton and his men raised their hands.

Below them in the cove the sleek grey form of an E-boat nosed into shore. This one carried a force of German soldiers. Clean, fresh-shaven and not so long from sleep, they leaped onto the beach. The sun was well up now. The light was golden, beaming down hot and glorious on a new day. It didn't feel so wonderful to those men who were sheltering up the beach in one of the caves.

The walking wounded had finally made it down to the beach, only to discover the MTB was still stuck fast. They'd taken refuge in the shadows of a cave. There, Graham Taylor clutched at his chest wound while drawing his revolver. Further back in the shadows lay the rest of the injured.

He glanced in the direction of the newly arrived German troops, who were forming up on the beach. 'Well, this is it. I suppose we'll have to fight it out here.'

Doc Gibson unleashed a salty burst of Canadian invective, grabbed Taylor's pistol and prised it from his grasp. He gestured at the sorry state of the occupants of the cave. The time for fighting was over, he told Taylor. These men didn't need to fight; they needed urgent medical attention. Reluctantly, Taylor accepted that Doc Gibson was right: surrender never came easily to such a man.

With his Red Cross satchel held prominently before him, Doc Gibson stepped out of the cave. The German troops rushed towards him. He was struck by their youth and by how clean and fresh they looked. By contrast, the bloodied and bandaged commandos resembled a band of piratical desperadoes.

He was shocked too at the Germans' reaction. They actually seemed to want to rally round the wounded British troops. Grasping the situation within seconds, the Germans helped the commandos to board the E-boat. Food and drink were conjured out of nowhere as the injured men were laid on the decks.

Graham Taylor required a stretcher to make the E-boat: the superhuman efforts of the last few hours had finished him. As he was carried across to the waiting craft, he could hear remarks addressed to him in broken English. The German troops were delighted at how the commandos had routed their Italian comrades. An atmosphere close to hysteria had broken out among the Italian defenders, and the Germans liked nothing more than to see their Axis allies humbled. They were taking huge pleasure from their discomfiture.

They assured Taylor that in spite of his seeping

chest wound he would survive with the benefit of German medical aid. As he was loaded aboard the E-boat, he could hear the pounding crack and thump of gunfire above him on the headland. At the villa the commandos were fighting on.

In spite of everything, he wished that he were with them.

At the battered and bullet-scarred villa, the commandos were resisting to the last, because resistance was what they knew and it was what they had come here to do. And they were not alone. From across the far side of the harbour the faint drift of small-arms fire reached them on the early-morning breeze: some of the marines at least had got ashore, and they too were fighting. Their fire was lessening, suggesting that their resistance was faltering, but those who could battled on. God bless them.

The sun was higher in the sky now. It bore down upon men who had had no shade or rest, and little water or food, for many hours. The sea beyond the headland stretched blue to the horizon, but it was deceptively placid. Out there equally deadly duels were being fought, as British warships attempted to repulse the warplanes sent after them.

While they had bullets in their guns the men at the villa would fight. They were commandos; they would battle on. Plus something else drove them on. The majority of the attackers were

Italians, and after the night of bloodshed on that headland, they felt certain the Italians would take their revenge in horrific ways.

The attackers fought with surprising tenacity and bravery. They were marines of the San Marco Battalion, one of the prisoners had revealed, an elite unit not dissimilar to the British commandos. In all directions the ground seemed alive with enemy troops, crawling, ever crawling, towards their isolated villa redoubt.

There was no way out.

Earlier that morning there had been a moment when they had believed themselves saved. They'd spotted a line of troops advancing from Tobruk harbour, moving purposefully in their direction. The strict discipline of that line, its very professionalism, had made them believe it must be British marines coming to their rescue. The first of the commandos had got to his feet, cheering. The answer was the ferocious death rattle of a Spandau. The line was made up of German troops.

Swinburn had split his force now, with eight men manning the sandbagged positions at the villa, and another group of similar size in an adjacent bunker, sandwiched between two metal sheds. That was their defensive line. And the line held. The men here felt certain that they were going to die. They fought for the man at their shoulder and for the chance to breathe a little more of the oxygen of life. It was never so precious as when it was about to be taken away.

The handful who fought found the nearness of death strangely exhilarating. The adrenaline was pumping; doubtless, it was all that was keeping them going. They laughed and joked as they crawled across one another in the cramped space, lighting the occasional cigarette for each other, before opening fire.

Someone remarked to his mates, 'You know what? This is better than bleedin' Butlins!'

Everyone laughed. They all got it.

The enemy crept closer. The commandos tried hurling grenades to drive them back, but the bombs couldn't clear the ridge that divided them from their attackers. One or two of the grenades rolled back and exploded near the villa's defences. That felt far too much like getting one's own back with interest and they stopped throwing the grenades.

Then SSM Swinburn had a flash of inspiration. It was a crazy idea, but nowhere near as mad as their present situation. He explained what he intended to one of his fellows. As they lay together in cover, that man held open the neck of an empty sandbag while Swinburn swiftly drew the pins from two grenades and dropped them inside.

An instant later Swinburn was on his feet, whirling the sandbag around his head. He let fly and it sailed over the ridge, exploding before it even hit the ground. The weighted bag had given him the extra range he needed. By rights, Swinburn shouldn't have survived that first attempt, or the next. Or the several more times that he repeated the slingshot exercise, as fire cut the air all around him.

Swinburn's sacks of grenades blasted their way along the ridge. The commandos let out a ragged cheer. Swinburn's exploits lifted their spirits greatly. There could only be one end to the heroic struggle under way here. But like the Spartans at Thermopylae, why would they ever seek to hasten their end?

A burst of heavy fire raked the villa's sandbagged bunker from end to end. A machine-gun crew had got themselves set up on a vantage point. Unless they could be dealt with, Swinburn's die-hards were done for. Again, the SSM seized the moment. He got to his knees, braced a Bren gun against his hip and let rip with a scything burst right down the throat of the enemy gunners.

Swinburn should have been dead many times over, but when he dived back down into cover somehow he remained unscathed.

The enemy machine gunners ceased firing. Swinburn's calm ferocity and quiet fearlessness were extraordinary to see. If he was worried about taking a bullet there was little sign of it. He was an inspiration to those who fought beside him, and because he showed no fear he inspired others to act likewise. Courage proved contagious, even in the face of overwhelming numbers.

Finally, the villa was overrun.

The defenders fell back to the bunker lying

between the two sheds. Still they would not give up. A German mortar team switched their attention to that last patch of resistance. A round crashed through the roof of the shed to one side of the bunker, ripping it to shreds. Another detonated on the opposite side of the sandbagged wall. A couple of feet either way and everyone inside the bunker would have been annihilated.

The enemy were close now. A German stick grenade came tumbling through the air, lazily, end over end. It landed against one of the men's feet. He couldn't move because he was sandwiched under a press of bodies. He closed his eyes and waited to die.

The grenade exploded. The soldier opened his eyes again. Somehow he still had his left leg and foot. No one else seemed hurt. It was unbelievable, but they had all witnessed the seemingly impossible happen with explosives before. Swinburn asked how much ammunition each man had remaining. The answer was dispiriting: no more than one or two rounds to each of them.

Everyone was looking at Swinburn now. Their heavily bearded faces were bathed in sweat, streaked with cordite burns and dirt and blood. For a moment Swinburn was reminded of the first time he had laid eyes on what he'd then seen as the ruffians of the LRDG.

Like those desert wanderers, these were some of the very finest warriors alongside whom a man could ever wish to serve.

CHAPTER 23

Just about every tree and clump of bushes had been strafed by the circling Falcons, which made it all the more remarkable that Jake Easonsmith's patrol had suffered so few casualties. But their position was utterly dire. Easonsmith had started out with seventeen vehicles, and of those only two Chevys and two jeeps had escaped destruction. More to the point, they still had an epic desert crossing ahead of them.

When the last of the Falcons seemed to have given up the hunt, he ordered whatever food, fuel and water could be saved to be loaded aboard one of the two usable Chevys. The other would be used to carry those with the worst injuries. Everyone else would need to move on foot, walking wounded included.

They were readying themselves for the off when a pair of Falcons dived out of the heavens unexpectedly. Their single propellers and 12.7mm Breda cannons were pointed directly at the Chevy piled high with stores. Bodies dived for cover as the fighters opened fire. The vehicle shook from end to end as long blasts tore into it. Within seconds it had been reduced to a burning heap of wreckage.

Figures dashed about, trying to save whatever precious fuel and water they could, but the heat proved too intense and they were driven back. The pair of Falcons zipped away, leaving the men to take stock: they had one truck remaining, loaded with the wounded, and two surviving jeeps, one of which had taken hits but was still mobile.

They were thirty-three, all told, and ahead lay a journey of well over 600 miles just to reach the sanctuary of the Kufra oasis. They would be heading into the wilderness of the desert woefully ill prepared, burdened by the wounded and still hunted by the enemy. It seemed beyond all possible limits of human endurance. It seemed crazy even to attempt it. But that was not the mindset of the desert warriors.

Easonsmith drew up roll calls for what he termed the driving and the walking parties. Those in the walking party packed whatever they could carry. The column was to stick together, moving at the pace of the slowest: that way, they would all have the benefit of the meagre rations now stored on the vehicles.

Doc Lawson would ride with the worst of the wounded in the one surviving Chevy, for they would need tending to. His party included Parker (shot through the guts), Wilder (shot through both legs), Popski Peniakoff (with a missing finger and knee full of shrapnel) and three other severely injured.

A jeep would travel with them and the wounded Peniakoff volunteered to drive it.

Frank Jopling – Wilder's navigator – would lead a walking party of nine, despite having been shot in the leg during that morning's ambush. Easonsmith would lead the rest of the men, accompanied by the other jeep, which was piled high with supplies and tommy guns.

Perhaps fittingly, the one surviving Chevy was *Te Anau II*, one of those that had spearheaded the Barce airfield raid, and which had rescued Wilder and Parker when their jeep had overturned.

There was one glimmer of light on an otherwise impossibly dark horizon: Bir El Gerrari. At this isolated outpost lying sixty miles south in the desert the patrol had had the foresight to leave one vehicle, packed full of water, fuel and supplies. It had been placed there, well hidden, for just such an eventuality. This was their initial objective. If they could reach it, the truck at Bir El Gerrari might be their salvation.

Doc Lawson flapped the buzzing swarms of flies away from bloodied bandages. Flies. Bloody flies. They were everywhere, especially around his wounded. And flies carried infections. He proceeded to give Parker, Wilder and the other severely injured a shot of morphine. It was to help them deal with the pain of what lay before them. Without it, every jolt of *Te Anau II* would prove unbearable agony.

That done, they set off into the bush.

They were not long into the trek when the first trouble hit. The jeep that had been partly shot up was in the lead, with the other vehicles following. It had a holed fuel tank, and the driver had to keep stopping to top up the petrol. Then it blew a tyre. It was clearly beyond salvation, so a time bomb was set and the vehicle abandoned.

They were now down to the trusty *Te Anau II*, plus the one jeep, with thirty-three men, many of whom were injured. As they set off once more, it was difficult to see how any of the Barce raiders would ever make it home.

Swinburn glanced from face to face. He smiled, a rare thing for the big sergeant. 'All right, lads, that's enough, eh. Let's pack it in now.'

With no ammuntion remaining the last of the villa's defenders had nothing left to fight with. Just like that, it was over.

On Swinburn's word, those who remained laid down their weapons. With their ammo exhausted, they were next to useless anyway. They crouched in cover, wondering what horrors would unfold once their attackers got hold of them.

Swinburn rolled over and proceeded to remove his shirt. It was very far from white, but it was the best that he could manage. He stood up, the shirt held aloft in surrender. A hail of gunfire met his gesture. He kept waving the shirt back and forth as the bullets slammed into the sandbags to left and right.

Eventually the firing petered out. The last echoes of gunfire died away, to be replaced by an unearthly, ringing void of silence. They had been fighting for close to fourteen hours now. Gunfire had become the backdrop and the baseline to their existence. And now it had stopped. It was somehow so ominous and eerie.

Wearied beyond belief the figures beside Swinburn clambered to their feet. Slowly, painfully, they raised their arms above their heads. At first there was no sign of movement amid the rocky terrain, and then the first uniformed figure showed himself. Another and another followed, as soldiers popped their heads out of cover, wondering at last if the British had finally surrendered.

When it was understood that they had, the trickle became a flood. From every direction figures rose from the ground and began to run. The first blood-thirsty screams and cries of abuse reached the commandos' ears. The Italians' faces were contorted by hatred and a wild, bloodthirsty fury.

The commandos bunched closer instinctively, but there was clearly going to be no defence against such a screaming horde. Yet a surprising figure was first to reach them. He was a big, fit-looking German officer. Even though the commandos could see that he was wounded, his first words all but bowled them over, so unexpected were their sentiments.

In near-perfect English the officer announced, 'It was a very good fight. Congratulations.'

Swinburn gave a slow nod. It had been a good fight for sure.

But behind the German came the screaming hordes of Italians. It was clear that they felt very differently. They came crowding in, faces distorted with rage. One smashed a blow across Swinburn's face. He just took it, standing there in mute defiance as the blood trickled from the corner of his mouth.

The Italians were yelling for revenge: these were the men who had slaughtered their comrades in the night. They gripped guns and bayonets as they jostled and fought with each other to be the first to get at a commando. The circle of vengeance closed, as Swinburn and his men readied themselves for the very last fight of their lives.

But just as the Italians were about to grab their first victim, a column of German troops pushed through the throng. They threw a protective line around Swinburn and his men – the few – yelling at their Italian comrades to back away. Every time the crowd surged forward, the German troops shoved them back again.

The inconceivable had become reality: the commandos were being protected by men who moments before had been their mortal enemies. For an hour or more the face-off continued, as Italian soldiers tried to break through and German soldiers forced them back.

At times the Italians looked poised to triumph. At others the Germans appeared utterly implacable.

Yet to Swinburn and his men, quite suddenly it didn't seem to matter any more. They were so utterly finished, they no longer had the energy to worry whether they lived or died. All they wanted was water and the chance to rest.

They slumped onto the nearest rocks, encircled by Germans, hands resting on their heads and eyes closed. Surely the Italians would win this battle eventually. They outnumbered the Germans many times over. Swinburn and his men waited for death to come, hoping it might be mercifully swift.

Gradually the Germans gained the upper hand. In time the Italians seemed to grow tired of the struggle and their bloodlust dissipated. It was replaced by a sullen, hostile acceptance that the commandos were not going to die, at least not today. The German soldiers crowded closer around Swinburn and his men. It was around midday, and it looked as if the little knot of men was going to live.

One of the German officers told them that they would need to move into Tobruk as quickly as possible. There was no transport available, so in spite of their obvious exhaustion they would have to walk. And so an odd procession set off: Swinburn and his men encircled by a protective ring of Germans, as the Italian soldiers milled about angrily and yelled their final words of abuse.

The walk was only a few miles, but it felt like a trek of epic proportions, especially as several of the men were wounded. It was also a walk plagued with the knowledge of defeat and dark worries about what might lie in the future.

The fighting at Sciausc Bay was over, but in the isolated ravines and wadis that surrounded the cove resistance was not.

On a landing craft salvaged from an MTB, Tommy Langton, Russell and several others paddled east along the shoreline in a desperate effort to escape. Bullets spat into the water, but still they managed to make landfall at an isolated ravine.

From there, they hoped to make for the hills and somehow break out of the Tobruk cordon. Their only hope of salvation had to lie in the open desert. Though exhausted from the night's combat, they climbed steadily, laboriously wending their way onto the higher ground and sticking to cover. They reached a ridge with a view into another ravine stretching inland.

Down in the bottom was a group of figures – more of their own men, as intent as they were on breaking out. Just as Langton and Russell went to descend into the valley, the enemy spotted the fleeing commandos. They raced down helter-skelter, as a hail of gunfire kicked up sand and dirt around their feet.

They reached the other party unscathed. It consisted of Big Bill Barlow, along with David Sillito and MacDonald, plus some twenty others. Though many were wounded, they'd broken out of the enemy lines encircling Sciausc Bay. They confirmed how Haselden had died. When MacDonald had run forward to rescue him, he'd believed him only wounded. It was the grenade that had finished Haselden off.

Their conference on the floor of that ravine was hurried and fraught. One thing was clear: they were painfully short of food, water and ammunition. They decided to push on as one party, climbing inland. Once they found a good place to hide they'd lie up for the day. Come night, they'd split into smaller parties, each officer leading two or three men, to try to break through the Tobruk perimeter.

They were all 'weary and broken in spirit', Langton remarked. 'We climbed up the wadi and onto the high ground and each hid himself as best he could. Barlow and I found a small cave and at once lay down to sleep fitfully . . . When we woke there were aeroplanes circling overhead, searching.'

The situation was dire. 'It was pretty grim,' Langton's account continued. 'We were more than 300 miles from our own lines, with nothing but desert and the enemy in between. At the moment we were trapped like rats, inside the perimeter defences of Tobruk.'

In hushed whispers, he and Barlow discussed how they might try to breach the perimeter.

'There's a lot of barbed wire,' Langton told Barlow. 'It'll be heavily manned and more than likely mined.'

Barlow nodded, gloomily. 'What's more they'll shoot us if they find us, which they're sure to do one way or another.' Now the fighting was over, he seemed uncharacteristically subdued.

The two men tried to distract themselves from their morbid thoughts by reminiscing about life back home. They were both keen rowers. They tried to bring to mind the Henley Regatta – the Mecca of the sport – but it seemed so distant and otherworldly. Right now their dark reality was hard rock, relentless sun, diving warplanes and the terror of being hunted at every turn.

Come nightfall, the little groups set off into the darkness. Bill Barlow led one party of three. Russell took another. David Sillito led a third, and MacDonald a fourth. They moved out at five-minute intervals. Some decided to head for the coast, seeking to link up with Royal Navy search patrols. Langton and Russell argued that was suicide. The shoreline would be scoured end to end, as the enemy watched like hawks. The only hope of safety lay inland: into the desert.

Langton's party was the last to leave. He had with him one of the surviving commandos, a private from the Fusiliers, plus Chunky Hillman of the SIG. In single file and moving in silence they scaled ridge after ridge, pushing inland. It was punishing going. At one stage a voice challenged them in Italian. Langton ignored it but the cry came again from the darkness, more threatening this time.

'*Deutches Mobilisches!*' Langton shouted back at him. It didn't matter how garbled was his German, for these were clearly Italian troops.

Still the challenger seemed suspicious. He cried out another challenge. When Langton didn't answer a shot followed; warning rounds unleashed above their heads.

'*Schiesse nicht!*' Langton yelled, as if angry. '*Schiesse nicht!*'

His German was awful, but it was the best he could manage. The Italian clearly didn't buy it. He fired again, this time in the direction of Langton's voice. The shots went wide and Langton dashed on for another hundred yards. He waited for the others to catch up. Hillman was the last and he didn't look very happy.

'You shouldn't have tried to talk German like that!' he objected.

Langton thought he was being sarcastic about his terrible German language skills. He wasn't. Hillman was simply desperate to hide all clues as to his real identity, in case he was captured.

'Well, why can't you keep up?' Langton retorted.

Hillman pointed to his right boot. The sole was torn half away and his foot was bleeding. He'd injured it trying to scale some barbed wire. Langton passed him a handkerchief and told him to bind the sole tightly to the boot's upper. He needed to keep up. It was crucial for when they came to try to cross the perimeter.

A little later they stumbled into four figures. It

was Bill Barlow and his little band of escapees. They decided to join forces for the attempt to cross the perimeter. Strength in numbers – if nothing else it was good for morale. They pushed ahead as one band, but all of a sudden there was a burst of machine-gun fire followed by grenades. The explosions tore apart the night.

Langton led the band into a narrow ravine, and they went to ground amid some thorn bushes. Whispers in the dark revealed that all were present save big Bill Barlow. No amount of searching or hushed calls of 'Bill! Bill!' could raise any kind of response. They waited for ten minutes, hoping he would appear, but no joy.

Finally, Langton decided they had to push on.

After a hundred yards he tumbled into a ditch in the darkness. It was a clean-cut tank trap, and he realized they must be on the very perimeter. The machine-gun nest must have been part of its defences. Langton signalled for the others to take cover in the ditch and he crawled on alone to check the way. He clambered out of the ditch into an entanglement of barbed wire.

He hissed to the rest to follow. Each would have to help the other. Prising apart the cruel strands and getting lacerated on the barbs, they braced themselves for the fire they felt sure would nail them on the wire. But instead, with torn and bloodied clothes, they scrambled through.

Langton and his war-ravaged band had broken free of the Tobruk perimeter.

They staggered on for another few hundred yards, exhausted, parched with thirst and desperate to find shelter. Langton stumbled upon a deserted bunker. They crawled inside before collapsing in a heap, seven bloodied figures trying to recover their breath and their spirits.

Langton glanced back the way they had come. He saw a line of lights that seemed to dance and shift in the thick darkness. He imagined a column of enemy troops with lamps, searching for him and his party. The lights were slowly advancing, but Langton was too finished to move.

Finally he realized the lights were passing the bunker by. He and his men weren't being hunted at all; it was simply a column of vehicles moving along the coastal road towards Tobruk.

The seven men took stock of their situation. Unfortunately, Barlow had been carrying what meagre rations the party had with them. That was all lost now. Between seven men they had one small tin of sweets, one bar of chocolate, four biscuits, a few squares of cheese and barely four pints of water. All were parched, famished and exhausted, and daylight couldn't be more than an hour away.

Langton tried to inspire the confidence and spirit in the men he was far from feeling himself. They got moving again. Just as it was getting light they found a small cave – little more than a shadowed overhang. The seven wedged themselves inside and prepared to wait out another blisteringly hot day.

A little further along the perimeter Russell – the Flying Scotsman – had also sneaked through the wire with his force of three. And Captain Henry Cecil Buck was also attempting his own breakout. A die-hard believer in the SIG's holy trinity of deception, bluff and trickery, he knew that it was no fault of theirs that the raid on Tobruk had failed. Their part in it had been played to perfection.

Indeed, Buck was convinced the deception that had got so many in could get a few good men out again. He set out heading *into* Tobruk, taking those who were willing with him. He intended to ride out of the enemy fortress in style. On the road ahead was an Italian camp. He planned to walk in the front gate, grab a truck and plenty of supplies, and drive off into the open desert in the pilfered vehicle.

He had with him the injured Rohr – one of the walking wounded – plus another member of the SIG and a handful of commandos, survivors from Major Campbell's assault force. Together, they struck inland making for the Italian encampment and the tantalising prospect of escape.

As he turned his back on Sciausc Bay, once more Captain Henry Cecil Buck was making for hostile lines dressed in the uniform of the enemy.

EPILOGUE

The stories of those who escaped from the raid on Tobruk are worthy of a book in themselves.

On Friday 13 November 1942, Lieutenant Tommy Langton made it back to British lines. He had with him some of those who'd crossed the Tobruk perimeter in his company, including Chunky Hillman of the SIG, who was still nursing his injured foot. It had taken them fully two months to make it back to Allied lines, a herculean task by anyone's reckoning.

Langton and his escape party had spent days moving only at night, and begging food from Arab villagers. They dodged enemy patrols, air attacks and the occasional hostile or treacherous locals. At one point they holed up with fellow escapees in a seaside cave, surviving off bony, indigestible fish for weeks on end, and getting bombed by Allied warplanes, who mistook them for the enemy.

Hillman – just nineteen years old – felt certain that the Germans would know his real name, due to the treachery they'd suffered at the hands of Bruckner, the Afrika Korps veteran who had trained the SIG. Accordingly he had everyone in Langton's little escape group address him as Kennedy. 'The Jerries knew his name, so we changed it in case he got caught,' Langton would remark of their escape. 'He'll always be known as Ken to us.'

Through no fault of his own Langton lost escapees along the way, mostly through dysentery, which plagued his small party and made many of them too weak to continue. Those who could not go on walked off alone to the coastal road, to get picked up by an enemy patrol. 'A tall, strong fellow as a rule,' Langton would write of one, 'he looked like a haggard old man when he left us.'

After several weeks Langton ended up with just three, including Hillman, who stubbornly refused to give up despite his injury. As they set off on their final push towards the Allied lines Langton and his party carried with them a map, several cans of bully beef, some goat meat and ten bottles of water. They pushed through a desert moonscape contorted by the recent fighting and littered with war debris.

They scavenged discarded food left by those who had perished and drank water from the radiators of abandoned vehicles, which was polluted with dirt and debris. Langton's notes from the time reflect the tortured nature of their existence: 'Thirst. Water (Petrol. Rat. Salt. Sand.) . . . Gradual change from physical to mental deterioration. Mental strain . . . But our amazing luck relieves . . . Our feast in the tank.'

In such a way they finally made contact with an Allied unit, at Himeimat, some thirty miles south of El Alamein. It was exactly two months since the fateful raid on Tobruk and the four escapees had covered some 375 miles on foot, moving through heavily occupied enemy territory and sun-blasted desert terrain.

Langton was awarded a MC for his role in the raid and subsequent escape. The citation reads:

> Lieut T. B. Langton was in command of a detachment of the S.B.S. which accompanied the land party to Tobruk on Sep 13th . . . The land attack was almost successful and two landing craft made for the shore . . .
>
> At dawn, when the raid had failed in its purpose, Lieut Langton collected all the men he could find and refused to give himself up even though he was within the perimeter of an enemy garrison. His very great courage and personal spirit enabled him to bring his party safely back to our own lines almost 350 miles to the east, even though they were often short of food and water during their walk of two months.

Following his almost superhuman endeavour Langton spent some time recuperating, before going on to command HQ Squadron of 21 SAS at D Day and to the end of the war. After the war he went to join his father, working as a Lloyd's underwriter, and he continued playing rugby and rowing with vigour. He had a distinguished business career, and also became involved in politics, standing as an MP.

His life is perhaps best summed up by his Jesus College Boat Club History entry: 'T. B. Langton, twice Head of the River, twice a rowing blue and President of the C.U.B.C., was the hero of an epic escape across the African Desert to Alamein.'

Hillman was also awarded a Military Cross for his part in the Tobruk raid and escape. His citation, which was penned personally by Lieutenant Langton, lists him simply as a member of the SAS Regiment.

> During the nine weeks during which we endeavoured to get back to our lines, Hillman showed courage, endurance and cheerfulness which was a great example to the rest of us. This despite the fact that the soles of his boots were torn off during the action and he tore his feet badly on the barbed wire . . . causing sores which were still open when he reached hospital nine weeks later.
>
> 'Whenever enemy positions were encountered Hillman showed the greatest calmness and courage. He was entirely responsible for persuading the Arabs to give us food etc. I have no hesitation in saying that without his example and help we would

have had very little chance of escaping successfully.

Hillman's MC citation ends with a note in parenthesis: 'No details of the above operations may be published owing to their secrecy and that fact that Pte Hillman was dressed in German uniform.'

Hillman went on to have a distinguished combat record with the SAS, winning a Military Medal the hard way, on missions behind the lines. He remained serving with the British army long into the fifties, where he was a popular character renowned for his somewhat 'crazed' sense of humour.

Five days after Langton and Hillman's extraordinary escape, Lieutenant David Russell also made it back to British lines. He was recommended for an immediate Military Cross, and his citation best records the extraordinary nature of his sojourn.

> This officer took part in a raid on Tobruk dressed as a German officer on 13 Sep 42. He exhibited great bravery and complete disregard for his own personal safety . . . by repeatedly organizing the Command Post against enemy attacks . . . When the Post was surrounded by the enemy and the commander ordered a withdrawal, Lt Russell put the wounded in the truck under heavy fire, and led a counter-attack to enable the party in the truck to withdraw successfully.

Later, he was responsible for arranging the escape of two officers and eight O.R.s from Tobruk.

His own escape was eventually carried out in face of enemy opposition and under extreme hardship; in one instance Lt Russell walked through two Battalions of Italian infantry. After hiding . . . he was finally picked up . . . on 18 Nov 42.

In circumstances of extreme danger and difficulty this officer displayed the highest courage, endurance and devotion to duty.

Opprower of the SIG had slipped through the Tobruk perimeter as part of Lieutenant David Russell's group of escapees. However, over the proceeding days he was shot when he and Russell tried to break into an Italian camp to steal food. In the stifling heat and with flies buzzing around his wound, he grew increasingly sick.

Lieutenant Russell tried to bolster Opprower's spirits and his resolution, but the young SIG operator was fading fast. After seventeen days on the run Opprower finally convinced Russell to leave him to crawl into an Arab encampment and seek his fortunes there. This Russell reluctantly did in an effort to save Opprower's life.

The Arabs didn't believe that Opprower was who he claimed to be. They feared he was a German agent provocateur and handed him over to the Italians. They in turn handed him to the Gestapo.

Opprower was tortured for several days. He was beaten unconscious in an effort to get him to admit to being a Jew and a 'renegade member of the SIG'.

At one point he was made to dig his own grave as a firing squad stood at the ready. Finally, an Afrika Korps officer intervened. He managed to secure Opprower's release from the Gestapo, followed by a transfer to a POW camp. Opprower had given the man his word that he was neither Jewish nor had anything to do with the SIG.

Private Rohr of the SIG – wounded at Tobruk while trying to go to the aid of the fallen Colonel Haselden – was also taken captive but would survive the war. In May 1945 he was in hospital in Surrey, having escaped from a German POW camp.

SIG member Maurice 'Tiffin' Tiefenbrunner did not take part in the raid on Tobruk. He continued serving with elite forces, being promoted to sergeant and taken into the SAS. In December 1942 he was on a thirty-vehicle SAS mission deep behind enemy lines, which planned to link up with the US 1st Army advancing from Tunisia. But his jeep broke down and he was captured, together with his driver.

Via Italy, he was sent to Stalag 351, a POW camp in Hanover, Germany. He claimed to be Maurice Tiffin, a French-Canadian born in Montreal, who'd been recruited into the British military in Palestine. His cover story must have been convincing: he was still at Stalag 351 when the camp was liberated by British troops in 1945. After the war, he discovered that both his parents had been killed in the concentration camps – his father in 1942, his mother in 1944.

Tiefenbrunner married in 1947, and went into the business of paper manufacturing. In 1962 he applied for and was granted British citizenship, along with his wife and four children. As part of his naturalization claim, he was asked why he wanted to become British. Tiefenbrunner pointed out that 'he had lived in this country for a long time and had fought side by side with British soldiers. He felt more British than anything else and intended to remain here for the rest of his days.'

That so many of the SIG operators who were captured actually avoided execution is perhaps testimony to the exhaustive preparation of their cover stories. Thankfully, in each of Opprower, Rohr and Tiefenbrunner's cases, Hitler's June 1942 order that any captured SIG members were to be 'mercilessly wiped out in battle', or those captured 'shot out of hand' was not carried out.

SSM Arthur Swinburn was taken into captivity in Tobruk. Weeks of semi-starvation and brutality followed, as his captors tried to break the man's 'commando spirit'. They did not succeed. Swinburn would survive captivity in both Italy and Germany, and would earn a Distinguished Conduct Medal (DCM) for his part in the Tobruk raid, the oldest

British award for gallantry. He returned to the UK to become a very active member of the Middle East Commando Historical Research Group.

Lieutenant Graham Taylor, who was shot through the chest during the Tobruk raid, was taken prisoner by the Italians. He survived his wounds and in the summer of 1943 was sent to Camp 47, in Italy, for bona fide Allied prisoners of war. He was transferred from there to Oflag 05A at Weinburg, in south-west Germany, where he spent the rest of the war.

Major Colin Campbell, the commanding officer of the SOE Commando, survived the injuries he sustained at Tobruk. When the villa headquarters was overrun the wounded major was taken captive. He survived the war, and in 1948 he would write to the *London Scottish Regimental Gazette*, expressing typically exacting soldierly pride and an eye for scrupulous detail.

He sought to correct any misapprehensions over how he came to be shot in the buttock. 'I can assure you . . . that I was neither shot by one of my own men nor running away, being engaged at the moment in collecting ammo, etc., from one of my officers who had just been killed – by the only party . . . we met who could shoot . . . That officer was Lt M. J. Duffy, of the Hampshires.'

David Lloyd Owen finished the war commanding the LRDG, despite being wounded several times in action. On one occasion he severely injured his spine and was told not to return to special forces duties. He bluffed his way past a medical board and was reunited with his beloved LRDG. The unit was disbanded at war's end, but its legacy endures.

For his wartime heroics Lloyd Owen was awarded both a Military Cross and a Distinguished Service Order. He went on to have a long career in the military, rising to the rank of major general. He would write two books about his time with the LRDG, which were well received.

Following his death on the Tobruk raid, Lieutenant Colonel John Haselden was recommended for his second MC (MC and bar), for 'gallant and distinguished services in the Middle East during the period May 1942 to October 1942'. And in June 1946 he was recommended for a Mention in Dispatches. The citation reads simply, 'Received in recognition of gallant and distinguished services in the field.' Both were awarded posthumously.

Months after Haselden's death the Eighth Army's newspaper would report his loss with the headline DEATH COMES TO SPY WHO FOUND ROMMEL – 'THE SECOND LAWRENCE OF ARABIA'. The article went on: 'He was a star of British Military Intelligence. The enemy would have called him a spy . . . if they had ever caught him. He was John Haselden, expert in Arabic and Balkan languages, tall, brown and hard-looking.'

His son Gerald would say of his sacrifice, 'My father was a brave man. He gave his life for his country . . . My father decided that he needed to drive the enemy back and he singlehandedly charged the German positions. They were forced back and the trucks managed to get through.' For a man who had been orphaned at a young age, Gerald Haselden betrayed an admirable lack of bitterness or rancour.

Following the Tobruk raid nothing was heard of Captain Buck, the founder of the SIG, for many weeks. As late as 9 December 1942 he was still posted as missing in action by the SOE. In fact he had been wounded while trying to escape from Tobruk, and following days on the run was finally captured.

From Tobruk Buck was shipped to Italy by submarine, where he was imprisoned first in the Certosa di Padula monastery, from where he subsequently escaped. He was recaptured and sent by train to Germany. During that journey he cut a hole in the floor of the rail carriage and escaped once more. Again he was recaptured.

He was branded a serial escapee, and was locked in solitary confinement for many days. He was next sent to Oflag V, in Heilbronn, a city in southern Germany, and from there to various other POW camps. At those he established a fencing club, ran Highland dancing classes and, typically, held study sessions on Indian mysticism. He also wrote a thesis while imprisoned, exploring the interface between Indian mysticism and Western philosophy.

Upon the liberation of the camps, Buck returned to Britain and was slated to deploy with the SAS for the unit's final wartime operations. SAS veteran Major Roy Farran, DSO, MC, wrote of Buck, 'Every effort must be made to get this officer for SAS Brigade.' The regiment's deployment to the Far East was being mooted, as the war ground on against the Japanese. That, of course, was made unnecessary with the dropping of the atomic bombs and the Japanese surrender.

In early November 1945 Buck married his childhood sweetheart Celia Wardle, who had served in the ATS during the war, at St Peter's Church, Yateley, Hampshire. Two weeks later Buck was one of twenty-two soldiers who took off in a RAF Liberator bomber from Merryfield airfield in Somerset, en route to Castel Benito, an aerodrome on the eastern coast of Libya. The mission of those aboard remains unclear, although the vast majority – eighteen – were wireless operators.

The Liberator crashed shortly after take-off, at White's Farm, near Broadway Pound, Somerset. All aboard, including Buck, were killed. The crash was put down to pilot error. 'Pilot failed to maintain straight course while climbing in cloud . . .' the accident investigator concluded. 'Had been briefed to climb to 1,500 [feet] before turning. Flight should not have been authorized as pilot was not sufficiently trained . . .'

As the Liberator was flying to Libya, Buck's life ended while he was on his way to where the SIG had begun its short but illustrious history. It was 22 November 1945. He was twenty-eight years old and he and his bride had not yet had their honeymoon.

Of the Barce raiders led by Jake Easonsmith, all who made up his walking and driving parties would escape with their lives, in an epic of endurance and survival that rivalled Langton and Russell's escapes from Tobruk. Some of the Barce raiders became lost in the desert, but all were traced and rescued. Lloyd Owen's LRDG patrol would carry out sterling work in helping locate and bring in those survivors.

The worst of Easonsmith's wounded were driven across the desert on the sole surviving Chevy, direct to LG 125. From there they were evacuated by a Bristol Bombay flying out of Kufra. It was 18 September, and all would survive their injuries, including Captain Wilder and his driver, Trooper Derek Parker.

Many of Easonsmith's remaining men made it back to Kufra under their own steam in the surviving vehicles. They reached the oasis on 25 September, having completed a 1,880-mile round journey. The Barce raid remains one of the longest – if not the longest – special forces overland mission of all time. It is also considered to be one of the most successful long-range beat-up attacks ever undertaken.

Easonsmith had lost ten men taken as POWs and had six seriously wounded. None of his force had been killed. That the desert raiders could strike so far and hard behind their lines proved a serious dent to Axis morale. It gave a corresponding boost to the Allies. One Military Cross, two Distinguished Service Orders (one to Captain Wilder) and three Military Medals (one to Merlyn Craw) were awarded to the Barce raiders, making this one of the most highly decorated special forces missions of the war.

Merlyn Craw and the other captives taken prisoner at Barce were subjected to intensive and often brutal interrogations. At one stage a stool pigeon – a former British soldier now working for the enemy – tried to trick them into revealing all they knew. That man, Private Theodore Schurch, would be tried for his treachery and executed.

In January 1943 the LRDG would be one of the first units to liberate Barce from Axis forces, as the Eighth Army scored a series of rapid victories against Rommel's Afrika Korps. Easonsmith's patrol was able to revisit the airfield in a victorious mood. The evidence of their 13 September 1942 raid was plain for all to see: burned-out wrecks of aircraft littered the fringes of the airfield.

Merlyn Craw survived the war and returned to his native New Zealand, as did Captain Wilder. Wilder's leadership qualities had been fully recognized during the war, when in 1943 he was appointed commanding officer of the New Zealand Divisional Cavalry, a unit then serving in Italy.

Sadly, John 'Jake' Easonsmith was killed in action during the Dodecanese campaign, on the island of Leros in November 1943. The 'Hero of the Desert' was then serving as the commander of the LRDG, and he was shot by a German sniper while carrying out a lone reconnaissance of a village. He was thirty-four years old.

Lieutenant Jock McKee, Buck's fellow April 1942 escapee, went on to join Force A, Lieutenant Colonel Dudley Clarke's specialist escape unit. He teamed up with the LRDG, seeking out Allied escapees deep behind the lines, serving on daring escape missions in North Africa, Italy and Austria. For such work he was awarded a MC. He survived the war.

Leah Schlossberg – the hitchhiking teenager who inspired Buck to form the SIG – met Yitzhak Rabin, her future husband at school in the British Mandate of Palestine. They married in 1948, the year Israel gained independence. Yitzhak Rabin became the prime minister of Israel in 1974. Leah Rabin died in 2000 aged seventy-two.

Bruckner, the former Afrika Korps sergeant who betrayed the SIG, went on to fight with the German military. He was captured by the Americans towards war's end. His treachery did not catch up with him. He was released, re-enlisted in the French Foreign Legion and served with that unit for many years. Apparently, fears of retribution over the Derna betrayal stalked him well into the sixties.

* * *

So much for the heroes – and the villains – of the story. What of the official assessment of the 13 September 1942 raids? A 15 September 'Most Secret' report drafted at Cairo headquarters summed up the confusion reigning in the immediate aftermath of the raid on Tobruk.

'No news of Haselden's party. We thought some MTBs might have them on-board, but it turned out they were left ashore. No suggestions to be made in the Press that anyone is left ashore or making a getaway by land, as we would like them to think that it is all over and there is no one left . . . Of the Marines, originally 360, all are missing except 60.'

In due course the total losses from the raid on Tobruk – including those of the Royal Navy, the Royal Marines, other landing forces, Haselden's men and the bomber crew shot down – would rise to approaching 750 men. Three British warships – including the destroyers *Sikh* and *Zulu* – had been sunk, and several smaller vessels lost.

The Germans reported taking 590 POWs. Elated over this setback to the Allies, Field Marshal Erwin Rommel flew into Tobruk. There he expressed his 'appreciation to the troops for the well-conducted defensive action they had fought'. The raid had caused 'no little alarm, for Tobruk was indeed one of our most valuable points'.

Admiral Sir Henry Harwood, the commander in chief of the Mediterranean Fleet, produced a somewhat more upbeat assessment of the raid.

'The stakes were very high, as a successful breaking up of Tobruk dumps and facilities would have had a big effect. Big risks were therefore deliberately taken . . .' He pointed out how the SIG and SOE Commando had played their parts to perfection, but lamented 'more than anything else that [they] did not receive their reinforcements due to MTBs not entering [Sciausc Bay]'.

Harwood's gist is clear: the SOE Commando – aided by the SIG – had done its job faultlessly in seizing the landing beach. Had the seaborne reinforcements arrived as scheduled, the outcome may well have been otherwise.

A 'Most Secret' 'lessons learned' document, drafted in the autumn of 1942, stressed the success of the SIG and SOE Commando ruse: 'The tactical planning for the attack on Mersa Umm Es Sciausc was sound in that surprise was achieved and bridgehead was formed in order to allow troops arriving by sea to land without opposition . . . In fact, the surprise that had been gained was lost due to the lapse of time.'

The War Cabinet's official history concluded: 'The raids . . . though they failed to achieve their immediate objects, were not entirely barren of result; and it became clear later that the indirect results had been considerable. The enemy sent back troops from the El Alamein position to the coast, and expended much air and fuel, of which they were short, in precautionary measures.'

That may have been so, but with proper and

realistic planning and execution, the raid on Tobruk could have set out to do much less and have achieved so much more. Had Buck, Russell, Haselden, Lloyd Owen and Stirling been given their heads, they could had done what was possible and necessary. Had they been left to raid the underground fuel dump at Tobruk and free a few thousand POWs, they could doubtless have done so, before melting back into the desert from which they had so mysteriously sprung.

But hindsight is a fine thing.

Rommel's forces were eventually driven out of Tobruk and the port fortress liberated. By 12 May 1943 the Afrika Korps had been defeated in North Africa, the campaign won by the Allies.

On 6 October 1944 Graham Taylor's father – Mr J. P. Taylor – wrote a letter concerning his son's part in the raid, which he'd just learned about from an escaped POW. He described it as a 'thrilling' escapade.

'Well now, no one got back, all were either killed or taken prisoner,' he wrote, 'so there is little hope of any records of this – to say the least what seems to be a very hazardous and daring raid, which was successfully carried out.' His letter was addressed to the War Office, but forwarded to the appropriate party, so that it could be filed as part of the official '1942 M.E. Commando diary'.

Desmond Duffy, the brother of Michael Duffy – the commando who was killed while fighting shoulder-to-shoulder with Major Campbell – also wrote of the Tobruk raid in similar upbeat terms. 'Force B achieved its objective. After a 1,500-mile journey across the desert they, undetected, entered Tobruk and disabled the coastal defence guns . . . Neither Lt Col Haselden, the leader of the expedition, nor Michael, have a known resting place. However, in the beautifully kept Tobruk Military Cemetery, all those who perished on 13th and 14th September 1942 lie together and any of a small number of graves marked "unknown" could be assumed to be Michael's.'

Perhaps theirs should be the last words regarding the 13 September 1942 raid on Tobruk. There is perhaps no better epitaph for the role played by the commandos and the SIG.

The raid on Tobruk sounded the death knell for two elite units, even though neither had failed in the tasks they were set on that fateful night. The SOE Commando had been decimated, and the SIG had been wiped out almost to a man. Those few who survived had been busy on other desert missions, and both the SIG's commanders – Russell and Buck – were lost. The unit was never reformed and those SIG operators who remained were subsumed into the SAS.

Though the SIG perished as a distinct unit as a result of the raid on Tobruk, the concept behind it did not. Its essence was taken into the SAS, SBS and related units. The use of bluff, deception and masquerading as the enemy continued. Anders Lassen, the only member of the British SAS ever to be awarded the Victoria Cross, was a master of such operations during World War Two, and the fate of Lieutenant David Russell, formerly of the SAS and the SIG, is also instructive.

In the autumn of 1943, Russell was deployed to what was then Yugoslavia, on a clandestine SOE mission code-named Operation Ranji, the aim of which was to organize and arm the local resistance. As part of the mission, Russell had to dress as a German officer in an effort to gain access to a high-security area. Old habits die hard and Russell had taken the lessons learned from the SIG into a new theatre of war.

On 4 September 1943 Russell was murdered in an isolated hut in the Yugoslav mountains by unknown assailants. He was twenty-eight years old at the time of his death. He was buried in the small churchyard at Vaciorova, near where he fell, and subsequently at the military cemetery in Bucharest. Some argued that Russell had been killed by thieves, who stole the gold sovereigns that all SOE operatives carried to pay informants and to buy their way out of trouble. This was discounted when the sovereigns were subsequently recovered. He'd been shot in the back of the head with a large-calibre pistol and it seems likely that he was targeted and murdered by his enemies.

Russell's role in Operation Ranji – if not his untimely death – proved how enduring was the legacy of the SIG. In more recent years special forces operations have again showed how such deception endures as a means to secure difficult and challenging objectives.

Consider Operation Tango. In July 1997 a NATO-sanctioned mission to seize suspected Serbian war criminals was executed in Bosnia. Four-man SAS teams were inserted by helicopter. Milan Kovacevic was one of two key targets. The former mayor of the Bosnian city of Prijedor, Kovacevic was wanted by international law enforcement agencies for the rounding up of Muslims to be sent to the notorious death camps.

Kovacevic was known to be the director of the Prijedor hospital. To gain access without arousing suspicion, the SAS team talked their way into the building by posing as officials from the Red Cross, their weapons concealed beneath their clothing. They arrested Kovacevic and spirited him away to a waiting US helicopter, which flew him out of the country. He was subsequently tried in the Hague for war crimes, and would die in custody from a heart attack.

In short, Captain Buck's unit, the Special Interrogation Group, bequeathed a legacy that endures until today.

ACKNOWLEDGEMENTS

In researching this book I was able to speak to and receive assistance from a number of individuals, many of whom were especially generous with their time. My special thanks and gratitude are extended to all, and my apologies to those that I have inadvertently forgotten to mention.

In no particular order I wish to thank the following, who assisted in many ways: research, proofreading, recollections and subject matter expertise. Martin Sugarman, author of books on the Jewish military and archivist at the Association of Jewish Ex-Servicemen (AJEX), for your invaluable insight into the SIG. Robert Sherwood for lending a forensic investigator's eye to this and related stories. Simon Winters, for insight into the subject matter presented herein. Tean Roberts, for your hard work and diligence, as always. Simon Fowler, for your expertise and inspiration, gleaned from the various archives. Paul and Anne Sherratt, for your perceptive comments and guidance. Anne's father, Captain Charles 'Ginger' Muir, served with the commandos in World War Two, as did Paul's uncle, Les Vaughan. Both saw action in the North African desert.

My very special thanks are extended to Jack Mann, SBS, SAS and LRDG veteran, for your invaluable insights and recollections from World War Two. Likewise, I'd like to thank Peter Forbes, who doggedly pursued me to tell the story of the the 'Keepers': you helped inspire the tale told herein, and, as you know, there is much more to be done!

Also, I'd like to extend my heartfelt gratitude to Jeremy Evans, the son of the late Harry Meirion Evans, for sharing with me your father's story of Bletchley and beyond. I hope I have done it justice in these pages. Matthew Johnston from New Zealand is also deserving of special mention, for your help and assistance from those islands that have produced so many foremost soldiers.

The staff at several archives and museums also deserve special mention, including those at the British National Archives, the Imperial War Museum, the Churchill Archive Centre at Churchill College, Cambridge, and the Camden Jewish Museum. Some files from the National Archives were made available to me as a result of Freedom of Information requests, and I am grateful to the individuals at the archives who made the decision that these files should be opened. I'm also grateful for the help provided by Thomas Gordon of the Royal Scots Regimental Museum in researching Jock McKee's wartime history, and to the staff at the Liddell Hart Centre for Military Archives, King's College London, for the same.

My gratitude also to my literary agent, Gordon

Wise, and film agent, Luke Speed, both of Curtis Brown, for helping bring this project to fruition, and to all at my publishers, Quercus, for the same, including, but not limited to: Charlotte Fry, Ben Brock and Fiona Murphy. My editor, Richard Milner, deserves very special mention, as does Josh Ireland. Your faith in my ability to tell this remarkable and important story is, I hope, rewarded in these pages.

I am also indebted to those authors who have previously written about some of the topics dealt with in this book and whose work has helped inform my writing. In alphabetical order they are: Norman Bentwich (*I Understand The Risks*), Johnny Cooper (*One of the Originals*), John W. Gordon (*The Other Desert War*), David Jefferson (*Tobruk: A Raid Too Far*), G. Landsborough (*Tobruk Commando*), Isaac Levy (*Now I Can Tell*), Eric Morris (Guerrillas in Uniform), Brendon O'Carroll (*Barce Raid*), John Sadler (*Operation Agreement*), Peter Smith (*Massacre At Tobruk*), Martin Sugarman (*Fighting Back*) and Ex-Lance Corporal X, QGM (*The SAS and LRG Roll Of Honour 1941–47*). I have included a full bibliography, which follows.

And of course, thanks are due as always to Eva and the ever-patient and wonderful David, Damien Jr and Sianna, for not resenting Dad spending too much of his time locked away . . . again . . . writing . . . again.

BIBLIOGRAPHY

R. A. Bagnold, *Libyan Sands*, Hodder & Stoughton, 1935

Norman Bentwich, *I Understand the Risks*, Scottish Country Press, 1950

Johnny Cooper, *One of the Originals*, Pan Books, 1991

Virginia Cowles, *The Phantom Major*, Grafton Books, 1958

M. Crichton-Stuart, *G Patrol*, William Kimber & Co., 1958

John W. Gordon, *The Other Desert War*, Greenwood Press, 1987

Oliver Hoare, *Camp 020*, Public Records Office, 2000

Malcolm James, *Born of the Desert*, Collins, 1945

David Jefferson, *Tobruk: A Raid Too Far*, Robert Hale, 2013

W. B. Kennedy-Shaw, *Long Range Desert Group*, Greenhill Books, 1989

G. Landsborough, *Tobruk Commando*, Greenhill Books, 1989

Isaac Levy, *Now I Can Tell*, Dalkeith Press, 1978

David Lloyd Owen, *The Desert My Dwelling Place*, Cassell, 1957

David Lloyd Owen, *Long Range Desert Group 1940–45: Providence Their Guide*, George G. Harrap & Co., 1980

Charles Messenger, *The Middle East Commandos*, William Kimber & Co., 1988

Eric Morris, *Guerrillas in Uniform*, Hutchinson, 1989

Brendan O'Carroll, *Barce Raid*, Ngaio Press, 2005

Brendan O'Carroll, *Bearded Brigands*, Ngaio Press, 2002

Vladimir Peniakoff, *Popski's Private Army*, Cassell, 1950

Public Records Office War Histories, *Special Forces in the Desert War 1940–1943*, Public Records Office, 2001

John Sadler, *Operation Agreement*, Osprey Publishing, 2016

Peter Smith, *Massacre At Tobruk*, William Kimber, 1987

Martin Sugarman, *Fighting Back*, Vallentine Mitchell, 2011

Arthur Swinson, *The Raiders Desert Strike Force*, Pan Books, 1968

Alastair Timpson, *In Rommel's Backyard*, Leo Cooper, 2000

Ex-Lance Corporal X, QGM, *The SAS and LRDG Roll Of Honour 1941–47*, SAS-LRDG-RoH, 2016